The Family Business Guide

Other Works by Frederick D. Lipman

International and U.S. IPO Planning: A Business Strategy Guide

Executive Compensation Best Practices

Corporate Governance Best Practices: Strategies for Public, Private, and Not-for-Profit Organizations

Valuing Your Business: Strategies to Maximize the Sale Price

Audit Committees

The Complete Guide to Employee Stock Options

The Complete Guide to Valuing and Selling Your Business

The Complete Going Public Handbook

Financing Your Business with Venture Capital

How Much Is Your Business Worth

Going Public

Venture Capital and Junk Bond Financing

The Family Business Guide

Everything You Need to Know to
Manage Your Business from Legal
Planning to Business Strategies

Frederick D. Lipman

First published in 2010 by
PALGRAVE MACMILLAN®
in the United States—a division of St. Martin's Press LLC,
175 Fifth Avenue, New York, NY 10010.

Where this book is distributed in the UK, Europe and the rest of the world, this is by Palgrave Macmillan, a division of Macmillan Publishers Limited, registered in England, company number 785998, of Houndmills, Basingstoke, Hampshire RG21 6XS.

Palgrave Macmillan is the global academic imprint of the above companies and has companies and representatives throughout the world.

Palgrave® and Macmillan® are registered trademarks in the United States, the United Kingdom, Europe and other countries.

ISBN: 978–0–230–10515–7

Library of Congress Cataloging-in-Publication Data

Lipman, Frederick D.
    The family business guide : everything you need to know to manage your business from legal planning to business strategies / by Frederick D. Lipman.
        p. cm.
    Includes index.
    ISBN 978–0–230–10515–7
    1. Family-owned business enterprises—Management. 2. Family-owned business enterprises—Law and legislation. I. Title.

HD62.25.L57 2010
658′.045—dc22   2010002984

A catalogue record of the book is available from the British Library.

Design by Newgen Imaging Systems (P) Ltd., Chennai, India.

First edition: August 2010

10 9 8 7 6 5 4 3 2 1

Printed in the United States of America.

To my brother, Harold Lipman, and to Charles S. Lipman and Beatrice Lipman, who were the founders of the author's family business

Contents

Acknowledgments

The author wishes to thank Phillip Clemens, Chairman and CEO of the Clemens Family Corporation, for educating me on some of the best practices used by family businesses that have survived for more than 100 years and for allowing me to reproduce his speech in this book.

The author received helpful suggestions from Professor John L. Ward. Professor Ward is the Wild Group Professor of Family Business at IMD, Lausanne, Switzerland, Professor and Co-Director, Kellogg School Center, and a founder of the Family Business Consulting Group International.

Larry Colin, the co-author of "Family, Inc.," made helpful suggestions for the book cover design.

The author wishes to acknowledge the assistance of the following attorneys at Blank Rome LLP in the preparation of this book: Bradford Clemens, Esq.; Lawrence S. Chane, Esq.; Lawrence Finkelstein, Esq.; Joseph T. Gulant, Esq.; Norman S. Heller, Esq.; Cory G. Jacobs, Esq.; Barry L. Klein, Esq.; Stephen E. Luongo, Esq.; Leonard P. Nalencz, Esq.; Joel C. Shapiro, Esq.; Raymond L. Shapiro, Esq.; Mary T. Vidas, Esq.; and Alan L. Zeiger, Esq.

Lawrence S. Chane, Esq., an estate planning attorney; Norman S. Heller, a matrimonial attorney; Barry L. Klein, Esq., an employee benefits and labor attorney; Leonard P. Nalencz, Esq., an estate planning attorney; and Alan L. Zeiger, Esq., a corporate and business attorney, served as coauthors of designated chapters, or portions of chapters, of this book, and their contributions have been duly noted in these chapters. The author acknowledges the helpful contributions of Raymond L. Shapiro, Esq. and Joel C. Shapiro, Esq., attorneys specializing in business restructuring and bankruptcy, to Chapter 9, "Family Businesses in Financial Distress."

Cheryl Halversen, a business research librarian at Blank Rome LLP, was also helpful in our research.

Finally, the author wishes to acknowledge the outstanding services of Barbara Helverson, who served as an editor as well as the typist for this book.

Introduction

This book addresses the following key questions for owners of family businesses and their advisors:

- What provision should be inserted into your Will to help ensure the continuation of the family business
- If you are married, why you should not have an affair after giving voting stock to your children
- Why it is important to take your young children to work
- Why you should insist that family members working in the business sign employee agreements
- How to protect your family business from claims by divorcing spouses of family members
- What are the worst practices in succession planning
- What are the best governance structures for family businesses
- What provisions for resolving family disputes after your death should be inserted into your corporate charter
- How to set the compensation of the family members who work in the business
- How to create equity-type incentives for key employees without giving up any equity
- How to get rid of troublesome minority shareholders
- Why infusing cash into a family business that is in financial distress is not necessarily a good idea
- Methods of minimizing gift estate and inheritance taxes
- How to sell your business to other family members and key employees
- The pros and cons of an initial public offering (IPO)
- And many other questions

This book is intended to provide a practical guide to best practices and worst practices for family businesses and should be read by all members of family businesses and their advisors. The author has drawn upon his own background as a member of a family business and as a lawyer/consultant to family businesses for almost 50 years. The book also distills the best practices for family businesses from over 200 primarily empirical academic studies.

In addition to presenting best practices, this book also analyses actual court cases involving family businesses to draw lessons about the worst practices that resulted in these courtroom battles. These family litigations occurred throughout the United States, including in courts in New York, California, Pennsylvania, Michigan, Ohio, New Jersey, Nebraska, New Hampshire, North Dakota, Massachusetts, Kansas, Alabama, Connecticut, Maine, Wyoming, and Rhode Island. Understanding and avoiding worst practices may be even more important than understanding best practices.

Sample legal agreements are included that will help you avoid some of the major risks, such as claims by divorcing spouses to shares of the business. The book also contains suggested provisions for articles and certificates of incorporation that will permit trusted independent directors to resolve irreconcilable family conflicts which threaten the business. Finally, the book suggests forms of phantom equity and stock option plans which will provide equity-type incentives to key employees (whether family or not) without actually making these key employees shareholders.

Overview of the Family Business

The family business is the dominant form of small business entity in the United States and throughout the world. It has been estimated that approximately 80 percent to 90 percent of the businesses in North America are family owned.[1] Indeed, even public companies whose majority owners are a single family can be classified as family businesses. A substantial percentage of the Fortune 500 companies are considered family firms and their founding families on average owned almost 18 percent of their equity.[2]

A family business is unique because it involves a mutual interdependence between a family and a business, two very different systems that are nonetheless closely and intimately interconnected. Changes in either system seriously affect the other. One academic researcher has found that the family's adaptability, including having a policy of open communication among family members, was significantly related to business success.[3]

The family business is the oldest form of multiparty business enterprise. In fact the world's oldest continuously operated family business, the Japanese temple builder Kongō Gumi Co., Ltd., began in 578, as discussed in Chapter 1.[4]

Outside the United States, of a total sample of 27,987 firms from 45 countries around the world, 894 family-controlled groups were identified with 2,734 different companies in, typically, emerging markets. The portion of listed firms belonging to family business groups is at least 30 percent in Chile, Columbia, Israel, Philippines, Sri Lanka and Turkey, and Sri Lanka is the largest at 64.10 percent. Chile's Angelini family, Denmark's Maersk-Moeller Group, Israel's Shrem, Fudim Group Ltd, Italy's Marco Tronchetti Provera Group, Korea's Lee Jun-Hee, the Philippine's de Ayala family, Singapore's Keswick and Weatherall families, and Turkey's Sabanci family all control more than 10 percent of their respective country's total stock market capitalization.[5]

Family businesses have been classified by ownership in the seminal book *Generation to Generation*[6] as follows:

- Controlling Owner—Ownership is consolidated in a single individual or couple (e.g., husband and wife copreneurs)[7] with only token holdings, if any, by other family members.
- Sibling Partnership—Two or more siblings have ownership and effective control. This is typically a second generation business.
- Cousin Consortium—Many cousins are shareholders. This is typically a third or later generation business.[8]

Family businesses can also be classified according to those that are managed by family members and those that are owned by family members but managed professionally,[9] by the size and maturity of the business, and by whether it is privately or publicly held.

The Organization of This Book

Chapter 1 deals with the extremely important topic of succession planning, which applies primarily to business that are family-owned and managed. The average family business lasts 25 years; only 40 percent go to the next generation; only 12 percent go beyond the second generation; and only 3 percent go to the fourth generation.

Chapter 1 presents the best practices to ensure the continuation of the family businesses as well as some of the mistakes and worst practices which should be avoided. Chapter 1 ends with the best practices of family businesses that have survived over 100 years, including Kongo Gumi, which survived over 1,000 years.

Chapter 2 discusses the necessity of having an agreement with each family member who becomes either an employee or a shareholder of the business. Many of the risks involved in operating a family business can be prevented through such carefully drafted agreements, which can cover such situations as family members leaving the business and then soliciting former customers. Since divorce is one of the main problems of the family business, this chapter also suggests methods of avoiding the pitfalls of the divorce risk with simple provisions in shareholder agreements and through irrevocable spendthrift trusts for gifts of family business equity. The use of prenuptial agreements, postnuptial agreements, and conditional gifts to prevent divorcing spouses from claiming equity shares in the family business are also discussed in this chapter. These legal agreements are not only crucial to the economic success of the family business, but they also help to ensure its survival for future generations and avoid costly redemptions of the equity of divorcing spouses. Finally, the chapter concludes with a discussion of shareholder liquidity programs.

Chapter 3 describes the best corporate governance structures and practices for the family business, including the use of independent directors who can both advise the founder and relieve him or her of the difficult task of setting compensation for family members. The independent directors can also serve as potential impartial tiebreakers in the event of family disputes, thus avoiding entangling the founder in the emotions generated by the dispute. This chapter emphasizes the need for frequent and open communication with family shareholders in order to build trust, including the use of family councils and annual shareholder meetings, particularly for cousin consortiums and other multigenerational businesses. Chapter 3 also describes a case from the Supreme Court of Pennsylvania that illustrates good succession planning through the use of independent directors who worked to resolve family disputes.

Chapter 4, "Worst Practices: What We Can Learn from Family Disasters," contains a detailed review of court cases throughout the United States involving the family businesses, particularly defective succession planning cases, with an analysis of how the litigation might have been prevented. The author believes that this may be the most valuable chapter in the book because it provides concrete examples of what family businesses should not do.

Chapter 5 deals with the difficult topic of compensating family members who are employed by the business and discusses best practices. The use of independent board members to help establish arms-length compensation, thereby insulating the owner from these difficult decisions, is recommended.. Since procedural due process is important to maintain family unity, it is recommended that independent compensation consultants be involved in establishing fair compensation levels for family members.

Family businesses must find ways to create incentives to hire and retain key employees who are not family members. Chapter 6 discusses the use of phantom equity incentives that permit the family business to compete for such key employees. Phantom equity incentives can also be given to family members who are employees of the business but not significant shareholders.

Chapter 7 analyzes relationships between the family business and inactive shareholders. We recommend methods of providing non-monetary rewards to inactive shareholders to enhance their commitment to the business. We also discuss the need to treat inactive majority shareholders fairly, such as by giving them the same investment opportunities that are available to active family members.

In Chapter 8 we discuss methods by which the family business can eliminate minority shareholders, either through voluntary sales or through involuntary methods such as reverse stock splits. This chapter discusses several litigations in this area, including an actual Ohio court case.

Family businesses periodically suffer downturns that should involve putting into place cost-cutting and other measures to preserve the business. In Chapter 9 we review the best practices for family businesses that are under financial distress.

The best practices for selling a family business are analyzed in Chapter 10, with an emphasis on the importance of advance planning, which helps to preserve and maximize the value of the family business. This chapter also covers selling to other family members and to an employee stock ownership trust (ESOP).

Chapter 11 contains both a summary of methods of preserving family wealth discussed elsewhere in the book and a few select methods of minimizing federal and state gift, estate and inheritance taxes for the owners of the family business.

More substantial family businesses may wish to consider going public. Chapter 12 contains advanced planning techniques and reviews the advantages and disadvantages of an IPO. The book ends with the worst practice of the founder of Benihana Restaurants, who managed to lose control of his public company by naming his new wife as his successor.

Appendix 1 of the book is a speech by the CEO of Clemens Family Corporation, which has survived for over 100 years, on the methods he uses to preserve the family business.

Appendix 2 contains a form of prenuptial agreement that is used in New York State.

Appendix 3 contains a form of an Irrevocable Spendthrift Trust, which is one of the best methods of protecting family business stock from the claims of divorcing spouses.

Appendix 4 contains a form of a Phantom Unit Agreement for Key Employees of the family business, which is discussed in Chapter 6.

Appendix 5 contains a form of Stock Option Plan for a family business, as discussed in Chapter 6, which permits the granting of stock options to key employees which options are only exercisable in the event the family business is sold or there is an initial public offering.

CHAPTER 1

Succession Planning

"The father buys, the son builds, the grandchildren sell, and his son begs."
—Scottish proverb

There is an old American saying attributed to Andrew Carnegie (1835–1919): "From shirtsleeves to shirt sleeves in three generations." Approximately 30 percent of family firms survive into the second generation of ownership, and just 15 percent survive into the third generation.[1] The rate of survival for a small family business is even lower, down to an average of five to ten years.[2]

Succession is one of the hardest decisions a family business can make but also one of the most important. A well-structured succession can preserve the business for future generations, while a poorly structured one can result in expensive litigation among members of the next generation—and the ultimate sale or failure of the business.

Succession planning may be significantly different for a first-generation, single-owner business than for a second-generation sibling partnership or a third-generation cousin consortium.[3] Nevertheless, there are best practices for each type of family business.

Note that for ease of reference, we will generally refer to the owner or owners of the business as the "owner," recognizing that there can be multiple owners. This chapter is written for the family-owned and family-managed business and does not apply to professionally managed family-owned businesses.[4]

Mentoring the Next Generation

Successful succession planning requires mentoring the next generation.

Succession is a process that takes time to develop and needs to be managed in order to be successful.[5] For a small family business to survive, it is essential that the founder engage in the process of transferring his or her knowledge and intellectual capital to the next generation.[6] Even though a successor may choose to reject some of the founder's business practices and judgments, it is, nevertheless, important for the founder to provide the successor with that intellectual capital. Founders who are extremely secretive about their knowledge will seriously lessen the likelihood that the family business will survive.

> **Best Practice**
>
> Early childhood experiences and the responsibilities imposed by parents play a significant role. Experience with other businesses is also helpful to successors.

In the following interview, American billionaire Ronald Perelman talks about his relationship with his father, Raymond, owner of Belmont Ironworks (now called Belmont Industries):

Q: I heard that when you were a kid your father used to put you in a tie and a jacket and take you to the board meetings of your family's business.

A: I don't know if he put me in a tie and jacket, but it was me wanting to go. I was always fascinated by the decision-making process and the managerial process and just business in general. So every opportunity I had to hang around with him, I did. Just watching him do his job—I mean, he's very good at his job. He's a very clear thinker. He was a great believer in decision-making. [in] making decisions. That if you don't make a decision, a decision's going to be made for you. He let me work on my own to a far greater extent than I should've been—just to learn as I was making my own mistakes.[7]

An academic study divided this knowledge into three categories[8]:

- Industry-related competencies (e.g., specific knowledge unique to the industry)
- Business competency (e.g., methods of operating the business, products and services, taking calculated risks, resolving problems and conflicts, etc.)

- Ownership competency (e.g., governance, maintaining a fair balance between various stakeholders, and adding economic value to the business)

The process of educating the next generation must begin in early childhood, with a particular focus on the responsibilities that parents give their children early on. One academic study of five small family businesses cited this type of early childhood education as a key to entrepreneurial success.[9]

A more recent study of six small family businesses found that positive parent-child and founder-successor relationships played a key role in successfully passing on the business to the next generation.[10] It included examples of a daughter who as a teenager enjoyed driving to work with her father, a son who cherished the extra days and years he was allowed to spend with his father after his father suffered several heart attacks, and a daughter who was trusted enough by her father to help with the business' accounting. In each case, the positive relationship began in the childhood of the potential successor and grew over time.

The same study found that owners should speak to their potential successors in balanced terms concerning both the positive and negative aspects of the business. If owners constantly complain about the business (lazy employees, rude customers, etc.), this is all that children or other potential successors will hear regarding the business and it tends to turn them off.[11] It is important that the founder instill in his or her children a sense of pride in the family business, while at the same time frankly discussing its risks and problems.

Dinnertime is an excellent occasion to discuss the family business. These conversations should begin as soon as the child is able to understand how the business works. However, many families have a "no business at the dinner table" rule with their children. While the author agrees that dinnertime conversation should not focus exclusively on the family business, banning the topic entirely is counterproductive to the mentoring process.

Dinner conversations should include interesting anecdotes that can give children a better understanding of both the benefits and challenges of operating a family business. The children will have a better sense of their future place in the world if the owner shares his or her pride in the family business. Of course, while the owner should give the child a feeling for the benefits and challenges of the business, this does not mean that he should limit or discourage his child from exploring careers outside of it.[12]

In addition to dinnertime conversations, the owner should, on occasion, bring the child to work and hire him or her to help with the business when it's appropriate.

Owners should also take advantage of some of the excellent outside resources that are available. As early as preschool, there are many games and children's and young adult books for parents to explore with their children. Parents should plan trips to Wall Street, or the relevant financial center where they live. Children should be sent to financial education camps where they spend time learning the basics of budgeting, saving, and investing.[13]

Once the child is older, about 14- to 18-years old, the family should begin career counseling and vocational aptitude testing, preferably through outside consultants. Some attempt should be made to distinguish between those children who are interested in the family business and have the appropriate aptitudes from those who have neither the interest nor the aptitude.[14]

Mentoring should continue through college. The owner should offer suggestions on possible majors (e.g., accounting) and degrees helpful to further understanding the operations of the family business. Although attending a prestigious business school is helpful, some children are not interested in pursuing a business degree, cannot qualify for acceptance to such a school, or would simply prefer a liberal arts education. Owners should always respect and support the decisions of their children. Ultimately, many kinds of education are useful to running a family business. For example, a background in English literature could offer keen insight into human behavior that ends up being more relevant to the business than some business courses.

It is not unusual for some children to be interested in art and music careers while in college and after graduation. But after pursuing these careers for a few years, they may decide that participating in the family business would be more rewarding. Therefore, if a child is an art or music major, it's important to suggest also taking accounting and other business courses.

Mentoring should continue throughout the post-college years for children participating in the family business. A number of the major business schools provide weekend and evening courses for adults as well as executive education programs.

It is helpful to have potential successors work in other businesses before joining the family business, even though this is rare.[15] This helps to build their self-confidence and gives them credibility when they do enter the family business. The child's experience in other businesses can be extremely useful in developing new ideas, practices, and procedures for the family business.

Mentoring involves more than just teaching the specific skills and methods needed in the family business. After all, the next generation may have completely different ideas about how to operate and grow the business, or may face challenges their parents never did. Mentoring therefore also requires asking hard questions and being prepared to allow the next generation to make a few mistakes that they can learn from.

Some family members may wish to start their own businesses, separate from the family business. Here the founder can play an important role, providing some of the family's intellectual capital for these newly minted entrepreneurs. In addition, a founder should be ready to offer some financial assistance when appropriate.

The founder's intellectual capital is the most important asset he or she can be transfer to succeeding generations. This must be done in a manner that is acceptable to the next generation, as they may have quite different ideas about how to operate a business. A wise founder makes himself open and available to give advice but avoids being didactic and authoritative, as these qualities tend to turn off younger people.

The founder must not only impart intellectual capital but also ethical norms to succeeding generations. Albert Boscov, whose remarkable story is recited in Chapter 9, is the co-owner of 39 retail stores called Boscov's. Albert's father, Solomon, a Russian immigrant, founded Boscov's as a general store in Reading, Pennsylvania. One of Albert's first jobs in his father's store was catching flies—he got a dime for 30 every week; just enough for a movie ticket. But it was hard for Albert to catch flies because he was so short. Since all dead flies look alike, he decided to concoct a scam whereby he would pass off the old flies from one week as newly caught ones for the next week. Solomon eventually discovered the scheme and took back Albert's dime. He also gave his son a long lecture on integrity. Albert apparently learned his lesson well: He would go on to earn an outstanding reputation for honesty. Because of that reputation and the friends he made over the years, he was able to obtain financing to buy back the family business after it filed bankruptcy in 2008.[16]

Develop a Written Strategic Plan That Considers Succession Issues

Many family businesses owners fail to develop a systematic framework for thinking about the future of their businesses. One survey indicated that close to 70 percent of respondents reported not having a strategic plan.[17] Many owners also fail to consider whether some of their children should *not* be involved in the business.

> ### Best Practice
>
> Develop a written strategic plan for the family business taking into account the issue of succession. It should include whether financial inducements should be given to family members to *not* participate in the business and whether different children should be given different business units to manage and to own.

Succession planning should be part of the strategic plan for the business. The process of preparing a strategic plan for the business that includes succession issues helps to focus your thinking on the future. There are a number of books that contain excellent discussions on how to prepare an integrated strategic business and family succession plan.[18]

It is important to involve the next generation in the strategic planning process. One academic study has indicated that involving potential successors in the process may play a critical role in building and reinforcing next generation's knowledge, particularly their industry and business knowledge, functional capabilities, and decision-making skills.[19]

Both advisory boards and boards of directors can play a significant role in the development of a strategic plan and succession planning, as discussed more fully in Chapter 3.[20]

Finally, a strategic plan that addresses succession issues should consider whether financial inducements should be given to certain family members to not participate in the family business and whether independent business units should be established for different family members, as described later in this chapter.[21]

Example:

Jack, Sr., age 65, is the founder of a family business that manufactures and sells swimming pool supplies. He would like to retire in five years, when he is 70. He has three children in the business: his oldest child, Alice, who is 40 years old, and two sons, Jack, Jr., who is 38, and Jim, who is 36. Jack, Jr. has had problems with both customers and employees and numerous conflicts with his siblings.

Because the swimming pool business is seasonal on the East Coast, Jack, Sr. recently purchased a small manufacturer of snowboards, and he also has real-estate holdings outside of the family business. Jack, Sr.'s strategic plan is to grow both the swimming pool and snowboard businesses over the next five years, gradually giving ownership of the swimming pool business to Alice, and to have his youngest son, Jim, who is an avid skier, manage and operate the snowboard business. The snowboard business is still small, and therefore significant capital is required to grow it to the point where it can support Jim. Jack, Sr. believes that he must get Jack, Jr. out of both businesses because of his conflicts with his siblings and difficulties with customers and employees. Therefore, his strategic plan contemplates increasing his real estate holdings outside of the family business and ultimately giving them to Jack, Jr. to manage and subsequently to own.

Periodically Review and Reevaluate Succession Planning

Succession planning is an evolving activity and requires periodic review as circumstances change—preferably at least once every five years. Failure to do so may result in a failed succession plan.

> **Best Practice**
>
> Succession planning must be reviewed and reevaluated, preferably at least once every five years. Difficult succession decisions should be reviewed with an independent board of directors.

An owner may initially think that his eldest son is the most capable of all his children of running the business. But five years later that owner might become disillusioned with this son's business judgment and begin to consider the capabilities of his second-oldest son. In another five years, when the owner's daughter enters the business, the owner might want to reevaluate the succession plan once again.

In the prior example, after operating under the strategic plan for two years, Jack, Sr. comes to the conclusion, with the advice of his independent directors, that the snowboard business is too competitive and cannot grow to the size needed to support his youngest son, Jim. Jack, Sr. sells it and uses the proceeds to grow the swimming pool business. He defers retirement to age 75 instead of 70, and he decides to make Alice the head of marketing for the swimming pool business and to bring Jim back into the swimming pool business as head of manufacturing. At age 70, he expects to make Alice president of the swimming pool business, and he would become chairman of the board.

Succession decisions are often very difficult to make. In one real-life example, a father had a son and a son-in-law who both wanted to take over the running of the business when he retired. The son-in-law was clearly the more competent of the two, and the father knew it. However, he was unable to choose his son-in-law over his own son, who had spent his life working in the family business. Ultimately, the company formed a board of directors that included independent members, and they selected the son-in-law to succeed the father.[22]

Consider Communicating Proposed Succession Plans to Family Members

Some owners of family businesses prefer to keep their succession plans confident. This is particularly true of first-generation single owners. Even in sibling partnerships and cousin consortiums, family relationships may already be strained and would be worsened by an open discussion of succession planning. Therefore, openly discussing succession is not necessarily appropriate for every business. However, at a minimum, serious consideration must be given to the desirability of communicating proposed succession plans to family members and receiving feedback.

> **Best Practice**
>
> If it is appropriate for the owner's situation, consider discussing proposed succession plans, either through family councils or otherwise, and receive feedback from family members.

It has been said that family businesses succeed when dreams of the younger generation are integrated with the dreams of the family.[23] It has also been suggested that there are more CEOs with lost personal dreams in family businesses than in any other type of business.[24]

Open discussions of succession planning within the family tend to identify these potential CEOs and their aspirations.

Frequent communication among family members is important to maintaining harmony, and it provides an outlet for airing any grievances resulting from succession planning. Since succession is one of the most important issues that will be addressed by the owners, they must be prepared for emotional reactions, comments, and recommendations. The owner's spouse plays an important role in this process, particularly if she is the mother, for it's the mother who acts as the CEO (chief emotional officer), equally committed to both family and business.[25] Indeed, the women who work behind the scenes of these businesses are often the "glue" that holds the family together.[26]

Usually, family businesses are not functioning democracies. After hearing all family views, it is the owner who ultimately makes the decision on succession.

Consider Retaining Control in the Owner's Surviving Spouse

Many owners die before developing a succession plan. Other owners have developed a succession plan but are not certain that it will be successful after their death. This is particularly true if the owner has more than one child in the business and it is not clear how well they will get along after his death.

> **Best Practice**
>
> If the owner's spouse has good business judgment, the owner should consider giving him or her the power to change the succession plan and should retain voting control for the owner's spouse during that spouse's lifetime.

If the owner of the family business believes the surviving spouse is capable of making good business decisions, he or she should consider giving that spouse the final say on succession.

Once the owner dies, there is typically a significant change in the family dynamic. While alive, the owner often plays an important role in preventing and resolving family business conflicts, and that owner's spouse may serve a similar role in resolving disputes outside of the business. Once the owner has departed, however, relationships among the children may change, sometimes for the worse. But should the owner's surviving spouse have good business judgment, he or she may see problems in the succession plan that were not present during the owner's lifetime. It may be desirable to give the surviving spouse the legal power to change the succession plan to reflect the reality after the owner's death.

If the owner gives the stock or other equity of the family business outright to his or her spouse, that spouse can maintain control of the business. If the surviving spouse wishes to makes gifts of the stock during her lifetime, she should retain voting control of the stock that is gifted to other family members. Voting control can be maintained either by an irrevocable spendthrift trust or a voting agreement or trust, or both, depending upon state law. This voting control will help to maintain family harmony and also permit the surviving spouse to reexamine the owner's succession plan.

For estate planning purposes, it is typical to not give a spouse the stock outright but have it held in trust for her during her lifetime. In this case, in his Will, the owner can give the surviving spouse the power to allocate the stock or other equity of the family business among their children. This permits the surviving spouse to give each child an equal share of the estate's assets, but allocates the equity and control of the family business to a single child while the other children receiving property of equal value.

The author has seen many Wills that fail to give such a power to the surviving spouse, even in situations where the spouse has good business judgment and is trusted by the owner. It is important that the owner's attorney review the estate planning to ensure this power of allocation of assets among the children is included in the owner's Will. The owner can stipulate that this power of allocation of equity in the family business would terminate upon the remarriage of the surviving spouse.

Example:

Patrick and his wife Maureen started and grew a substantial business, and at the same time raised five children. Of their sons, Sean was the eldest, followed by Daniel, then Ryan, and then Kyle. Their fifth and youngest child was their only daughter, Shannon. Each of the children got jobs in the business. During Patrick's lifetime Sean was his parents' clear favorite. Patrick died at age 70 and was survived by Maureen, who lived another ten years. During this time, Sean became president of the company. Initially, he did a good job. But following a messy divorce, Sean began drinking and fighting with his brothers over both business and personal issues. The other brothers also began to have conflicts about business and personal issues, including over which of their children should be hired by the business and how much to pay them. At the same time, Shannon began to blossom in her executive abilities, and she often served as peacemaker during her brothers' many fights. Patrick's Will had given all of the stock ownership in the company to Maureen during her lifetime. Upon her death, all of his assets would be divided equally among the five children, including Patrick's substantial real estate holdings.

The Will gave Maureen the power to designate which children would receive specific assets upon her death. Following infighting among her sons after her husband's death, Maureen determined that, upon her death, Shannon would become the controlling shareholder of the company and also its chief executive officer. She stipulated that 51 percent of the equity of the company would go to Shannon, and the remaining 49 percent would be divided equally among the remaining children. To make up for Shannon getting the larger share of the business, Maureen further stipulated that a greater share of the real-estate holdings would go the remaining four sons than would be received by Shannon.

If Maureen had not had such power, each of the children would have received 20 percent of the equity of the company, and it was likely that there would have been substantial conflict among the equity holders.

Will Provision

The following is a simple Will provision that accomplishes the purpose described above. It is assumed that the Will of each spouse will create a testamentary trust for the life of the surviving spouse for tax planning purposes and that the provision that appears below will be included in each Will as a provision of each testamentary trust.

> Upon the death of the survivor of myself and my spouse, the principal shall be distributed to, or held in trust for the benefit of such person or persons among the issue of my spouse [insert name of spouse], and me and upon such estates and conditions as my said spouse shall appoint by Will, making specific reference to this power. Any unappointed property shall be divided into as many equal shares as there are children of mine then living and children then dead, leaving issue then living. Thereafter: . . .

If the Business Will Be Divided Equally between Two Children, Provide for an Independent Impartial Tiebreaker

The best succession plan for a family business is to have only one child, akin to the "one-child policy" in China. However, this is not practical for most owners. Therefore careful succession planning is necessary to preserve the family business for future generations.

If the family business is to be divided equally between two children, it is important to have an independent impartial tiebreaker. The tiebreaker can be a trusted friend or a member of the board of directors. Many of the litigations that involve family businesses result from clashes that occur after the death of the founder between two children who each own 50 percent of the business.

Best Practice
If equity ownership is divided 50/50 in the next generation, provide for an independent impartial tie breaker.

Example:

Vito, an Italian immigrant, starts a small manufacturing business. When he dies, the business is given to his only son, Anthony. Anthony and his wife, Carmella, grow the business substantially. Their daughters, Isabel and Angela, are also active in the business and help to expand it even further. However, the two sisters are both very strong-willed, with completely different personalities. While Anthony is alive, he is able to resolve the conflicts that arise between them. When Anthony and Carmella pass away, each sister received 50 percent of the equity of the business. Isabel and Angela try to divide the functions of the business between them, but they are constantly in conflict. One sister runs the West Coast operation, and the other runs the East Coast operation. Their conflicts threaten the business enough to that the sisters seek counseling. But the counseling does not go well. Ultimately, the business has to be sold.

Anthony's mistake was failing to recognize that the constant fighting between his two daughters would threaten the business once he and Carmella were not in the picture.

Since Vito, Anthony's father, only had one child, the transition to the second generation had been very simple. However, the transition to the third generation by Anthony was much more complex.

The answer to Anthony and his problems would have been to establish tiebreaking mechanisms—like an independent board of directors—within the company during his lifetime. Anthony could then have selected one or possibly three of the directors to serve as impartial tiebreaker after his death.

It should be noted that independent directors should not be given legal authority to make decisions except when the family is in disagreement. As long as they are in agreement, the family should run the family business.

How Does a Tiebreaking Provision Work?

Tiebreaking provisions can include a specific individual to break ties or a legal mechanism that goes into effect after the death of the owner of the business and/or that owner's spouse. Many surviving spouses do not have the business acumen to break ties, and even if they have good business judgment, do not want to be placed in the position of having to favor one child over another.

A person chosen as an impartial tiebreaker should be someone close to the owner, preferably someone who has served on the owner's board of directors and is very familiar with the business (see Chapter 3). This is always preferable to doing the job yourself. And there are many other legal mechanisms for creating impartial tiebreakers, such as using a panel of trusted business persons or letting that panel pick the impartial tiebreakers.

The following case in the Supreme Court of Wyoming illustrates the benefit of an impartial tiebreaker, in this case between two trustees.[27]

This case, and the two others with which it was consolidated, arose from a squabble among siblings over control of the family business following their father's death. Raymond Woods started Imperial Homes, Inc., a company engaged primarily in residential construction. Before his death, Raymond had established the W. R. Revocable Trust and had transferred into it his majority Imperial shares. After his death, the trust remained the majority shareholder, and the other shares were divided among Raymond's four children and his brother. The trust documents provided that sons Steven and Roger would be successor co-trustees; however, their disputes led Roger to file a lawsuit against Steven for an accounting and declaratory judgment. After various procedural skirmishes, the district court ordered the removal of both brothers; Norwest Bank Wyoming was named sole successor trustee. (The bank later merged with Wells Fargo.) Norwest exercised the trust's rights as majority shareholder and served on Imperial's board of directors. A bank trust officer was eventually named president of the company.

The Mistake: Raymond Woods' W. R. Revocable Trust should have provided for a trusted person to be the impartial tiebreaker in the event of a dispute between Steven and Roger. This friend could have then hired a competent president to run the company, and the tiebreaking director could have avoided much of the later litigation that occurred between the sons and the company. The failure of Raymond Woods to include an impartial tiebreaker provision in his succession plan resulted in a bank trust officer ultimately running his family business.

> **Worst Practice**
>
> Divide the family business 50/50 between two siblings and fail to provide for an impartial tiebreaker in case of a dispute.

Dividing the Business

Some businesses are by their nature divisible geographically, horizontally, or vertically. An example of geographic divisibility would be a retail operation with stores on both the East Coast and the West Coast. An example of a horizontal divisibility would be a food wholesale distribution business that included two divisions, one for supermarket sales and one for institutional sales. An example of a vertically divisible business would be a manufacturing company that also owns retail stores in which it sells its products.

When there is more than one child involved in the business, upon the death of the owner it is tempting to divide that business among the children geographically, horizontally, or vertically. Supposedly this avoids conflicts among the children since each has a separate business to run.

There is no clear best practice in this area. Dividing the family business may not always be practical, particularly if the individual units are too small. Sometimes dividing a business works well, but at other times, it merely leads to conflict between independent businesses each owned 100 percent by a single child. For example, the child who owns the West Coast retail stores may decide to come to the East Coast, and visa-versa. The owner should not be in the position of limiting what each child can do with the business after the owner's death.

If the Business Is Easily Divisible into Separate Businesses, Give Each Child 100 Percent of the Equity in Each of the Separate Businesses

If the family business is divisible into separate businesses, some succession plans will provide for either equal ownership among the children of the founder or majority ownership, with one child in the majority and the other child or children in the minority. This type of division tends to sow the seeds of future discord.

We have already discussed what happens when ownership is equally divided. However, even if majority ownership is given to a single child, conflict with those children in the minority should be anticipated after the death of the owner and the owner's spouse.

Best Practice

If a business is to be divided after the death of the owner and the owner's spouse, each child should preferably receive 100 percent of the equity of each separate business.

If a business is to be divided between two or more children, each child should preferably receive 100 percent of the equity of each separate business to be run by such child. The owner should attempt to avoid creating minority interests of one child in another child's business, for example, giving one child 51 percent of the equity and dividing the remaining 49 percent among those children who may also own separate businesses. A minority interest tends to lead to conflicts in the next generation.

This is easier said than done. Most owners would prefer to give each child equal value upon the owner and his spouse's death. The businesses to be divided among the children may have unequal value, and there may not be sufficient assets (e.g., real estate) to equalize each one's shares, thereby necessitating giving other children minority interests in one child's majority-owned business.

The following actual court case illustrates why it is a bad idea for the family to give a minority interest to two siblings in each others business.[28]

Jerry James is the majority shareholder in Franklin Homes, Inc., owning 57 percent of the stock. His brother Thomas is one of three minority shareholders, owning 31.11 percent of the stock. Thomas was the majority shareholder of Indies House, Inc., owning 56 percent of the stock, while Jerry, as one of two minority shareholders, held

41.5 percent. The James family had held the stock in both corporations since their incorporation, and Jerry and Thomas were involved
each business. During the trial, the Indies House was facing financial
troubles and had to be sold

At trial, Jerry introduced evidence indicating that Thomas had
paid himself excessive salaries, had paid members of his family excessive salaries, had bought automobiles for his children with corporate
funds, and had used excess corporate cash to finance loans while personally retaining the interest paid on those loans. Jerry argued that
the amount he had received from the liquidation ("sale") of Indies
House was less than it should have been because of his brother's mismanagement and theft. Since Jerry's interest in Indies House was
41.5 percent, his expert suggested an amount of damages by taking
the total amount Thomas claimed to have lost in each act of wrongdoing and multiplying it by .415. At the conclusion of the trial, the
jury awarded Jerry James the sum of $4,213,283.10 against Thomas
James, and the jury's verdict was for the most part upheld on appeal.

The Will of the Owner and the Owner's Spouse Should Provide Legal Mechanisms to Resolve Family Disputes if Equity Interests Are Given to More Than One Child

If the succession plan contemplates giving equity interests in the family business to more than one child, owners should anticipate disputes
among their children. In the absence of a legal mechanism in the Will
of the owner and the owner's spouse to resolve such issues, these
future conflicts may materially damage the family business.

Best Practice

If equity interest in the family business must be given to more
than one child in order to equalize inheritance valuations, the
Will of the owner and the owner's spouse should include legal
mechanisms that insure against destructive conflict among the
siblings.

As noted previously, once the founder of the family business passes
away or retires, it is not unusual for disputes to occur among his or
her children, grandchildren, or other relatives who are involved in the
business. Indeed, sensational litigation between family members is
very common. Such litigation is extremely expensive, diverts the

management's time away from the business, and often results in the sale or failure of the business.

Family businesses are particularly susceptible to disputes because business issues and emotional personal issues get intertwined. When sibling rivalry mixes with genuine business disagreements, the results can be disastrous.

There are many causes of family conflict. Family businesses encompass two competing systems, business and family. The business contacts encourage productivity and profitability whereas the family contacts encourage nurturing and acceptance. These different values make it difficult to manage the complex roles and relationships of family and business. A few of the focal points for conflicts are differing visions concerning the business, succession, jealousy, poor communication, poor conflict management skills, and inequality in rewards.[29] Very wealthy families have been known to have extreme conflicts over philanthropy decisions.

Many family businesses do not last beyond the second or third generation because of this heady mixture of emotion and business. They are usually sold, liquidated, or end up in bankruptcy.

These unfortunate results can be avoided if the founder, while still in control of the business, establishes a dispute resolution mechanism using independent directors to resolve the disputes. An example of a dispute resolution mechanism that was upheld by the courts, involving Hanover Foods Corporation, is discussed in Chapter 3.

Many family disputes are the result of poor succession planning by the prior generation. Chapter 4 describes four litigations involving family businesses that were the result of defective succession planning. Three of the litigations were the result of failing to provide an impartial tiebreaker for next-generation disputes, and one was the result of the failure to provide reasonable severance and a clawback mechanism (i.e., a provision that the family members lose their severance payments if they litigate their employment termination) in the succession plan.

The legal mechanisms in the Will can include impartial tiebreaker provisions and put and call provisions that are given to both the majority and the minority equity holders. Under a put and call provision, a majority equity holder has the option (the "call") to purchase the minority interests at an independently appraised value, with payments spread over a number of years plus interest.

The minority equity holders could be given a "put," i.e., an option to force the company to buy back the minority equity, with yearly payments (plus interest) limited to a small percentage of cash flow from operations (as determined by the independent accounting firm), in order to avoid burdening the cash flow of the business, along with other payment-limiting protections. For example, if the minority equity holders decide to exercise the put, they are limited to yearly payments (plus interest) not to exceed 10 percent of cash flow from operations, and in no event can the payments cause a default under any bank or other financial institution loan to the business or otherwise cause the business to become insolvent, as determined by its board of directors.

If the child with the minority interest is also employed in the business, consideration should be given to protecting that child from termination by the provision of a generous severance arrangement. The severance arrangement should be subject to a clawback, i.e., forfeiture, if that child brings legal suit to challenge the employment termination. (See Chapter 4 for the Squabbling Brothers litigation.)

Dispute Resolution Mechanisms in Charter

Dispute resolution provisions placed solely in shareholder agreements or in Wills may not necessarily be specifically enforced by the courts. The courts may decide that the sole remedy for violating the dispute resolution mechanism in a shareholders agreement or in the Will is damages.

> **Best Practice**
>
> Establish tiebreaker and other dispute resolution mechanisms in the charter of the family businesses which is automatically effective once the founder dies or retires.

The best practice is to establish tiebreaker and other dispute-resolution provisions in the charter of the family business, which would automatically become effective once the founder dies or retires. In the case of a corporation, the articles or certificate of incorporation is the charter, and in the case of a limited liability company, the certificate of organization and the operating agreement are the charter. Dispute resolution provisions that are placed in the charter of the family business are much more likely to be specifically enforced by the courts.

Pruning the Family Tree

> **Best Practice**
>
> Family members who do not share common values with the rest of the family should be eliminated from the business. Multigenerational family businesses should consider simplifying its structure ("pruning the family tree") by reducing the number of family shareholders, splitting up the business, reducing the number of family managers, and otherwise simplifying the governance structure.

It has been suggested that family members who do not share common values with the rest of the family should be pruned from the business in order to eliminate destructive conflict.[30] This prevents the family from becoming fractionalized, leading personal relationships within the family business on a downward spiral.

Multigenerational family businesses are inevitably confronted with greater internal complexity. They tend to have large numbers of inactive shareholders and to be engaged in a number of different businesses that can be split between family members. Likewise, these multigenerational family businesses may have a complex governance structure and a large number of family managers.

There are advantages and disadvantages in simplifying these advanced-stage family businesses. For example, purchasing the equity of inactive shareholders may simplify the business but may also deprive it of capital needed for expansion.

At a minimum, the issue of "pruning" should be considered by all multigenerational family businesses.[31]

Family Businesses More Than 100 Years Old

The author has interviewed the members of a number of family businesses that are over 100 years old. Although each one is unique, they share many of the following characteristics, the first of which is the most important:

- The family business presents a good economic opportunity for family members compared to their alternative careers.
- The family business typically involves a staple product or service such as food manufacture or distribution or, in the case of Kongo Gumi (see article below), Buddhist temple construction.

- The family has developed mechanisms to resolve disputes within the family, including purchasing equity from unhappy family members without resorting to major litigation that ruptures family ties and leads to selling.

Appendix 1 of this book contains a speech by Phil Clemens, the Chairman and CEO of Clemens Family Corporation, which is well over 100 years old. His speech contains insights as to how Clemens Family Co. has survived as long as it has.

There are even family businesses that have survived over 1,000 years, as illustrated by the *Business Week* article, "The End of a 1,400-Year-Old Business" by James Olan Hutcheson. The article's headline reads: "What entrepreneurs starting family businesses can learn from the demise of Japanese temple builder Kongo Gumi":

The world's oldest continuously operating family business ended its impressive run last year. Japanese temple builder Kongo Gumi, in operation under the founders' descendants since 578, succumbed to excess debt and an unfavorable business climate in 2006.

How do you make a family business last for 14 centuries? Kongo Gumi's case suggests that it's a good idea to operate in a stable industry. Few industries could be less flighty than Buddhist temple construction. The belief system has survived for thousands of years and has many millions of adherents. With this firm foundation, Kongo had survived some tumultuous times, notably the 19th century Meiji restoration when it lost government subsidies and began building commercial buildings for the first time. But temple construction had until recently been a reliable mainstay, contributing 80% of Kongo Gumi's $67.6 million in 2004 revenues.

Keys to Success

Kongo Gumi also boasted some internal positives that enabled it to survive for centuries. Its last president, Masakazu Kongo, was the 40th member of the family to lead the company. He has cited the company's flexibility in selecting leaders as a key factor in its longevity. Specifically, rather than always handing reins to the oldest son, Kongo Gumi chose the son who best exhibited the health, responsibility, and talent for the job. Furthermore, it wasn't always a son. The 38th Kongo to lead the company was Masakazu's grandmother.

Another factor that contributed to Kongo Gumi's extended existence was the practice of sons-in-law taking the family name when they joined the family firm. This common Japanese practice allowed the company to continue under the same name, even when there were no sons in a given generation.

So if you want your family business to last a long time, the story of Kongo Gumi says you should mingle elements of conservatism and flexibility—stay in the same business for more than a millennium and vary from the principle of primogeniture as needed to preserve the company. The combination allowed Kongo Gumi to survive some notable hard times, such as when it switched temporarily to crafting coffins during World War II.

Burst Bubble

The circumstances of Kongo Gumi's demise also offer some lessons. Despite its incredible history, it was a set of ordinary circumstances that brought Kongo Gumi down at last. Two factors were primarily responsible. First, during the 1980s bubble economy in Japan, the company borrowed heavily to invest in real estate. After the bubble burst in the 1992–93 recession, the assets secured by Kongo Gumi's debt shrank in value. Second, social changes in Japan brought about declining contributions to temples. As a result, demand for Kongo Gumi's temple-building services dropped sharply beginning in 1998.

By 2004, revenues were down 35%. Masakazu Kongo laid off employees and tightened budgets. But in 2006, the end arrived. The company's borrowings had ballooned to $343 million and it was no longer possible to service the debt. In January, the company's assets were acquired by Takamatsu, a large Japanese construction company, and it was absorbed into a subsidiary.

To sum up the lessons of Kongo Gumi's long tenure and ultimate failure: Pick a stable industry and create flexible succession policies. To avoid a similar demise, evolve as business conditions require, but don't get carried away with temporary enthusiasms and sacrifice financial stability for what looks like an opportunity. These lessons are somewhat contradictory and paradoxical, to be sure. But if sustained success came easy, then all family businesses would have a 1,428-year run.[32]

Chapter 2 of this book discusses family employee agreements and shareholder agreements that are important not only in succession planning but also in the protection of the business during the lifetime of the owner.

CHAPTER 2

Family Employee Agreements and Shareholder Agreements[1]

Many family businesses suffer from the failure to have legally effective and well-drafted family employee agreements and family shareholder agreements.

The purpose of this chapter is to discuss best practices relating to two types of agreements:

- An agreement with family members who become employees of the business, whether or not they own equity in the business.
- A shareholder agreement with family members who own equity in the business.

The discussion of shareholder agreements will also review best practices for avoiding the problems that result when family members who are shareholders divorce. Finally, we will consider shareholder liquidity plans for family businesses that provide cash to shareholders in the event of certain emergencies or other pressing needs.

Utilize Family Employee Agreements

Many family businesses hire family members without requiring them to sign an employee agreement that restricts their right to use confidential information (such as customer lists) and prevents them from soliciting customers or employees of the family business in the event that their employment is terminated. This failure can result in significant harm to the family business if a family member leaves it.

Best Practice

No family member can become an employee of the business until first signing an agreement protecting the business against the use of confidential information, solicitation of customers or employees, or accepting orders from customers for a period of time after employment termination.[2] A similar employment agreement should be signed by the owner.

It is a best practice for every employee of any business to sign an employee agreement prior to and as a condition of commencing employment. Depending upon the nature of the business, the agreement should contain, at minimum, the following:

- The employee agrees to maintain the confidentiality of nonpublic information obtained during the course of the employment, such as methods of doing business, trade secrets, customer and employee lists, and so forth.
- The employee agrees to transfer to the company any inventions made during the course of the employment, whether during working hours or otherwise, which directly or indirectly relate to the business.
- The employee agrees to be restricted from soliciting former customers or employees and from accepting orders from former customers for a one- to two-year period following termination.

Family-owned businesses that require all non-family employees to sign an employee agreement often do not require employed family members to sign such an agreement. This is a bad practice and can boomerang against the family business.

Example No. 1:

Ben starts and grows a business that employs 20 people and has over $5 million in sales. Ben and his wife, Sarah, have three children, one boy and two girls. The oldest is David, the second oldest is Esther, and the third is Elizabeth. When David graduates from college at age 23, he joins the family business. Although Ben believes in employee agreements, he considers David exempt because he loves his son and does not believe that David would do anything to harm the family. David is put in charge of a customer relations function and is very helpful in growing the business, to the point where the revenues are over $15 million. At age 29, David marries Beverly. But Beverly comes from a wealthy family and soon grows unhappy with her standard of living. She presses David to either increase his annual salary to at least $500,000, with a significant equity stake, or leave the business. Ben tries to alleviate the issue by increasing David's salary to $300,000 and giving him 30 percent of the business, keeping in mind his two other children who may wish to enter the business. But this doesn't satisfy Beverly, who envies the high standard of living enjoyed by her friends. Family relations become strained. Ben's wife has taken to referring to her daughter-in-law as "Beverly the Bitch." Ultimately, a rival offers David $500,000 per year and a 49 percent share of the company, provided that he brings over the customers he served while working for his father. David accepts. The family business is severely injured by the loss of major customers as a result of his defection.

The failure to get David to sign an employee agreement was the result of Ben's bad decision to treat employed family members differently than other employees. He assumed he was protecting his family by exempting David from an employee agreement, when, in fact, he was disregarding the rest of his family's interests, jeopardizing the business.

Example No. 2:

Soon after David joins the family business at age 23, Ben has the opportunity to hire a hotshot salesperson, George. Ben successfully negotiates with George for salary and benefits. However, George is unwilling to sign an employee agreement that restricts his right to solicit customers of the business after termination of his employment. George cites the fact that neither David nor Ben has ever signed an employee agreement. Therefore, he sees no reason why he should be subjected to a nonsolicitation of customer clause just because he is not a member of the family.

It would have been helpful in negotiating with George had Ben and David signed employee agreements when they first began working at the company. Since Ben owns the company, the employee agreement signed by him is more symbolic of the culture of the company than legally binding. Ben could always waive the provisions of the agreement by virtue of his control of the board of directors. Nevertheless, establishing an employee agreement that must be signed by everyone, regardless of the family relationship, is important to protecting the family business.

Obtain Employee Agreements from Existing Family Employees by Coupling the Employee Agreement with a Phantom Equity Grant

Family businesses cannot force an existing employee (whether a family member or not) to sign an employee agreement after they have commenced employment. Therefore, some mechanism should be used to induce current employees to sign an employee agreement, such as coupling their signature with a phantom stock grant.

> **Best Practice**
>
> If the family business has not uniformly required an employee agreement to be signed by all family and non-family employees, it should consider methods to obtain one by coupling it with a phantom stock grant to employees—or at least to key employees.

It is essential that the employee agreement be signed at the commencement of employment. In general, many state laws will not enforce an employee agreement relating to post-termination solicitation of customers or employees unless there was some consideration initially given at the time of execution. That consideration can be in the form of a job for a new employee. However, for existing employees it can also take the form of a significant pay raise or bonus, a transfer to a new and more important position, or the grant of equity compensation such as a phantom stock grant. As described in Chapter 6, a phantom stock grant can be structured to be settled in cash and not stock, thereby maintaining 100 percent equity ownership in the family. Also noted in Chapter 6, a phantom stock grant can have a provision that prevents vesting unless certain events occur, such as a sale of the business or an initial public offering.

Since many family businesses fail to establish an initial requirement for employee agreement, they may still obtain the same result by coupling an employee agreement with a phantom stock grant.

Why Does the Employee Agreement Not Restrict Competition?

It is generally easier to get employees to sign an agreement restricting them from soliciting or accepting orders from the customers of the business than it is to restrict them from competing altogether. Salespeople will typically resist a restriction on competition, as most are concerned about finding another job in the same industry if their employment is terminated (either voluntarily or involuntarily).

Sometimes it is possible to obtain a noncompetition agreement applicable only if the employee quits voluntarily. However, even that more limited noncompetition provision is usually very difficult to obtain.

Can an Employee Agreement Backfire?

In our example, we suggested that it was a best practice for Ben, the founder, to personally sign an employee agreement to demonstrate to his employees that everyone has signed such an agreement. Can this backfire? Yes, if he loses control of the board of directors or the board of managers of the business.

Example:

Ben has an affair with Zoe, his bookkeeper. His wife Sarah finds out about it and is so distraught that she divorces him. Under applicable state law, Sarah is entitled to half of Ben's equity in the business. Since Ben has given his son David 30 percent of the voting stock, Ben is left with 70 percent of the voting stock and must give 35 percent to Sarah. Now holding the majority of the voting stock, David and Sarah take control of the board of directors and fire Ben. Ben tries to start a new business but has signed an employee agreement that prohibits him from soliciting his own customers.

Of course, Ben's biggest mistake was having an affair with Zoe. From a legal perspective, however, his mistake was not signing the employee agreement but giving 30 percent of the voting stock to David. Had he given David non-voting stock or given the stock subject to a voting trust in his favor, Ben would never have lost control of the board of directors.

Since a divorce and subsequent property settlement are always possibilities, it is dangerous for a founder to give away even as little as 1 percent of the voting stock to a family member without a voting trust in the founder's favor. If there is a subsequent divorce and property settlement, that 1 percent could, when added to 50 percent of the founder's remaining shares, be used by the founder's spouse to deprive the founder of control.

No Family Member Should Receive Equity in the Family Business without Signing a Shareholder Agreement

If stock or other equity in the family business is given or sold to a family member without requiring the member to sign a legally enforceable and well-drafted shareholder agreement, the business is subject to major legal risks. These risks, discussed below in more detail, include the possibility of the stock or other equity being transferred to people outside the family, such as creditors of the family member.

Best Practice

No family members can become owners unless they first sign a shareholder agreement (or operating agreement in the case of a limited liability company) that protects the family business and its other shareholders.

No family member should be given equity in the business unless he or she has first executed a shareholder agreement. A shareholder agreement should protect both the family business and each of the other shareholders against the following threats and risks (among others):

- Sales, gifts, or other transfers to non-family members (The best practice is to completely prohibit such things).
- Pledges of the equity that include, but are not limited to, pledges to third persons such as banks and other financial institutions as collateral for loans, which can, in the event of a loan default, result in the foreclosure of the equity by the lender and its sale outside the family or retention of the equity by the lender in partial or full satisfaction of the loan (The best practice is to completely prohibit pledges of equity).
- Transfers that destroy the tax status of the family business, such as a transfer that destroys the Subchapter S status of the family business, or refusals to join in execution of documents necessary to preserve the tax status of the family business (The best practice is to prohibit such transfers).
- Refusals to cooperate in the formation of a holding company for the family business that has been approved by the business' board of directors (The best practice is to require the transfer of stock to the holding company in exchange for holding company stock if such transfer has been approved by the board of directors).
- Refusals to join in any sale of the stock of the family business that has been approved by its board of directors or exercising dissenters rights of appraisal in connection with a merger approved

by the board of directors (The best practice is to insert a so-called drag-along clause in the shareholder agreement which would require such joinder and provide that exercise of dissenter's rights of appraisal creates an offer to sell the stock below the market price).

- Exercising the shareholder's right of inspection of books and records under state law that may reveal confidential information (The best practice is to prohibit such exercise and provide that any such exercise creates an offer to sell the stock at a below market price).
- Taking hostile action against the family business, such as establishing a competing business, soliciting employees or customers to leave the family business, bringing claims and law suits against the family business, etc. (The best practice is to prohibit any such hostile action and to provide that any such hostile action creates an offer to sell the stock below the market price).
- The threat of divorce, which is discussed below (The best practice is to use irrevocable spendthrift trusts to protect against divorce).

Each of these threats and risks to the family business can be ameliorated by provisions in the shareholder agreement. For example, the shareholder agreement can contain a noncompetition agreement and provide remedies for the breach of that covenant, such as the right of the family business to either buy back the equity of that shareholder at below market price or cause the forfeiture of the equity of that shareholder.

The need for a so-called drag-along clause in a family business shareholder agreement is supported not only by actual experiences but also by academic studies of sales of control blocks in family firms.[3] The studies indicate that families are not monolithic and that their ties can be insufficient for insuring that the interests of all owners coincide.[4]

It is important to use an attorney familiar with the threats and risks facing the family business to draft such a shareholder agreement.

In addition to the threats and risks cited above, the owners of the family business must decide whether to permit formerly employed family members who either left voluntarily or were fired for cause to remain shareholders. If they are not to remain shareholders, one possible solution is to provide that a voluntary quit or termination for cause creates an offer from the family shareholder that the family business can, at any time accept based upon some valuation formula. The valuation formula need not be actual fair market value but a net book value or other agreed value formula that would apply when the offer was accepted. The shareholder agreement should indicate whether or not a minority and illiquidity discount should be applied in determining the value of shares to be repurchased by the company or its other stockholders pursuant to any such offer. In the absence of a specific provision in the shareholder agreement, experts in valuation would typically take a minority and illiquidity discount.

Do Not Require a Unanimous Vote to Amend a Shareholder Agreement

Shareholder agreements need to be amended from time to time as circumstances change. It is important to avoid provisions that require unanimous consent of all family shareholders for any amendment to the agreement. A unanimous consent clause gives each family member a complete veto over any amendment, even if the majority of the shareholders might favor it.

> **Worst Practice**
>
> Requiring a unanimous vote of all family shareholders in order to amend a shareholder agreement.

It is important to make the shareholder agreement amendable by a vote of the shareholders with the majority of the voting stock. Typically this will give the founder, who usually owns a majority of the voting stock, the power of amendment. Occasionally, a higher percentage than a bare majority is considered desirable, such as two-thirds or three-quarters. Regardless of the percentage used, it is important to avoid a unanimity requirement except in unusual circumstances.

Consider a Shareholder Agreement Provision Requiring Minority Shareholders to Sell Their Stock

A common cause of conflict in family businesses is disagreements among the shareholders. Using best practices should permit a reasonable resolution of these disputes. However, as discussed in Chapter 1, there are a few occasions when it is best to remove a minority family shareholder for the sake of the business (i.e., a "pruning the family tree"). Since this is an extreme measure, it should be reserved for extreme cases.

Best Practice

Consideration should be given to inserting a provision in shareholder agreements that permits the board of directors to force the sale of stock by minority shareholders back to the family business or to other shareholders at the stock's current fair market value. Appropriate protection should be given in the event the business or its stock is sold at a higher price in the future.

Consideration should be given to a provision in the shareholder agreement that gives the board of directors the power to force minority shareholders to sell their stock in the business. It is preferable to limit this power to the founder of the business during his or her lifetime and then to the independent members of the board of directors after the death of the founder. In appropriate cases this power can also be given to the founder's surviving spouse. Indeed, many widows do extremely well in managing the family business after the death of their husband.[5]

Because this is a drastic remedy, the purchase price should be very fair to the minority family member. Therefore, the shareholder agreement should provide that, in valuing the stock of the minority shareholder, there be no minority or illiquidity discount and a nationally recognize independent appraiser determine the purchase price. Furthermore, the agreement should provide that if the business or its stock is sold at a higher price within a reasonable period thereafter, the selling minority shareholder would receive the benefit of that higher price. Because this provision forces the minority shareholder to sell at the option of the company (acting through its board of directors), the purchase price should be paid in cash at closing and not in installments.

The disadvantage of this provision is that it permits the controlling shareholder to force a sale of the stock by a minority shareholder. Because of the dangers for abuse in this provision, the ability to force such a sale should be stringently limited. For example, it might be limited to inactive shareholders (i.e., shareholders not employed in the family business).

Not every family business will adopt this type of provision, nor should they. However, it is very useful for ridding the family business of obstreperous or litigious minority shareholders. The best practice is to at least *consider* such a provision in the shareholder agreement.

Shareholder Agreements Should Protect the Family Business from the Risk of Divorce

Divorce is the enemy of family businesses. It has been estimated that approximately 50 percent of all modern marriages today will end in divorce.[6] The stock of the business may be considered a marital asset, depending upon state law. In a property settlement, family members who own stock in the business may, depending upon the state law, be required to transfer up to one-half or more of their stock to the divorcing spouse.

Best Practice

Shareholder agreements should attempt to protect the shareholders and the family business from the risk of divorce.

Having a former spouse as an equity owner of the business can create all sorts of problems, including the following:

- Ex-spouses who are shareholders of the corporation typically would have the right to review books and records of the family business.
- Ex-spouses who are shareholders of the corporation would have the right to receive dividends from the business and profit from the appreciation of the equity of the business.
- Ex-spouses who are shareholders of the corporation may be able to commence legal actions directly against the directors, officers or majority shareholders for breach of fiduciary duty.
- Ex-spouses who are shareholders of the corporation may have the right to bring derivative action on behalf of the corporation against its directors and officers and possibly against its majority shareholders.

Example:

In the example given earlier in this chapter, suppose David resists Beverly's demand that he leave the business. Infuriated, Beverly moves out of their house and ultimately divorces David. Under state law, the 30 percent of the equity of the business owned by David may be considered a marital asset, and Beverly may be entitled to become owner of 15 percent of the equity of the business. Ben and Sarah decide that there is no way that "Beverly the Bitch" is going to own a part of their business and are forced to pay an excessive amount of money to induce her to sell that 15 percent. This result could have been avoided by the kind of well-structured shareholder agreement discussed below.

Shareholder Agreements Should Require Forfeiture of Equity if a Prenuptial Agreement Is Not Signed

Family equity owners may marry without having their intended spouse sign a legally effective and well structured prenuptial agreement. The failure to obtain such an agreement could result in the spouse owning equity in the business after the divorce, equity that must be redeemed for cash by the family business.

Example:

Suppose that, in the prior example, the 30 percent equity had been given to David before he married Beverly. Unless Beverly signed a prenuptial agreement waiving her rights to the equity of the business, she would, upon marrying David, receive certain rights to the stock depending upon state law. Some states would not treat the equity owned by David as a marital asset to be divided with Beverly, some would treat only the post-marital appreciation of the equity as a marital asset (depending on whether or not the appreciation was the result of post-marital efforts, in some states), and some (e.g., Connecticut, depending upon the circumstances) might treat even premarital assets, such as the equity, as part of the assets to be divided. State laws keep changing and there is no one answer that is true throughout the United States.

> **Best Practice**
>
> A shareholder agreement must provide for a forfeiture of the equity of the family business if the family member does not enter into a valid prenuptial agreement waiving any rights of the spouse to the equity of the business.

There are four methods of protecting equity given to a family member from the risk of divorce:

- Prenuptial Agreements with the intended spouse[7]
- Postnuptial Agreements with the spouse
- Irrevocable Spendthrift Trusts for the benefit of the family member and their issue (see "Irrevocable Spendthrift Trust" later in this chapter); and
- Conditional gifts

The gold standard for protecting the family business from the risk of divorce is to transfer stock or other equity of the business through an Irrevocable Spendthrift Trust. This technique only works if the shares or other equity have not already been previously transferred outright to a family member. If the shares or other equity have been previously transferred, the divorce risk should be covered in the shareholders' agreement For example, the shareholders' agreement could provide for forfeiture of the family member's equity interest if that family member does not enter into a legally effective prenuptial agreement prior to marriage, or if already married, does not enter into a valid postnuptial agreement (to the extent permitted by state law).

Assuming that the intended or existing spouse is willing to sign either a valid prenuptial or valid postnuptial agreement, why should the shareholders' agreement continue to require a forfeiture of equity if such an agreement is not obtained in the future? Simply because people marry more than once.

Example:

When David receives his 30 percent equity interest in the company, Beverly agrees to waive her marital rights to the equity. Subsequently, David and Beverly divorce. David then marries Kathleen. Unfortunately, David did not obtain a prenuptial agreement from Kathleen before the marriage. Kathleen and David subsequently divorce and Kathleen claims her right to 15 percent of the equity of the business.

Some leaders of family businesses might view the remedy of equity forfeiture for failing to obtain a prenuptial agreement as excessive. The author can assure the readers of this book that this is the dominant view of domestic relations lawyers with whom the author has spoken. Anything short of forfeiture permits equity to be owned by ex-spouses who are not necessarily friendly to the business and invites harassing law suits by their lawyers to extract excessive payment from the business.

The shareholder agreement should provide that the prenuptial agreement be in form and substance satisfactory to the company. The company should issue a written approval if the prenuptial agreement is satisfactory in form and substance.

Protecting Against Invalid Prenuptial Agreements

In a contested divorce case, it is not unusual for one spouse to challenge the validity of the prenuptial agreement. There is always a risk that a court will invalidate a prenuptial agreement.

Best Practice

The stockholders' agreement must protect against a subsequent judicial declaration that a prenuptial agreement is invalid.

To protect the family business from this event, the stockholders' agreement must provide for automatic forfeiture of the equity if there is a judicial decree invalidating the prenuptial agreement as a whole or as to the waiver by the spouse of the rights to equity in the family business.

Each state has its own criteria for invaliding a prenuptial agreement. The most typical defense to a prenuptial agreement's validity is the failure to make full disclosure of assets to the spouse waiving his or her rights. However, there are many other defenses.

For example, Connecticut has enacted its version of the Uniform Premarital Agreement Act, which applies to any premarital agreement executed on or after October 1, 1995. Under this law, premarital agreements can be set aside in the following circumstances, among others, because:

- "Such party did not execute the agreement voluntarily."
- "The agreement was unconscionable when it was executed or when enforcement is sought."
- "Before execution of the agreement, such party was not provided a fair and reasonable disclosure of the amount, character and value of property, financial obligations and income of the other party."[8]

- Such party was not afforded a reasonable opportunity to consult with independent counsel.
- There was a finding of duress.

In a case decided by the Connecticut Supreme Court, the court held that the spouse against whom the premarital agreement is to be enforced must be afforded sufficient time before execution of the agreement to consult with an attorney other than the attorney representing that party's future spouse.[9]

At some time in the marriage, the parties may have resided in a state that traditionally favors upholding prenuptial agreements. However, the parties may subsequently move to a state more ready to nullify prenuptial agreements.

Given the ambiguities of state law, it is important that the shareholder agreement provide for an automatic forfeiture of the equity in a family business if, at any time, there is a judicial decree invalidating the prenuptial agreement as a whole or the provision waiving the rights to equity in a family business.

A form for a New York Prenuptial Agreement is contained in Appendix 2.

A Side Benefit of a Shareholder Agreement Containing a Forfeiture Clause

When two people are in love, it is very difficult for one of them to ask the other to sign a prenuptial agreement. It causes a breach in trust.

However, if obtaining a prenuptial agreement is required in order to permit one of the spouses to retain equity ownership in the business, it may be an easier sell. For example, if David were to say to Beverly before the marriage that he would forfeit his equity in the family business if Beverly did not sign a prenuptial agreement, Beverly would have to think twice about this difficult choice. David might say that he loves Beverly so much that he would be willing to sacrifice all of his equity in the business in order to marry her, thereby giving Beverly the choice of permitting David to retain or lose this equity. Since this equity could be very valuable for Beverly in the future, it might induce Beverly to consent.

Having said this, there is no assurance that Beverly would ever sign a prenuptial agreement, even if her failure to do so forced David to forfeit his equity under the terms of the shareholder agreement. In addition, David may ask his father Ben to waive this requirement in the shareholder agreement. As is typical in most family situations, there is no perfect solution.

Transfers after Marriage and Postnuptial Agreements

The following are the facts in an actual court case that illustrate a typical problem in making a direct gift to a child after marriage. In 1980, Kent Jardine married Julie McVey. During their marriage, Julie's father, John, gave stock to Julie in all three of the family corporations. In 2003, Kent filed for divorce. In the property settlement agreement, Kent received payment for the one-half interest he claimed in the stock held by Julie in the family corporations.[10]

In the court case, John titled the shares solely in Julie's name. However, Kent nevertheless received payment for a one-half interest in the stock.

Kent and Julie were married for twenty-three years. How would John feel if they were married for only two years and then divorced, with Kent receiving payment for a significant interest in the stock?

In the event of divorce, it can be very difficult to obtain a legally effective postnuptial agreement waiving the right of a spouse to receive a portion of the equity of the family business that was gifted after the marriage. The courts will examine the disclosures made to the spouse in detail to determine if full disclosure was made and the spouse was properly represented by separate independent counsel when fully negotiating the arrangement. Also, some states do not enforce postnuptial agreements (e.g., Connecticut) or require consideration (e.g., New York).

Although transfers of equity by parents to children through gift and/or sale after the marriage of a child can be conditioned on the child's spouse giving written consent to forfeit certain spousal rights, there is no guarantee that this waiver would be legally upheld in every state. In fact, as noted above, it is normally harder to enforce postnuptial agreements than prenuptial agreements. This is particularly true if the stock is sold to the child using jointly owned funds to pay the purchase price.

However, execution of a written waiver of spousal rights to the stock may be seen not as a postnuptial agreement, but as a condition imposed upon the gift by the donor. Thus, if John donated equity to his daughter conditioned on a waiver of spousal rights by Kent to the gifted equity, it is more likely that this condition will be enforced, subject to two caveats. First, in the event of a divorce and property settlement, Julie may have to use more of her non-business assets to compensate Kent, as some state laws provide for a distributive award instead of the division of certain assets in kind. But this is not a terrible result since it still protects the family business. The second caveat is that there is no guarantee this condition will be upheld by the courts. Accordingly, the gift should contain the condition that in the event of a judicial decree invalidating the waiver of spousal rights, the equity would be forfeited.

Irrevocable Spendthrift Trusts

Depending upon state law, John could have protected the stock he gifted to Julie by transferring the stock to an irrevocable spendthrift trust for the benefit of her and her issue, instead of transferring the stock to her directly. The trust would protect the shares from the claims of Julie's creditors, which might include her husband after the divorce.

In addition, the irrevocable spendthrift trust could contain a right of the trustees (which trustees could have included John's spouse, but not John) to change the beneficiary from Julie to her issue if the spendthrift provision was legally ineffective to protect against claims by Julie's ex-spouse. This provision may not work in every state, but it is certainly worthwhile reviewing with an attorney before making gifts to family members.

An example of such an irrevocable spendthrift trust is contained in Appendix 3 of this book. Unfortunately, an irrevocable spendthrift trust cannot reserve voting rights to the owner/settlor of the trust without creating an estate tax issue upon the death of owner/settlor. Therefore, it is best to transfer non-voting stock to the irrevocable spendthrift trust in order to avoid compromising the control of the owner of the family business.

Conditional Gifts

Depending upon state law, gifts of equity can be made to family members subject to a condition (a "condition subsequent") that the gift will be forfeited (possibly to another family member) if the recipient of the gift does not obtain an effective prenuptial or postnuptial agreement to waive any marital rights to the gifted equity. Since state laws vary as to the validity of a condition subsequent and it is difficult to determine what state law will ultimately apply, the irrevocable spendthrift trust is generally a better mechanism to protect equity of the family business from the divorce risk.

Again, it is preferable to make a gift of non-voting stock in order to avoid compromising the control of the family business.

Example:

If, in the prior example, David received his 30 percent equity interest in the business *after* marrying Beverly, the stock transfer to him (typically either by gift from Ben or a combination of gift and sale) could be conditioned in a postnuptial agreement (if permitted by state law) in which Beverly waived her spousal rights to the equity. If Beverly did not waive her spousal rights, the gift (or gift/sale) would not be completed.

However, even if Beverly waived her right to the equity, that would not affect the right of any future spouse of David after his divorce from Beverly to obtain rights in the equity owned by David. The only way to protect against that risk is to not give the stock outright to David but instead transfer the stock to an irrevocable spendthrift trust or to use the forfeiture provisions in the shareholder agreement previously discussed.

Shareholder Liquidity Programs

Stock or other equity of a family business is not a liquid asset and cannot normally be sold. Many family businesses do not declare dividends on their equity except to the extent required to pay income taxes for tax flow-through entities, such as Subchapter S corporations and limited liability companies. A major source of conflict in family businesses is the desire for liquidity of family shareholders, particularly inactive ones (i.e., those who are not also employees of the business). Even active shareholders need liquidity from time to time.

> **Best Practice**
>
> Family businesses should maintain a liquidity fund to provide, on a voluntary basis, liquidity to shareholders through sale of some of their stock back to the company or to other family members.

Although shares of a privately held business may appreciate in value over time, there is no market for these shares or any other method of realizing this appreciation apart from a liquidity fund.

A liquidity fund permits shareholders to receive some money while defusing shareholder demands for higher cash dividends or the sale of the family business. Since not every family business can afford such liquidity, any purchases of shares by the company should be voluntary. There should be no legal requirement in a shareholder agreement for a liquidity fund.

Shareholder liquidity programs should permit limited sales of the shares by family members back to the business in order to fund the purchase of a home, college education, or other emergencies affecting family shareholders.

In the next chapter, we review corporate governance structures for family businesses that are not only important to succession planning but also help resolve family conflicts within the business.

CHAPTER 3

Governance Structures for Family Businesses

T his chapter describes the best corporate governance structures for a family business. Family firms range from very small "mom and pop" businesses to multigenerational, advanced-stage companies with many shareholders. The best practices recommended in this chapter must be tempered by the size and stage of development of the family firm.

For example, a very small family business consisting of a husband and wife may not want a board of advisors or a board of directors, whereas this is clearly the best practice for a larger, more advanced family business. However, even a small husband and wife business should consider having an impartial advisor to resolve spousal business disputes and should also consider a more formal structure (either a board of directors or a board of advisors) if and when children are to be admitted into the family business.

No single corporate governance structure will fit every family business. Therefore, each business must develop its own structure to suit its needs.[1]

Establishing Governance Structures

Many family businesses exist without a formal governance structure. The owner makes decisions and never consults anyone else. The owner never obtains impartial advice from qualified third persons who can help settle business conflicts and also help the business to grow and expand. As a result, many family businesses suffer from a lack of fresh ideas.

> **Best Practice**
>
> Create a board of advisors or board of directors with independent persons of outstanding credentials.

Successful family businesses establish effective governance structures that separate personal issues from business problems. One such governance structure is a board of advisors or board of directors, which should be considered by every family business except the very smallest, as noted above.

Independent directors are the sole actors at the highest level of firm governance with the capacity to bring appropriate detachment to bear in resolving difficult questions that implicate both family ties and business necessity (e.g., management succession and external threats to the firm's position and separate existence). Independent directors may help assure the board focuses on pertinent issues despite the distracting influence or overhang of frictions within the founding family.[2] The board can also be helpful in analyzing and developing a strategic plan and a succession plan for the business, both of which are critical to its success.[3]

Establishing a board of directors that includes independent directors helps insulate and protect the owner, who must make difficult decisions that can adversely affect some family members. If the owner must reduce the compensation of a son or terminate his employment for the good of the business, independent directors can provide some cover for the owner within the family. The mother of the son who is terminated (typically the father's current wife) may give her husband a great deal of flack for his decision. But if the decision is made unanimously by independent directors he obtains some protection from emotional backlash from his family.

Likewise, a succession question can be turned over to the board because, regardless of how clear the qualification of a particular successor, it is "absolute torture" for the founder to pick one child over another.[4]

In addition, the board of directors can provide benefits to the family business, such as:

- providing valuable business advice;
- offering access to external resources such as information, expertise and networks;[5]
- providing industry expertise;

- providing fresh business ideas; and
- assisting the business to establishing new and beneficial customer or supplier relationships.

If the right persons are on the board of directors, they can serve as a sounding board for difficult business decisions and provide helpful critique to the owner.

Finally, after the death of the owner and the owner's spouse, outstanding members of the board of directors can serve as tiebreakers in case of conflict among the siblings or cousins of the next generation.

It is preferable to have a majority of independent directors on the family business' board of directors. The owner would also be a director. The owner could control the board of directors by having multiple votes as a director to the extent permitted by state law. Even if state law does not permit multiple director votes by the owner, almost all state laws allow the holder of a majority of the outstanding voting stock to remove directors without cause (assuming the board is not classified as to terms of office). Therefore, the owner should not be concerned about losing control of the board of directors.

It is preferable not to have family member employees other than the owner on the board of directors, since the board will be making compensation decisions that could affect other family members.

Board of Advisors versus Board of Directors

Many outstanding individuals do not want to serve on a board of directors because of the potential legal liability. This problem can usually be solved by either obtaining director and officer (D & O) liability insurance or establishing a board of advisors. Most people believe that serving on an advisory board does not carry the same legal liability as serving on a board of directors. Accordingly, if the owners are not willing to pay for D & O liability insurance, they should establish a board of advisors.

The board of advisors may have one advantage over a board of directors. Board of advisors members may believe their lack of fiduciary duties allows them to be more candid when dealing with the founders and owners of the business.

Obtain D & O Insurance for Family Businesses

Family businesses may be unable to obtain qualified independent persons to serve on a board of directors or advisors without director and officer liability insurance. Even without a board of directors or a board of advisors, the owner of a private family business should consider D & O insurance since it protects the owner as well as the relatives who are directors and officers from third party lawsuits.

Best Practice

Private family businesses should consider obtaining D & O insurance, including coverage for employment practices liability claims and fiduciary liability claims.

Many suits against private companies are employment-practices liability claims. In the Towers Perrin 2008 Directors and Officers Liability Survey, it was reported that 44.9 percent of all claims made in the last ten years against the private companies included in the survey were made by employees. Many D & O insurance policies for private companies include employment practices liability insurance, which covers claims from employees (including potential and former employees) alleging a variety of wrongful acts (e.g., discrimination, harassment, wrongful termination, etc.).

Fiduciary liability insurance should also be purchased either as a stand-alone policy or as an endorsement to the company's D & O liability policy. According to the Towers Perrin survey, 50 percent of privately owned companies purchased such coverage. Fiduciary liability policy insures against claims under ERISA (Employee Retirement Income Security Act) and similar charges against the directors and officers who serve in a fiduciary capacity in connection with employee benefit plans.

In the Towers Perrin survey, shareholders made the third most frequently filed claims against directors and officers of privately held companies. Such claims constituted 11.9 percent of all claims against the privately held companies included in the survey. In a family business it is not unheard of to have a family shareholder, particularly one who is not active in the business, claim a breach of fiduciary duties by other family members who are its directors and officers.

A family business can also subject itself to claims against directors and officers under federal and state securities laws, such as when it sells stock to, or repurchases stock from, family members. Both federal and state securities laws can create personal liability for control persons of private companies, such as directors, officers, or majority shareholders. Having a D & O policy with securities law coverage can insure against these claims.

Directors and officers of privately held companies should insist upon obtaining Side A coverage as part of their D & O policy, which insures directors and officers personally and typically contains no deductible. If a bankruptcy petition is filed with respect to the family business, Side A coverage will permit the directors and officers to continue to draw on the policy without concern that the bankruptcy court will enjoin the coverage based on the claim that the drawdown depletes an asset of the bankrupt estate. Some companies obtain only Side A coverage and not Side B coverage (which insures the company to the extent it is required to indemnify directors and officers under its charter or by-laws) or Side C coverage (which insures the company for its own liability).

It is also helpful to have a so-called Excess Side A/Difference in Condition (DIC) policy that provides even broader coverage than the traditional Side A policy. DIC coverage provides "drop down" first dollar coverage if (a) the insured company is in bankruptcy and the proceeds of the D & O policy cannot be accessed, (b) the insurance company fails to pay the claim as a result of the insurer's own insolvency, or (c) the company fails to otherwise indemnify the director or officer. DIC policies should preferably be purchased from an insurer that is not providing the underlining D & O coverage since it protects the family business from the insolvency of the underlying D & O insurance carrier.

It is also preferable to purchase D & O insurance from well-capitalized insurance companies even if the premium is somewhat higher.

Any D & O insurance should be carefully reviewed by an attorney who specializes in the area.

Compensating Directors

It is difficult to attract outstanding individuals to a board of advisors or directors without providing some compensation for that role. After all, cash is nice. A cash fee can be paid for each meeting. Alternatively— and preferably—a small phantom equity grant can be made to the director payable in cash after some vesting period or upon the retirement or death of the director (see Chapter 6). Sometimes a combination of cash and a small phantom equity grant is used.

Selecting Board Members

Ideal independent directors are persons with executive skills who are knowledgeable about the industry in which the family business operates. It is important to select people who do not simply take refuge in a CEO's decision but are willing to get more deeply involved in making that decision.[6] Persons who want to serve on the board of directors merely for the prestige should be avoided.

People who know the business well (i.e., suppliers, customers, professionals, and business contacts) can provide referrals to chief executive officers, entrepreneurs, and business owners with the good business judgment and leadership experience family business owners need.[7]

Retired CEOs of companies in the same industry can be very helpful to a family business. However, most retired CEOs of public companies are looking for more lucrative board positions in other public companies and it may be difficult for a family business to compete for them. A director of a public company can easily make over $100,000 per year even with small public companies. Most family businesses do not want to pay that much to attract directors.

The owners of other private businesses in the same industry who have sold their business and are not subject to a non-compete agreement can also make excellent directors.

If the owner cannot attract candidates with specific industry experience, he or she should look for people with analogous industry experience. For example, if the family business is a manufacturer of women's clothing, candidates with experience as wholesalers or retailers of women's clothing or manufacturers of men's clothing can be helpful.

Professionals in whom the owners have confidence are also helpful. This includes accountants, attorneys, business consultants, and so on.

At the end of the day, the owner has to be comfortable with the person selected. Sometimes the only way to know this is to try that person on the board for a year and see how it works.

If the company is considering the possibility of going public, it should select persons who qualify as independent directors under the rules of the NASDAQ Stock Market, Inc. and the New York Stock Exchange.

Clemens Family Corporation, which is discussed in Appendix 1, is over 100 years old and uses the following criteria in selecting board members:

All Board members must meet the following criteria:

1. Currently a senior management individual (or recently retired) from a successful business. We prefer the individual to be the President or CEO.

2. Strong financial background and clearly understands the need and value of business metrics.
3. Unquestionable ethics and integrity.
4. Embraces the vision, values and culture of the Corporation.
5. Does not have a conflict of interest with any of the CFC businesses.

"Our philosophy is to have a Board consist of a majority of outside individuals. Both outside and inside directors (inside being defined as either they or their spouse own stock in the Corporation) must meet the same criteria. Board members are elected for a 1-year term with no limitations. We generally prefer that Board members agree to serve a minimum of three years and prefer that the service does not exceed 10 years."

Board Committees

Once a board of directors containing independent directors has been created, it should establish compensation committees and audit committees consisting solely of independent directors.

The compensation committee can help establish arm's-length compensation for family employees.

The audit committee should select the independent public accountant and oversee the management's preparation of the financial statements of the business. Financial statements should be prepared according to generally accepted principles, particularly if there is a possibility of a sale or an initial public offering. The audit committee is also responsible for determining the adequacy of internal controls, since these are essential to the integrity of the financial statements.

Define Roles of Chairman of the Board and CEO or President

Many family businesses use the title "Chairman of the Company" to refer to the founder or his or her successor as the leader of the business. This title tends to obscure two different functions: (1) the role, duties, and authority of the Chairman of the Board and (2) the role, duties, and authority of the Chief Executive Officer or President.

The failure to segregate and identify the specific duties of these roles can lead to conflict within the business once the founder installs a successor (whether or not in the family) in the position of Chief Executive Officer or President. The founder may believe that as Chairman, he or she can still establish major business policies for the company, while the Chief Executive Officer or President believes that this is his or her role.

> **Best Practice**
>
> The board of directors should assist in defining the role, duties and authority of the Chairman of the Board and the CEO or President.

One important function of independent directors is to better define the respective roles, duties, and responsibilities of the Chairman of the Board and the CEO or President once these positions have been filled by different persons. Thereafter, it is better to use the more specific "Chairman of the Board" rather than "Chairman of the Company" to distinguish it from the position of CEO or President.

Use the Board of Directors to Help Develop a Long-term Strategic Plan Utilizing Competitive Advantages

Professor John Ward believes that family businesses perform better than other businesses because,[8] among other reasons, they plan long-term and use unconventional strategies to succeed against their competitors.[9] Ward believes that capital constraints force many family businesses to develop unorthodox business strategies to obtain revenues and profits.

A knowledgeable board of directors can be useful in sharpening the thinking of the family business owner toward these unconventional strategies, as well as challenging any false assumptions he might hold. This give and take process helps focus the long-term strategy of the family business. An independent board can also prevent the natural tendency toward nepotism from over influencing a strategic succession plan.

> **Best Practice**
>
> The board of directors should assist in the development of a long-term strategic plan for the family business that incorporate the both competitive advantages of the business and succession planning.

Risk Analysis, Prioritization, and Amelioration

Very often, family business owners do not take time to critically analyze the risks of either their businesses or the industries their businesses are part of. As a result, they are unpleasantly surprised when some of these problems occur. Since they have not thought ahead and developed contingency plans, these owners have no immediate method of dealing with such problems when they happen.

> ### Worst Practice
>
> Fail to take the time to critically analyze risks to the family business and develop plans to ameliorate such risks.

Either directly or through committees, directors and management should identify the major dangers facing a family business, prioritize them, and establish internal controls and a compliance program to help ameliorate them. A good way of identifying risks is to review the problems of other private and public companies in the same industry.

If another company in the same industry is the subject of a government investigation, directors and management should inquire as to whether the practices being investigated are also being practiced by the family business.

Since some risks are insurable, any risk analysis should include existing insurance coverage of the family business. This may require a legal review of insurance policies in cooperation with the business' insurance broker to determine what coverage is missing or inadequate.

One family business, namely Grato and Sons Trucking Company, Inc. in Palisades Park, New Jersey, learned about the importance of insurance the hard way. One of its trucks was involved in a serious accident in New York; the total potential liability was from 10- to 12-million dollars. Unfortunately, the company only had a million dollar's worth of insurance, and the owners had to dissolve their business and form a new one.[10]

> ### Best Practice
>
> Attempt to segregate in separate legal entities the assets of the family business while it is prosperous, so that in the event the business suffers financial reverses, its assets are protected from creditors.

One method of risk amelioration is to segregate the assets of the family business into separate legal entities so that all these assets are not subject to the claims of all creditors of the business. This segregation may involve transferring assets out of the operating company into another legal entity that is not subject to the claims of creditors of the entire family business. For example, if the legal entity that operates the family business owns real estate, consider transferring that real estate (to the extent it can be transferred tax efficiently) to another legal entity. If the real estate is used in the family business, the legal entity owning the real estate can lease it to the family business. Other transferable assets include excess cash, intellectual property, life insurance with cash value, and so on.

Many family businesses have more than one service or line of products, so it would be wise to transfer these multiple businesses to different legal entities.

Using different legal entities to operate a business can increase accounting, legal, and administrative costs. Moreover, it is not effective against banks or other financial institutions that require all the legal entities to guarantee debt. However, it is effective against trade creditors and other suppliers of the family business. Of course, this assumes that the legal entities are strictly respected by the family business, do not intermix their operations except pursuant to arm's-length agreements, and preferably, are managed and controlled separately.

Transferring business assets to other legal entities will be subject to legal challenge under fraudulent transfer and conveyance state and federal laws if the transfer is made in fraud of creditors, leaves the company with insufficient assets to pay its debts in the ordinary course of business, or renders the company insolvent. Therefore, the transfers must be made at a time when the company is prosperous and does not have any large contingent claims.

Whistle-Blower Policy

The independent audit committee should also help establish a whistle-blower policy that would permit the confidential submission of employee complaints about illegal or unethical activity. Complaints should be made confidentially to the chair of the audit committee. The independent audit committee has the responsibility to investigate serious allegations of wrongdoing and protect the whistle-blower from retaliation by family members or other parties.

According to a 2004 survey by the Association of Certified Fraud Examiners, fraud is detected 40 percent of the time through tips.

Utilize Independent Directors to Resolve Family Conflicts

> **Best Practice**
>
> Although conflict is inevitable in any business, a fair and impartial process of dispute resolution can help to eliminate family conflicts and reduce the high mortality rate for family-owned firms.

Conflict in a family business can exist on several levels. Visible conflicts are usually the ones described by the family members. However, there may be underlying animosities of which some family members may not even be conscious.[11]

A procedurally fair process of resolving disputes can help eliminate conflict.[12] When family members believe that they have been afforded procedural justice by an impartial body, they are more likely to accept its decision even though they may be disappointed by the resolution. It is important to take the necessary measures for establishing a respected process of conflict resolution, as internal conflict is one of the major reasons why family businesses do not survive.[13]

One of the significant advantages of well-respected independent directors is their ability to serve as an impartial body to address family conflicts. It is harder for a father or mother to resolve conflicts involving children and still be viewed as impartial.[14]

For independent directors to be viewed as providing a fair procedural process, they must permit a full airing of grievances from all sides of the conflict before rendering a decision. It is important that these independent directors not express any opinion before fully hearing from all parties involved.

Both the perception and actuality of procedural due process help prevent conflict even in situations where there are deep divisions within the family business. However, it is still not a cure-all for all family disputes.[15]

Insert Provisions into the Corporate Charter to Use Independent Directors to Resolve Conflicts

As discussed in Chapter 1, it is important to develop methods for resolving family deadlocks. One mechanism that has been approved by the courts is to insert a provision into the charter of the family business that provides for independent directors to resolve family disputes. This was achieved in the case of Hanover Foods Corporation (HFC) and subsequently approved by the Pennsylvania Supreme Court.

Best Practice

Insert dispute resolution provisions into the charter of family business, using independent directors to resolve the dispute after the death of the founder.

HFC is a vertically integrated processor of food products located in Hanover, Pennsylvania. It has ten plants in Pennsylvania, and it also has plants in Maryland, Delaware, New Jersey, and Guatemala. HFC is involved in the growing, processing, canning, freezing, freeze-drying, packaging, marketing, and distribution of its products under its own trademarks as well as other branded, customer, and private labels.

During the relevant time frame, the Class B common stock of HFC was owned generally by fewer than 40 members of the Warehime family and was the only voting stock of the company. HFC's Class A common stock was non-voting and publicly traded on the NASDAQ Bulletin Board.

Alan Warehime, arguably the founder of both HFC and its sister company, Snyders of Hanover (Snyders Pretzels), had three children: John, Sally, and Michael. In 1987, as part of his estate planning, Alan established a ten-year voting trust, expiring in 1997, to vote a majority of the Class B shares of HFC. Ten years was the maximum period for voting trusts then permitted under Pennsylvania law. Upon Alan's death, John, his oldest son, would become the sole voting trustee; Michael would be given control of Snyders of Hanover; and all the children would be given equity in each family business.

When Alan died in 1991, John succeeded him as sole voting trustee of the Class B common stock of HFC. Disputes soon arose between Michael and Sally on the one hand and John on the other concerning HFC. Until the voting trust expired in 1997, John had all the voting power, but it became clear that once it did expire, Michael, Sally, and John would be embroiled in a free-for-all fight for control that would likely result in the company being sold.

Alan had wisely created an independent board of directors for HFC. In 1996, the HFC independent directors decided to hire their own counsel (namely, the author). The board also hired an investment banker and other outside advisors to assist in evaluating the strategic alternatives for HFC once the voting trust expired.

After extensive deliberations, the independent directors decided to install a dispute-resolution mechanism in the articles of incorporation of HFC before the voting trust expired. This mechanism permitted the independent directors to cast approximately 80 percent of the votes of all Class B shareholders in the event of a dispute among the members of the Warehime family. This gave the independent directors the power to settle most Warehime family disputes unless the remaining shareholders overwhelmingly favored a certain side.

The specific dispute resolution mechanism used was to create a special class of voting stock which, for a five-year period, had 35 votes per share in the event of a family dispute and could be voted by the board in their capacity as trustees of the HFC 401(k) plan trust. This special class of shares was then contributed to the HFC 401(k) plan trust.

Despite significant litigation over the dispute resolution mechanism, it was upheld by the Pennsylvania Supreme Court in two separate cases.[16] As a result, HFC remains an independent company.

Similar dispute resolution mechanisms can be established in other family businesses prior to the death or retirement of the founder, preserving the business for the future.

Family Mission Statements or Family Constitution

> **Best Practice**
>
> Develop a family mission statement or family constitution.

A growing number of families are drafting mission statements and constitutions.[17] According to Stephen R. Covey:

> By creating and living by a mission statement, families are gradually able to build moral authority in the family itself. In other words, principles get built right into the very structure and culture of the family, and everyone comes to realize that principles are at the center of the family and are the key to keeping the family strong, together, and committed to its destination.[18]

The concept of a family mission statement or constitution derives from the idea of a corporate mission statement, which "engenders a company with a sense of purposefulness ... serves to unify people in a company ... provides the company and its employees with a sense of identity," and "*provides a foundation* on which the company can build its future."[19]

The process of preparing a mission statement or a constitution helps to clarify the thinking of family members about the role of the family business. It also helps to define the enduring core values of the family business.[20]

Establishing Family Councils

All family businesses face the challenge of sharing and accommodating the different expectations and desires of family members. Some consultants believe that establishing a family council to air these issues is desirable because it encourages participation and planning, problem solving, decision making, and "gaining consensus on critical family business issues."[21]

> **Best Practice**
>
> Where appropriate, establish family councils, but control the agenda for meetings of the family council.

Some of the suggested purposes and tasks for the family council are as follows:

- Interview candidates for the independent board of directors.
- Transmit family values and the family vision.
- Offer a family forum for sharing ideas.
- Encourage family participation and commitment.
- Support the family's ownership education programs.
- Develop family leaders from the next generation.
- Monitor family and business interactions.
- Implement family plans and programs.
- Create venture capital funds for entrepreneurial activity of family members.
- Provide financial support for family members who do not want to participate in the family business and decide to become poets or artists.
- Establish and maintain family charitable foundations.

The author does not believe that a family council should automatically be established for every business. The disadvantage of a family council is that it enables disgruntled family members to air their grievances and sometimes causes conflict rather than resolves it. Some would argue that creating a forum for airing grievances is desirable. However, permitting one family member to complain sometimes fosters in other family members negative attitudes toward the owners, who will be forced to defend themselves in the family council.

Owners should permit grievances to be aired by individual family members, but privately instead of in a room full of relatives.

If a family council is established, it is important for the owner to control the agenda for its meetings. Meetings should be used to discuss core family values,[22] stimulate next-generation entrepreneurship, provide family business education programs, and establish family philanthropy programs. Family councils are not an appropriate place for complaints.

There is some disagreement among family-council advocates about whom should be invited to council meetings. One group says that only adults and blood relatives should attend. Another believes that all family members—including teenagers, spouses, significant others, and in-laws—should attend. There is no best practice in this area. However, it is preferable to initially have a smaller family council before deciding whether to expand the group of invitees.[23]

The Clemens Family Corporation has 229 family shareholders and a very elaborate role for the family council called the "Owners Advisory Council" (see Appendix 1). The council established annual expectations for the business, including financial metrics.

Regularly Communicate with Shareholders Concerning the Family Business

Many family businesses fail to communicate with their shareholders concerning the status of the business. Failure to do this generates suspicion, particularly in passive shareholders who may believe that they should be receiving greater dividends from the business.

Best Practice

The board of directors should establish a system for regularly communicating with shareholders concerning the business.

The key to avoiding family conflicts is regular, candid communication concerning the business. Communication establishes a level of trust within the family, which is essential for family unity, as was discussed in Chapter 1. The board of directors must establish processes for regular communication with shareholders.

Establish an Open Culture

Owners of family businesses, particularly founders, tend to be very secretive about the business with the family members employed in it. New ideas are not encouraged. In fact, may be discouraged by the actions of the owner. As a result, the business may suffer from rigid adherence to the founder's methods of doing business.

> **Best Practice**
>
> The board and management of a family business must maintain an open culture that is receptive to new ideas and adaptable to changes in the business environment.

Family businesses must develop and maintain an entrepreneurial culture that promotes change and innovation. This requires an open attitude that supports new ideas and challenges to old methods of doing business. The board of directors and management must promote such a culture.

When the current generation does not allow the new generation to present new ideas, change is stifled and the very survival of the family business is put in jeopardy.[24]

Chapter 4 reviews judicial cases that are typically the result of using the worst practices in family businesses, particularly with respect to succession planning.

CHAPTER 4

Worst Practices: What We Can Learn from Family Disasters

This chapter examines actual court cases involving family businesses to determine what mistakes were probably made that led to the litigation. Each of these court cases not only resulted in substantial legal expenses and the disruption of the business involved but also demonstrated what can happen within a dysfunctional family. The author is aware of how easy it is to criticize a family business using twenty-twenty hindsight and apologizes to the families involved in these litigations for doing so.

Nevertheless, court cases are a useful way to learn what not to do in a family business. Court rulings will typically recite the facts of the case, at least to the extent proven in court, and therefore constitute a helpful learning tool. In the case below, the court decided the matter based solely upon the allegations of the plaintiff and assumed that those allegations were correct.

Defective Succession Planning: One Brother Freezes Out the Other Brother

Worst Practice

Gift a controlling position in a family business to another family member without a contract from the donee that continues any salary or employment relationship enjoyed by the donor and other family members.

When the brothers Townsend and Charles Thorndike took over the family corporation, each was supposed to have all the rights and privileges of equal ownership. Then Charles started to freeze out Townsend. Eventually Townsend got tired of the way his brother was treating him and sued, but he waited too long. In *Thorndike v. Thorndike*,[1] the Supreme Court of New Hampshire upheld the ruling of the trial court that Townsend's action was barred by the statute of limitations. Townsend's allegations are described below.

The corporation, Annalee Mobilitee Dolls, Inc. (AMD), which produces and sells collectible dolls, was founded by the brothers' parents. In the early 1970s, Townsend and Charles started working for the business. Up until 1992, all major business decisions had been made unanimously by all Thorndike family members.

In 1992, the parents gave each of the brothers 48 percent of the company's voting shares, retaining 2 percent for each parent. Then in 1995, the parents gave day-to-day control of the company to Charles with an agreement among themselves that Townsend would retain a directorship—a significant management position—and that the brothers would continue to share equally in the income of the business.

But once Charles got control things began to change. After Charles took over day-to-day operations, he and his parents added people who were neither shareholders nor Thorndike family members to AMD's board of directors. The parents also transferred their voting stock to a voting trust that was under the control of one of the new board members. Charles and the new board members then removed Townsend from his position as a director and from any management role in AMD. *Charles reduced the salaries of his parents and Townsend to zero, due to losses suffered by the company, but continued to pay himself and the outside directors.* The losses that began after Townsend's removal from management totaled in the millions of dollars. In 1997, AMD's financing bank terminated AMD's loans. In response to these losses, Charles invested some of his own money into AMD. In exchange, he and the new board members caused AMD to issue notes to Charles that were convertible to voting stock and would, if converted, increase his voting powers and decrease Townsend's.

Finally, on February 18, 2005, Townsend filed a suit claiming a breach of fiduciary duty by his brother, the majority shareholder, in freezing him out. However, Townsend's complaint was dismissed because the statute of limitations barred the suit.

The Mistake: Assuming Townsend's allegations were correct, the company did not start losing money until after he was removed from management. The parents of Charles and Townsend apparently believed that Charles was the stronger manager of the two brothers. Still, they failed to protect both their own and Townsend's salary. But the parents could have protected theirs and Townsend's salaries by providing, in consideration of the transfer by each parent of their 2 percent of the shares to the voting trust, that both they and Townsend would receive a salary and/or dividends so long as the company had sufficient cash flow from operations in the future to afford such payments and limited Charles' salary increases to cost-of-living adjustments together with a bonus based on the financial performance of the company.

In any event, we suspect that Charles would have vigorously disagreed with his brother's allegations had he been able to present his side of the case before Townsend's complaint was dismissed

Defective Succession Planning: Brother vs. Brother in a 50/50 Ownership Family Business

> **Worst Practice**
>
> A father gives each of his two sons 50 percent the equity of the same business without creating an impartial tiebreaker.

This case[2] occurred in the Supreme Judicial Court of Maine.

Over the course of 60 years, Lewis Rosenthal, patriarch of the Rosenthal family, established a large real estate and business complex in and about Maine. Beginning in the mid-1950s his sons, Robert and Theodore, assisted in the development of the family's many enterprises. Theodore began working with his father after high school and a stint in the military. Robert went on to Colby College and Harvard Business School before he started working in the family business. The family began its business in textiles, but with the decline of that industry in Maine branched out into real estate and the ownership and operation of shopping malls and hotels.

The Rosenthals created a considerable number of closely held corporations that were generally completely owned by family members. The most successful of their corporations was Bo-ed, Inc., which owned and operated the Holiday Inn at Cooks Corner in Brunswick, Maine. Unlike most of the family's corporations, Lewis played no direct role in that business. Theodore and Robert each held a 50 percent interest in Bo-ed's 100 shares of stock until 1972 when Robert transferred one share to his wife Rona. Thereafter, the company's board of directors comprised its three shareholders. The Rosenthals also owned extensive real estate that they placed in trusts, with some family members serving as trustees while others, including grandchildren, were beneficiaries. The family corporations then leased real estate from those trusts.

To assist with the overall organization and management of the family's business concerns, one of its corporations acted as a management company. It paid salaries to family members for work they performed in any of the family businesses and also billed the individual entities for services provided them by the other businesses. The Rosenthals maintained a long-standing policy of inter-company loans, through which the more successful operations would loan money as needed to less successful entities. This cash flow allowed their various business units to expand when opportunities arose, in keeping with the family's long-standing strategy to maximize business growth through extensive borrowing against their real estate. Little money was paid out to the family in the form of profits.

In the summer of 1975, after Theodore returned to Maine from a stay in Florida, the brothers began to disagree sharply about the proper financial policies of the Rosenthal business. As a result, the family members entered an agreement in November 1976 that attempted to set forth a policy on reinvestment and the payment of profits that would please all of the principal actors. However, this agreement failed to resolve the growing controversy between Robert and Theodore.

The events immediately precipitating the dispute before the court unfolded in 1978, when Theodore, then in charge of the operations of Bo-ed, Inc., became concerned about the payment of his 1977 and 1978 federal income taxes that arose out of profits attributed to him from the Rosenthal businesses. In circumstances sharply disputed by the parties at trial, at Robert's urging Theodore borrowed money from the bank to pay his 1977 taxes. Shortly thereafter, Theodore drew $105,000 from Bo-ed as a personal loan to cover his earlier personal bank loan and pay his future taxes. In response to Theodore's action, at a Bo-ed directors meeting in August 1978, Robert and his wife Rona voted to require two signatures instead of one on all future Bo-ed checks and to compel Theodore to repay the money he had withdrawn from the company.

Those disagreements over the family's business policies, brought to a head by Robert and Rona's votes in that 1978 meeting, led Theodore to decide to sell his entire interest in the Rosenthal enterprises. After complex negotiations between Theodore and the other family members involved in business operations, with both sides fully represented by counsel, Theodore agreed on March 31, 1979, to sell the family his full interest in all Rosenthal businesses in exchange for cash payments and other benefits, including the family's commitment to pay all his taxes arising out of the transaction. The total consideration received by Theodore under the agreement was estimated to amount to about $1.4 million. The letter of counsel memorializing the March 31, 1979 agreement also stated that

> [t]he obligations which [Theodore] has to any of the Rosenthal enterprises or to any Rosenthal family member will be herewith discharged as of this date except for obligations which arise as a result of this arrangement. The obligations which [Robert] has to [Theodore] will be terminated and discharged as of this date except for those which arise hereunder.

In 1983, with some dispute remaining about whether the family had fully paid Theodore's tax liabilities arising from the 1979 sale, Theodore filed a multicount suit against his brother and others. The parties tried three claims to the jury: that Robert had wrongfully interfered with Theodore's advantageous business relations in the family enterprises, that he had violated a confidential relationship with Theodore, and that he and Rona had violated their fiduciary obligations to Theodore in the context of the Rosenthal family businesses. In his brief to the court, however, Theodore had described as the "true crux" of his case against Robert and Rona that through their breach of fiduciary obligations to him "he was improperly forced out of the family businesses and then . . . sold his share of those businesses at an unfairly low price." During trial, Theodore abandoned any claim to be reinstated in the family business. In defending against the suit, Robert and Rona both contended that not only that their conduct had not been wrongful but also that the March 1979 agreement constituted a full accord and satisfaction of all the claims Theodore was asserting.

After a three-week trial, the jury found specially that the agreement did not constitute an accord and satisfaction, that Robert and Rona had violated their fiduciary obligations toward Theodore, and that Robert had abused a confidential relationship with Theodore. The jury held against Theodore on his count for wrongful interference with advantageous business relations by finding that he suffered no damages. On his successful claims, the jury awarded Theodore $2,800,000 in damages. The Supreme Judicial Court of Maine reversed the jury verdict because of an erroneous jury instruction and sent it back to the lower court for a new trial on the claim that Robert and Rona wrongfully froze Theodore out of the business in breach of their fiduciary duties.

The Mistakes: This case illustrates the typical mistakes in succession planning. The primary mistake of Lewis Rosenthal was creating a family business in which each of his sons owned a 50 percent interest without creating an impartial tiebreaker. A wise tiebreaker could have found a way to separate the two brothers in a fashion that would have prevented litigation. Ultimately, Robert found a method of breaking the tie by giving his wife Rona a board seat.

There is also the question of why the company paid Theodore $1.4 million without getting a full general release, which would have precluded Theodore subsequently raising the breach of fiduciary duty argument. Obviously, this was a mistake, by twenty-twenty hindsight if not foresight.

Defective Succession Planning: 50/50 Cousins Consortium Litigation

Worst Practice

The widow of a founder fails to retain voting control over stock given to her children during her lifetime in a 50/50 cousins consortium.

This case[3] occurred in the Superior Court of New Jersey.

Inman is a closely held family run business, incorporated in New Jersey in May 1986. Its sole asset is real estate in the Township of Woodbridge, New Jersey, on which is situated a shopping center consisting of two buildings housing about ten tenants and a parking lot. The company was founded by two brothers, John and Nicholas Trimarco, whose equal shares upon their death devolved to their widows, who in turn each transferred their 50 percent shares equally to their three children, respectively. After John's death in 1993, his widow Anne functioned as Inman's de facto president while her son Richard, to whom Elizabeth (the plaintiff) was married, assumed responsibility for day-to-day management of the company. Richard and his siblings, John Jr., and Phyllis, therefore owned 50 percent of

Inman and their cousins—Nicholas' children—Kenneth, Laura, and Judy (the nondefendant Trimarcos) owned the remaining one-half. At the time the non-defendant Trimarcos were completely passive shareholders and not involved in the company operations.

In January 2002, Richard died. Elizabeth inherited his one-sixth share, sharing management of Inman with her sister-in-law, Phyllis, pursuant to an employment contract, fixing her annual salary at $40,000 with medical benefits. But six months later, Elizabeth was terminated by her mother-in-law, Anne. According to Elizabeth, during her short tenure as Inman's co-manager, she had uncovered evidence of misconduct, corporate malfeasance, and improper use of company assets by the Trimarco defendants in their management of Inman, and had been fired as a result.

Consequently, in July 2002, Elizabeth filed suit against Inman and the Trimarco defendants (namely Anne, her brother-in-law, John Jr., and Phyllis) alleging both wrongful termination and, on behalf of the shareholders, derivative claims of corporate misconduct. As to the latter, count three of Elizabeth's nine-count complaint sought relief for statutory oppression of a shareholder due to the Trimarco defendants' breach of fiduciary trust based on their "misconduct and mismanagement of Inman" for their own "pecuniary gain to the exclusion of Inman's other shareholders." The Trimarco defendants answered, counterclaimed, and filed a third-party complaint against, among others, Richard's estate, alleging misconduct.

Discovery ensued through August 2003. Pursuant to court order in the interim, in July 2003 a shareholders' meeting was held, at which time the nondefendant Trimarcos allied themselves with Elizabeth and voted to oust the Trimarco defendants as officers and members of Inman's board of directors. Elizabeth was temporarily elected president. In that capacity, Elizabeth attempted to use $263,647.92 in corporate funds to pay her law firm's outstanding counsel fees and to reimburse herself for monies she already expended in legal fees on behalf of Inman.

The Mistakes: After the deaths of John and Nicholas Trimarco, the family business became a cousin consortium. The children of Nicholas Trimarco (the "non-Trimarco defendants") were 50 percent shareholders but were not active in Inman. Anne, the widow of John Trimarco and their children (the "Trimarco defendants") were active in the business but collectively only owned 50 percent of the equity. When Anne gave her three children, Richard, John, Jr., and Phyllis the stock of the corporation outright, she set up the possibility of losing control of the business. If Anne, in connection with transferring the stock to her three children, had instead retained the right to vote the stock during her lifetime, control of the company would not have passed to the combination of Elizabeth (Richard's widow) and Nicholas' children, who were not active in the business. By not retaining voting rights when she transferred the stock to her children, Anne exposed herself and her side of the family to the takeover by Elizabeth and Nicholas' children (the nondefendant Trimarcos.). When Anne fired Elizabeth as an employee, this risk was realized. (This commentary is apart from whether or not there was in fact any misconduct or mismanagement at Inman.)

Another Defective Succession Planning Case: The Squabbling Brothers

Worst Practice

Fail to provide reasonable severance for one of the owner's children in case other siblings terminate that child's employment in the family business, with a clawback clause in case the terminated child chooses to sue the family business.

A case decided in the Supreme Court of Nebraska is a good illustration of defective succession planning.[4]

The case involved a familiar story: squabbling among the children of the founder of a family business after his death. The plaintiff was Michael Johnson, a shareholder of Western Securities, a Delaware corporation. Michael's father, Dick Johnson, had incorporated Western Securities and was originally its sole shareholder and director. In 1975, Western Securities acquired Modern Equipment, a Nebraska corporation, and Dick became the sole director of that business as well. At the time of Dick's death, Michael was a vice president of Modern Equipment.

In 1998, Dick transferred 25 percent of his stock in Western Securities to his five children in varying amounts. Dick's stated intent was that his son Richard, one of the defendants, would succeed him as president and CEO of Modern Equipment and that Michael would in turn succeed Richard. Dick promised Michael and Richard that he would devise his remaining Western Securities stock to them in equal shares. After October 3, 2000, Western Securities and Modern

Equipment each had three-member boards, composed of Michael, Richard, and Dick.

Dick became ill in March 2001 and resigned as president of Modern Equipment in October. Dick, Richard, and Michael elected Richard to succeed Dick as president. Dick died on November 6, 2001. His Will provided that Michael and Richard were each to receive one-half of his Western Securities stock. Richard was appointed personal representative of his father's estate.

After Dick's death, Richard appointed Modern Equipment's vice president of manufacturing to fill vacancies on the boards of Western Securities and Modern Equipment without notice to, meeting of, or the knowledge or consent of the other shareholders. On August 28, 2002, Richard fired Michael and barred him from the premises of Modern Equipment. Thereafter, Michael was denied any participation in the operation of Modern Equipment and has not shared in its earnings. Modern Equipment's before-tax profits declined precipitously in the year following these actions; at the same time Richard's salary increased by 22 percent.

In February 2003, Michael notified the corporation's attorney of Richard's conduct. Shortly thereafter, Michael received notices of the shareholder and board meetings at Western Securities and Modern Equipment. At those meetings, Richard, in his capacity as personal representative of Dick's estate, voted all the shares of stock then still held in the estate to ratify what the court stated was Richard's poor conduct. Dick's Western Securities stock was finally distributed by his estate in 2004, after which Richard held approximately 48 per cent of the stock and Michael approximately 44 percent.

The Mistake. Dick Johnson clearly favored Richard over Michael as his immediate successor. Dick should have anticipated the possibility of conflict between Richard and Michael and provided protection for both sons. The protection could have been an impartial tiebreaker. It might also have included a generous severance agreement so that Michael would have had a source of income after his employment was terminated. This severance agreement could have been coupled with a so-called clawback clause that provided that Michael would lose the generous severance (but limited to a small percentage of cash flow from operations, with a limit on Richard's compensation) if he started suit against the company in connection with his employment termination. Dick Johnson also might have indicated to Michael that he would be prepared to help him finance a new business.

Father and Son Conflict over Employment Agreement

> **Worst Practice**
>
> Terminate the employment of a close family member who has been a long-term employee of the business without providing a generous severance arrangement, which would be forfeited in the event of litigation.

This case occurred in the Court of Appeals in Michigan and the facts found by the court are as follows[5]:

Robert Franchino began working at Franchino Mold and Engineering Company (FMEC) in 1974. Four years later he and his father, Richard Franchino, signed an employment contract in which they agreed that Robert could only be terminated by the unanimous agreement of FMEC's board of directors. From 1978 until 2001, Robert and Richard were the company's only board members, as well as its only shareholders, with Robert holding 31 percent and the Richard holding 69 percent. Robert and Richard were also parties to two stock-purchase agreements, one related to a family company called Franchino, Inc. and the other to FMEC. Under the FMEC agreement, Richard was required to offer his shares first to the corporation and then to Robert before they could be offered to anyone else, including Richard's daughters. The Franchino, Inc. agreement required Richard to offer his shares to his children in proportion to their current holdings. (Robert and both of his sisters held shares in Franchino, Inc.)

The father-son relationship deteriorated over the years they worked together. Lois Franchino, Robert's sister, testified that Richard had talked about firing Robert in recent years and that she had begged Richard not to take action against Robert until their mother passed away, which she did in September 2000. Furthermore, Richard became concerned that his estate would be "cannibalized" by estate taxes if the buy-sell agreements remained in place. In May 2001, Richard's attorney sent a letter to Robert stating that Richard wanted to set aside the buy-sell agreement for Franchino, Inc. and that if Robert was unwilling to agree, Richard was prepared to have it set aside by operation of law. A second letter stated that Richard planned to merge Franchino, Inc. into a new entity if the agreement was not set aside by mutual consent. Richard verbally fired Robert on August 21, 2001, ostensibly for yelling at another FMEC employee.

Robert then sued to prevent Richard from merging Franchino, Inc. with newly formed Franchino Holdings, and the trial court granted a preliminary injunction prohibiting the merger.

Robert then filed a complaint alleging that his father had breached his fiduciary duties to FMEC by terminating Robert's employment in retaliation for Robert having sued him over the buy-sell agreement. Richard responded, with the aid of his attorneys, by holding a special FMEC shareholders meeting to remove Robert from the board and to amend FMEC's bylaws to provide for additional directors who need not be shareholders. After the meeting, Robert amended his complaint to include allegations of willfully unfair and oppressive conduct. Both parties moved for summary judgment and the trial court ruled in favor of Richard. It concluded that the statute to protect the interests of shareholders applied only in their capacity as shareholders. Furthermore, it rejected Robert's attempt to recover under the theory that his reasonable expectations to remain on the board, remain employed, and share in FMEC's profits had been violated.

The Mistakes: The existence of the employment contract between the company and the son reflects the long-term poor relationship between the son, Robert, and the father, Richard. Presumably the son did not trust his father and insisted upon an employment agreement for himself that could only be terminated by the unanimous agreement of the board of directors, which consisted only of the father and the son. Robert presumably thought he was safe from being fired by his father through this requirement of "unanimous agreement." Unfortunately for the son, the "unanimous agreement" clause was easily avoided by restructuring the board of directors to remove him from the board.

The first mistake Richard made was to listen to his daughter's advice and wait until his wife died to terminate his son's employment. His relationship with Robert had clearly been poor for many years. Rather than allow his son to proceed on his own, with help from Richard, the situation was allowed to fester for many years. During those years Robert could have been building a business and a life separate from the father.

The Richard's second mistake was in failing to provide a generous severance payment in the employment contract (but limited to a small percentage of cash flow from operations) in the event his son was involuntarily terminated. The length of the severance would have assisted Robert in starting his own business or developing his own career. The agreement could have also stipulated that the severance would be forfeited if Robert legally challenged his employment termination. Such a clause is sometimes called a "clawback" clause and is very helpful in creating incentives to avoid litigation.

Terminating a relative who is both a long-term employee of the company and a significant shareholder should only be effected after consultation with an attorney who can help structure the termination in a manner designed to ward off litigation.

Some Family Businesses Should Not Exist

> **Worst Practice**
>
> If the key members of a family business cannot get along with each other, hire expensive law firms and litigate instead of selling the business to each other or to an unrelated third party.

Some families start businesses and find that they cannot get along with each other. Instead of selling the business, which would be the best practice, they litigate with each other. If the key members of the family business cannot get along, they are better off selling the business to one or the other of the family members or to an unrelated third party. The alternative is continual disputes and litigation, which is not in the interest of the family.

Sometimes it is clear from the beginning that a family should not be in business together. Taken from an actual court case, the following is a perfect example of a family business that should have been sold immediately.[6]

Rocco vs. Luigi

In the summer of 1994, Rocco and Luigi, two brothers, together with Giuseppe and Umile formed a corporation known as 4-D Rose, Inc. (the "corporation"). The corporation issued 300 shares of common stock. Giuseppe and Umile each received 24 shares, while Luigi received 126 shares. In an effort to shield the remaining 126 shares from Rocco's pending divorce proceedings, the shareholders agreed that those shares would be issued in Luigi's name and be held by him for the benefit of Rocco. Shortly thereafter, the corporation purchased real property known as 42 Dean Place in Bridgeport, Connecticut (the "property"), which consisted of forty residential rental units and was the primary asset of the corporation.

Although the parties initially managed the property jointly, disputes soon arose. In exchange for maintaining and managing 42 Dean Place, Rocco occupied an apartment at the property without paying rent. Thereafter, he granted himself a monthly salary of $3,500 over the objection of Luigi. Luigi subsequently questioned Rocco's management of the property, alleging a series of corporate wrongs, including Rocco's failure to provide financial documentation and to prepare timely management reports, his refusal to allow Luigi to participate in business decisions regarding the property, and his refusal to account for the income generated by the property.

Thereafter, the parties proceeded to expensive litigation.

The Mistake: It was clear from the beginning that Rocco and Luigi would not get along. They should have sold the family business as soon as that became clear to both parties, rather than enriching their respective law firms.

Chapter 5 discusses best practices in compensating family members and should be read in conjunction with Chapter 6, which analyzes the benefits of creating long-term equity incentives for key employees for both family and non-family members.

CHAPTER 5

Compensating Family Members

There is no uniform practice among family businesses for compensating family members who become employees of the business. Some owners overcompensate family member employees. They do this for several reasons, including the following:

- To permit the family member to enjoy the same lifestyle the family member was accustomed to while living in the family home
- To permit young grandchildren of the family business owner, who are the children of family member employees, to enjoy a better lifestyle
- To permit disguised gifts that are tax deductible by the company because they are characterized as employee compensation

Some family businesses take the opposite tack, underpaying family member employees—particularly new ones—to provide them with an incentive to work harder or to help them understand what it means to be poor. The owners sometimes justify undercompensating family employees on the ground that they will ultimately inherit the business and should thus be patient about obtaining the fruits of the business.

Pay Fair and Arm's-Length Compensation to Family Employees

The bond between employed and nonemployed family shareholders depends upon trust. That trust can be destroyed if there is a perception that the shareholders who are active in management are enjoying excessive compensation at the expense of the family members who are not active in the business. Resentments are easily aroused when the active shareholders enjoy perquisites that are not enjoyed by inactive family shareholders, such as country club memberships and low-interest loans. This can be true even if the overall compensation level, including perquisites, is competitive.

> **Best Practice**
>
> Family members should neither be overpaid nor underpaid. Instead, they should be paid a fair arm's-length compensation.

The best practice is to pay family employees a fair arm's-length compensation,[1] also called the "market value approach" to compensation.[2] This is particularly true if there are family shareholders who are not active in the business. Inactive shareholders can feel betrayed if the active family shareholders take advantage of business opportunities that are not made available to the inactive shareholders.

However, let us assume that there are no inactive family shareholders. A second problem with overpaying family employees is that it can create jealousy and resentment among the non-family employees performing the same job and unrealistic expectations by family employees about the nature of their jobs. Many businesses must employ non-family employees in key roles. Nothing is more destructive to esprit de corps among key employees than when family members are paid a greater salary than family members for doing the same job. Although some owners assume that they can keep the compensation paid to family employees confidential, this information tends to leak out.

A third problem with overcompensating family employees is that they develop a lifestyle that is unsustainable outside of the family business. Should the business be sold, it is likely that the buyer will not be willing to continue paying the same high compensation level to family employees.

> **Worst Practice**
>
> Pay family members an amount sufficient to maintain their lifestyle without regard to their contributions to the business.

When selling a family business, many sellers insist that an employment contract for family employees be part of the sale contract to maintain the high compensation for family employees for a period of time. While this will protect a family employee for a period of time, the overpayment of compensation to that employee may well result in a decreased purchase price for the business. Moreover, the buyer will typically not continue the compensation overpayment after the employment contract expires. Furthermore, the buyer may resent the requirement to overpay family employees, resulting in the termination of their employment as soon as the buyer is legally able to do so.

When overpaid family members are no longer employed in the business and attempt to obtain other employment, they are in for a culture shock. An overpaid family employee will find it difficult to accept employment at more realistic compensation levels. They will have to reduce their standard of living, which is extremely difficult. Moreover, some overpaid family employees find it hard to adjust to receiving more realistic compensation, with consequent harm to their self-esteem as well as their standard of living.

As noted, some family business owners purposely underpay family employees. While this avoids all of the disadvantages recited above for overpaid family employees, it can create hostility toward the family business owner. The author has seen situations where the family employees cannot wait for the owner to retire or die in order to obtain more realistic compensation. This practice tends to lead to bitterness and is hardly conducive to creating a positive culture within the company.

Develop Job Descriptions

If you ask an independent compensation consultant to establish a fair and equitable compensation structure for a family member, they will typically ask you for a job description. Without a complete description of a family employee's duties and responsibilities it is very difficult to establish arms-length compensation levels. This is particularly true in a business where family members serve multiple roles of varying importance.

> **Best Practice**
>
> Require each family member to create a job description for their position in the business.

One of the unique strengths of a family business is the typically unconventional roles that may be played by different family members.

One family member may be responsible for multiple tasks, such as accounting, operations and human resources.[3] Another may be solely responsible for sales to a particular customer group. Thought must be given to breaking down the specific duties of each family employee.

The job descriptions of family employees permit the owner to better evaluate the importance of each to the business.

Equal Compensation Policies Are Acceptable Only if They Are Fair to All Family Employees

Some businesses provide equal compensation for all the family employees who are at approximately the same level within the business. The purpose of the equal compensation rule is to avoid disputes within the family as to who is more valuable. Though not the best practice, it can be an acceptable one if—and only if—the compensation levels are within a fair and arm's-length range of what would other businesses would pay for the same position. There is usually a significant range of what is fair compensation for a particular position, so it should not be that difficult to compensate family members equally within that range.

Best Practice

If there is more than one family member employed in the business, equal compensation should be paid to them only if they have the same level of responsibility and importance in the business, and such compensation is at arm's-length levels.

The author is aware of businesses in which all family employees are paid the same amount of compensation, regardless of their responsibility or importance to the business. The owners justify this on the ground that it avoids having to make difficult judgments about the actual value of family employees to the business. These owners also argue that because differentiating the compensation levels of siblings and other close family members creates family jealousy and resentment, it is better to just give everyone equal treatment. Moreover, these owners believe that paying the same compensation to each family member creates esprit de corps among the family employees.

Although there is some truth to these arguments, there are also substantial counter arguments. If there are two children in the business of approximately equal age, and one is extremely industrious while the other is barely works nine to five, paying them the exact same compensation can create resentment in the more industrious child. This child may decide to leave the business rather than be unfairly compensated compared to his or her sibling. Some owners argue that they can handle this resentment through councils and other mechanisms that help reconcile family conflicts. Other owners would keep the compensation base the same for both children but attempt to reward the more industrious child with a larger year-end bonus.

Paying the more competent and industrious family member a higher compensation level is clearly in the best interest of the business. However, unequal compensation may not be in the best interest of the family. Accordingly, there is no single best practice that is in the best interest of both the business and family harmony. Each family must adopt the compensation practices best suited to its personal culture and business.

Use an Independent Compensation Committee to Establish Compensation

Owners tend to set the compensation of family employees and other employees of the business. Family employees who believe they are underpaid may interpret the perceived underpayment as a lack of respect within the family. The effect of the owner's compensation decisions may cause jealousy and rivalry with other siblings whom the family employee believes are overpaid. The owner's compensation decisions can create problems both for family unity and the business.

> **Best Practice**
>
> Use an independent compensation committee of the board of directors to recommend compensation for key employees, both family members and non-family members.

A compensation decision by the head of the family is not just a business decision. It is a personal decision that can produce emotional reactions in family members (*Does my father love me less than my brother since he gave my brother more money?*). Therefore, a best practice is to obtain the recommendation of independent directors for compensation of family members who are key employees, as well as non-family key employees. This removes some of the emotional element involved in compensation decisions made by the head of the family. We discussed in Chapter 3 how to form a board of directors for a family business that contains an independent compensation committee.

> **Best Practice**
>
> The compensation committee should have the authority to retain independent compensation consultants, counsel, and other advisors to provide the committee with independent advice.

The compensation committee should use independent experts to establish reasonable compensation for family members, and it should have the authority to do so at the expense of the business. Family employees tend to respect the decisions of the compensation committee if they have sought and accepted independent advice from compensation experts.

Some corporate governance experts believe that all companies should embrace the two compensation-consultant models. That is, executive compensation should be set by the board with the help of a consultant hired by the board, and all other compensation should be set by management using a separate consultant and not duplicating the same work. The purpose of the two-compensation-consultant model is to insure the independence of the compensation consultant.

Likewise, some corporate governance experts believe that compensation consultants should be rotated every five years.

Use an Independent Compensation Consultant if There Is No Independent Compensation Committee

Many family businesses do not have or do not wish to have a formal board structure, including an independent compensation committee. Therefore, the owner's compensation decisions lack the imprimatur of an impartial third party.

> **Best Practice**
>
> Even if the family business does not have an independent compensation committee, the owner should use independent compensation consultants in establishing compensation for family member employees.

If the business does not have an independent compensation committee, the best practice is for the owner to use an independent compensation consultant in order to obtain the respect of family employees for the fairness of the owner's compensation decisions. Following the advice of the compensation consultant provides cover for the owner.

Communicate to All Family Members the Elements of Their Compensation

Many family businesses provide nonmonetary compensation to family members, such as picking up the tab for country club dues, automobiles, health, life, and disability insurance. In addition, the family members may receive equity incentive compensation (either phantom stock or real stock) and dividends on their stock. However, family members may not appreciate the full value of what they receive from the business unless it is fully and clearly spelled out for them.

> **Best Practice**
>
> Communicate on a confidential basis to each family member the value of each of the elements of their personal compensation.

It is important that once a year the owner privately spell out for family members the value of each element of their compensation. Each element, including fringe benefits, should be specifically valued and fully explained to the family member. All the elements should be totaled so that the family member understands the full extent of what he or she is deriving from the family business.

Our next chapter deals with creating long-term incentives for both family employees as well as non-family employees by utilizing phantom forms of equity compensation.

CHAPTER 6

Creating Phantom Equity Incentives for Key Employees, Both Family and Non-Family

---

Best Practice

Give key employees who are not family members long-term phantom equity incentives that do not provide them with actual stock and do not compromise the confidentiality of the business' financial information. A similar plan can be established for family members who are key employees.[1]

A number of family business owners have no family successor-in-waiting and no family member who is willing and qualified to run the business.[2] These businesses should find ways of creating incentives that will attract and retain key employees who are not family members to become the future leaders of their business. These incentives should preferably be long-term to best align the interests of the key employees with the interests of the owner. Unfortunately, according to one academic study, many family businesses that are not professionally managed provide only short-term incentives to their employees.[3]

Many key employees who work for public companies are typically given long-term equity incentives to bind them to the company. A private family business must be able to compete for key employees who may be crucial to the growth and prosperity of the family business.

However, in order to maintain complete family ownership, key non-family employees should generally not receive stock in the business. Apart from the desire to maintain complete stock owner-ship, giving stock to non family members affords them certain legal rights that a family business might consider undesirable. For example, a stockholder of a family business corporation typically has the right under state corporation laws to inspect books and records. This right is inconsistent with the desire of a family business to maintain confi-dentiality. Moreover, stockholders can bring so-called derivative law-suits against the board of directors and potentially direct lawsuits against management and controlling shareholders.

Therefore, it is generally undesirable to permit non-family mem-bers to become stockholders in a family business. Similar arguments can also be made for preventing non-family members from becoming holders of equity in limited-liability companies.

The challenge is to create "phantom equity" incentives (also some-times called "synthetic equity" incentives) for non-family key employ-ees that do not reward with actual equity but pay only cash. A plan that provides only a cash reward, but is measured by equity growth or other equity performance metrics, is called a "phantom equity" incentive.

Any phantom equity incentive plan established by a family busi-ness should require the reward to be paid with money. To avoid adversely affecting the cash flow of the company, the plan should limit the total amount of the cash payment each year to all key employees to a small percentage of either the cash flow from opera-tions from the family business or EBITDA.

Phantom Equity Plan

A phantom equity plan is a notional plan that typically consists of a document that creates an equity equivalent award to the executive of the family business that is payable in cash. A bookkeeping account is typically maintained for each award. The phantom equity equivalent award is usually subject to vesting conditions and, when vested in whole or in part, is settled by payment in cash. The payment may be subject to payout limitations to avoid adversely affecting cash flow. The vesting conditions may just involve the continuation of the employment of the executive for a specific time period. A form of a phantom equity plan for a family business corporation is contained in Appendix 4.

Recipients of awards under the phantom equity plan are not con-sidered stockholders or other equity holders of the company. Phantom equity awards may be given to both nonemployees and employees.

The accounting for phantom equity awards is described in the Accounting Standards Codification, Topic 718.

Vesting Conditions

There are two basic types of vesting conditions that can be inserted in a phantom equity plan.

- Time-vesting conditions
- Performance-vesting conditions

Time-vested phantom plans reward the executive merely for continuing employment with the family business, without regard to the accomplishments of either the executive or the family business. The typical time-vested phantom plan does not require the payment of any exercise price by the executive, as would occur in a stock option.

A time-vested phantom plan (similar to a time-vested restricted stock award) rewards the executive even if there has been no appreciation in the equity since its grant. The reward is solely given for continuing employment with the family business.

Phantom plans can also contain performance conditions, as can stock options and stock appreciation rights (SARs). For example, the phantom plan may require as a condition to vesting not only that the executive remain with the company but also that the company or the executive achieves certain financial goals. Phantom plans can also be made similar to a SAR or stock option by rewarding the executive only for appreciation in the stock value after the grant date.

A typical vesting date could be five years after the award is granted. However, some family companies would not want to pay out any cash until there is an exit event (also called a "liquidity event"), such as a sale outside the family or an initial public offering (IPO). In this case, the vesting should be conditioned upon the sale outside the family or an IPO, and if neither occurs within the period of the phantom equity award (typically five or ten years), the award becomes valueless. The vesting period should extend at least six months to one year after the sale outside of the family or an IPO in order to encourage the employee to remain with the company.

Best Practice

Phantom equity incentives provided to executives should be tied to the strategic plan of the company and should be consistent with the company's culture and compensation philosophy.

The terms of the equity incentive that is chosen should be tied to that strategic plan. For example, if a company expects a sale outside of the family or an IPO exit within ten years, the vesting of the equity incentive should coincide with the expected exit date or at least be accelerated by the exit event.

The phantom equity plan must also mesh with both the culture and compensation philosophy of the family business. For example, the number of phantom units in the award should be sufficient to motivate the employee based upon his or her compensation level.

Phantom equity grants that provide payment over time are likely subject to Section 409A of the Internal Revenue Code. Section 409A imposes a strict regime of restrictions on deferred compensation and the executive who is the recipient of a phantom equity grant that does not comply with Section 409A is subject to substantial additional taxation. If a phantom equity grant is subject to Section 409A, the payment terms must be fixed at grant and payment may be triggered only as a result of the executive's termination of employment, death or disability, a change in control, or the specific date or dates scheduled at grant.

Measuring Equity Growth

Phantom equity plans can reward the executive for the equity growth of the family business.

The question arises as to how to measure the equity growth of the family business on which the cash incentives are based. Since family businesses need confidentiality, it is important that the plan prevent access to the financial records of a company. One method of resolving this issue is to use growth in net book value as the measurement for the equity incentive and permit the board of directors to determine this growth number. The plan would provide that the good faith determination of the board of directors or its outside accountants as to the amount of equity growth would be final, binding, and conclusive.

For example, the phantom equity incentive plan could provide that the non-family key employee receives 1 percent of the growth in the net book value of the business over the vesting period (i.e., the period that the key employee must remain with the business before receiving any reward). The dollar amount of the equity growth would be determined by company's the board of directors or its outside accountants, and their decision would be final, binding, and conclusive.

The board of directors could then advise the key employee each year during the vesting period as to the dollar value of 1 percent of the growth in net book value during the year in order to keep the employee up to date on the value of the award. This creates "golden handcuffs" between the employee and the family business. Once the key employee's award has been vested, he or she would receive in cash 1 percent of the growth in the net book value as determined by the board of directors from the date of the equity award until the vesting date. However, this payment would be subject to limitations on the amount of cash paid each year so not to adversely affect the business' cash flow.

Other Metrics

The phantom equity plan does not have to be tied solely to the growth in the net book value of the family business. The plan can be tailored to create incentives for the growth in sales revenue, cost reduction, or a variety of other metrics. The actual metrics can be established by the family business to satisfy both its business objectives and its strategic plan.

For the family business to be able to attract and retain a key high level executive, it may be necessary to use metrics that are based upon the increase in the value of the business as measured by independent appraisal. Typically this would only be offered to an urgently needed key executive for whom the business was competing.

Dividend Equivalent Rights

Many phantom plans also contain so-called dividend-equivalent rights. This is a bookkeeping entry that credits the executive with additional phantom units based upon cash dividends (exclusive of tax reimbursement dividends for Subchapter S corporations and limited liability companies) that are paid by the company prior to vesting. This is a desirable clause for companies with a high dividend payout that reduces the potential appreciation of the equity.

Advantages and Disadvantages of Phantom Equity

The phantom equity award helps to bind the non-family key employee to the company for the vesting period and until any vesting conditions are satisfied. It also aligns the interest of key employees with the interests of the shareholders. Its greatest advantage is that it does so without giving non-family executives the rights of shareholders. A similar plan could even be adopted for family members who are key employees if no other incentive compensation structure for them has been established.

A phantom plan results in the deferral of federal income taxation for the recipient of the phantom equity award until cash is actually delivered to or constructively received by the recipient (except that payroll taxes may be due upon vesting). The family business employer generally receives a federal income tax deduction at the same time and in the same amount that the key employee realizes ordinary income.

However, a phantom plan may have tax disadvantages when compared to restricted stock grants and stock options. A recipient of restricted stock may make a "section 83(b) election," in which case the executive would recognize federal income tax at grant in the amount of the fair market value of the stock (discounted significantly for lack of liquidity and control) and any post-grant appreciation is taxed as capital gain. A nonmarketable stock option results in the deferral of taxation until it is exercised or later in the event of an "incentive stock option" (see below). Moreover, because of the nature of a stock option, the executive may decide when exercise (and taxation) will be.

The disadvantage of phantom equity is that once the vesting conditions have been satisfied, payment must be made in cash. However, by limiting the yearly payments to all phantom equity holders to a small percentage of cash flow from operations, the business can avoid being adversely affected by the payments.

Some family businesses establish so-called rabbi trusts after the phantom equity grant, funding those trusts each year with the accrued but unvested benefit under the phantom equity grant. This avoids a large cash outflow in a single year. It also has the benefit of creating greater assurance for the beneficiary of the grant since the employee can see that the money has been placed in a trust of which he or she is the beneficiary, subject to compliance with the vesting conditions.

It is possible that a key employee could legally challenge the computation of an equity growth or other metrics despite the contractual provisions making the board's good faith decision final, binding, and conclusive. A legal challenge might occur if, for example, the business were sold for a sale price that substantially exceeded the equity growth figure determined by the board. In any such lawsuit, the holder of the phantom equity would probably be able to access the books and records of the business.

One method of discouraging such a legal challenge is to insert the so-called clawback clause in the phantom equity grant. The clawback clause would provide that if there were a legal challenge to the board's decision, the holder of the equity would receive nothing and would have to pay back any reward that they had received.

In general, the advantages of phantom equity awards typically outweigh the disadvantages by enabling the business to attract and retain key employees who are not family members.

Exit-Event Stock Options

A stock option gives the holder the right to purchase stock of the family business at the fair market value after the option becomes exercisable during its term. An exit-event option is only exercisable if during the option period there is an exit-event for the family business (i.e., a sale outside the family or an IPO). A form for an Exit-Event Option Plan for family businesses appears in Appendix 5.

The use of an exit-event option plan requires a determination of the fair market value of the family business at the grant date, preferably by an independent appraisal firm. The option price for the number of option shares granted to a specific employee would be computed from this appraisal. If the option price is less than the fair market value of the option shares at the grant date, the employee could have tax problems under Section 409A.

An exit-event option can work for a family business because once the business is sold outside the family or there is an IPO, it is no longer a business completely owned by the family. In the event of a sale outside of the family, the option form requires the holder of the option to remain with the buyer, if so requested by the buyer, for up to six months in order to be able to exercise the option. This permits the seller of the family business to provide incentives to key employees to remain with the business after its sale, thereby making it more valuable to the buyer. Of course, the six-month period can be changed to one year or possibly longer.

What happens if the family business is neither sold outside of the family nor subject to an IPO during the option period? The option expires unexercised since it has never vested.

ISOs Versus Non-ISOs

There are two types of exit-event stock options may be granted under the Code: incentive stock options (ISO) and non-incentive stock options (Non-ISO). The grant of a stock option that has an exercise price at least equal to the fair market value of the option shares at the grant date is generally not subject to federal income tax, regardless of whether it is an ISO or Non-ISO. The exercise of an ISO is generally not a taxable event for federal income tax purposes (except for alternative minimum tax as described below). However, the exercise of a Non-ISO typically results in ordinary income taxable to the optionee equal to the option profit (fair market value of the stock acquired less the option price paid) for federal income tax purposes, is subject to payroll withholding, and is deductible by the company.

The advantage of an ISO is that it permits the key employee to achieve long-term capital gain treatment on the appreciation of the stock after the grant date, provided two requirements are satisfied:

1. The stock is not sold or otherwise disposed of in a "disqualifying disposition" for two years after the option grant and for one year after the exercise date.
2. The option holder is an employee of the company at all times from the grant date until three months prior to the exercise of the stock option (one year in the case of death or "disability" as defined in the Code).

Section 422(d) of the Code limits the amount of long-term capital gains that an employee can receive on an incentive stock option. The limitation is measured each calendar year by multiplying the option price of the incentive stock options received by the optionee by the number of option shares that first become exercisable during that calendar year. To the extent that this multiplication exceeds $100,000 in any calendar year, the excess numbers of shares are not entitled to long-term capital gains investments.

Most employees will not satisfy the one-year holding period on ISOs because they cannot afford to hold the stock for one year after paying the exercise price. And while many highly paid executives can afford to keep the stock for the one-year holding period, doing so may subject them to alternative minimum tax applied to ISOs. To avoid paying this tax, many executives make disqualifying dispositions of stock acquired under ISOs in the year of exercise.

Consequently, by granting an ISO, the company can give an employee the *potential* of long-term capital gains treatment, but in most cases that is not the reality. When an employee makes a sale or other disqualifying disposition of the stock within one year after option exercise, the company (and/or the shareholders of an S corporation or the equityholders of a limited liability company) will generally obtain the same federal income tax deduction as if the employee originally received a Non-ISO.

Moreover, if an employee receives a Non-ISO and exercises it, the company will have to withhold on the exercise date an amount sufficient to pay the employee's federal income tax withholding and the employee's share of other payroll taxes on the share appreciation (unless the shares are subject to vesting conditions, in which case the tax is postponed until the vesting conditions are satisfied or a Section 83(b) election is made). Using an ISO avoids the result, since there is no withholding tax upon an employee's exercise of the ISO.

In general, it is preferable to grant an ISO to key employees even though they may not ultimately realize long-term capital gains treatment on the appreciation, since the ISO at least gives them the potential of receiving such tax treatment.

Our next chapter analyzes some of the problems and best practices in dealing with inactive shareholders.

CHAPTER 7

Dealing with Inactive Minority Shareholders

Communicate Regularly with Inactive Shareholders and Provide Them with Rewards

Many family disputes are the result of conflicts between inactive family shareholders and active family shareholders. The inactive family shareholders who do not receive adequate information about the business may feel estranged and this can result in family disputes. Without effective communication, inactive family shareholders may view the employed family shareholders as receiving all the benefits and rewards of the business and perceive that they are being treated unfairly.

> **Best Practice**
>
> Develop methods to enhance the unity and commitment of family members who are not active in the business through regular communication and various rewards.

The key to dealing with minority shareholders, whether active or inactive, is regular communication concerning the business. This establishes a level of trust that is essential to maintaining family unity. The communication must be open and frank, including not only the successes of the business but also its problems and failures.

According to academic studies,[1] what gives family businesses the inner strength to successfully develop and grow through several generations is the unity of its family members with both each other and the business, as they make up the community of persons that constitutes the company. Successful multigenerational businesses include a significant number of family members, by birth and by marriage, who do not work in the family business.

These academic studies suggest that rewards should be given to these inactive shareholders to enhance their commitment to the business. The following nonfinancial rewards have been suggested to complement the financial rewards (such as dividends, growth policy, and shareholder liquidity facilities for emergencies):

- Create status or image for nonemployee shareholders. This may involve the company publicizing the names of shareholders (with their permission) in the media or internal publications and publicizing shareholder contributions to the company. Nonemployee shareholders may also be given opportunities to be recognized for the efforts they make to the company or to family through their appointment to positions of responsibility in the family council, the committee of a foundation promoted by the family business, and so forth.
- Create training, such as seminars to help nonemployee shareholders expand their business knowledge by attendance at trade and family business conventions, and at seminars that provide specific training to take on board responsibilities.
- Provide nonemployee shareholders and their children with assistance in their career development, such as offering internships in the family business to younger family members.

Worst Practice

Fail to create an atmosphere of trust within the family, particularly with respect to inactive shareholders.

The enemy of family unity is secrecy. Secrecy causes distrust among family members, particularly inactive shareholders.

In 2004, Liesel Pritzker, a nineteen-year-old actress, and her brother Matthew accused their father, Robert Pritzker, of illegally moving money from trusts that were in their name into the Pritzker family foundation that benefited their cousins. The case threatened a separate secret legal agreement among 11 cousins to divide up the family assets, including the Hyatt hotel chain, the 60-plus companies in the Marmon Group, and a network of 2,500 trusts, many of which finance charitable activities. The case was subsequently settled, but represented the unraveling of a 124-year family dynasty that began when Nicholas Pritzker emigrated from a Jewish ghetto near Kiev.[2]

Hold Annual Meetings for Family Businesses with Large Numbers of Inactive Shareholders

As family businesses grow through the generations, they may accumulate a large number of inactive shareholders.[3] In this situation, communication must be more formalized to avoid dissention and misperceptions among the inactive shareholders about the business.

Best Practice

If there are a large number of inactive shareholders, such as in a late-stage cousin consortium, hold annual shareholder meetings and other family-unity events, but control the agenda for these meetings.

Once a family business has become a large cousin consortium with a significant number of shareholders, typically after a number of generations, different methodologies should be used to communicate with family shareholders, many of whom will not be active in the business and will need information concerning it.

This information can be supplied to the family shareholders through quarterly or more frequent newsletters and annual shareholder meetings. The Clemens Family Corporation, with 229 family shareholders, sends out shareholder information on a monthly basis. The newsletter should cover such topics as current events affecting the business, news that will impact the business and their investment, and, if there is a shareholder liquidity program (see Chapter 2), the value of the stock. The newsletter should also emphasize core family values.

Annual shareholder meetings should be conducted to maintain in-person communication. However, it is important to control the agenda at these meetings. Honoring key employees of the business is one way of helping to set a proper tone at the end of a meeting.

In addition to the annual shareholders meeting, the Clemens Family Corporation has a very elaborate informational meeting each year that is run in a fun and entertaining way. All shareholders over the age of fourteen are invited to attend, and the presentations are geared to a teenage audience. Multi-generational stories are emphasized. Some of their annual information meetings include a Christmas dinner at a local Salvation Army shelter where they feed underprivileged families and pass out gifts.

Provide Fair Treatment for Inactive Minority Shareholders

The courts have ruled that the majority shareholders in a closely held corporation have a fiduciary duty to the minority shareholders to act fairly, whether or not those minority shareholders are family members.[4] The courts have stated that majority or controlling shareholders in a close corporation have a heightened fiduciary duty to minority shareholders, and if they utilize their majority control to their own advantage without a legitimate business purpose, they can be sued directly by the minority shareholders.[5]

The controlling shareholders of a family business can set their compensation at such an unreasonably high level that there is no income available for the distribution of dividends to minority shareholders. In effect, the compensation includes a disguised dividend that is not shared with inactive minority shareholders.

Unreasonably high compensation levels are sometimes established in order to minimize payments of federal or state taxes, particularly those based upon income of the family business. However, establishing an unreasonably high compensation level can be challenged by federal and state taxing authorities and result in penalties and interest to the family business.

Best Practice

Treat inactive minority shareholders fairly. This is not only a best practice but also a legal requirement to avoid a charge of minority shareholder oppression. Fair treatment includes establishing reasonable compensation levels for active family members and having only arm's-length transactions with the family business.

Another tactic that can oppress minority shareholders is when the controlling shareholders engage in transactions with the family business that are not on arm's-length terms. For example, they may purchase property or services from the business for less than the fair market value, or they may sell property or services to the business at an inflated valuation.

Continuation of this conduct invites lawsuits from minority family shareholders, as illustrated in the following court case.[6]

Riverview Golf Course, Inc. ("Riverview" or "the corporation"), a Pennsylvania company incorporated in 1961, owns and operates the Riverview Golf Course. The golf course was built on a reclaimed strip mine along the Monongahela River in Elizabeth, Pennsylvania. The eighteen-hole course consists of approximately 150 acres and includes a clubhouse, driving range, practice green, and pole barn for the golf carts. The water for the golf course is pumped directly from the Monongahela River at no cost to the corporation.

Initially the corporation had four shareholders, including William B. Ford ("William"), husband of Margaret B. Ford ("Margaret"), and the father of Margaret L. Ford ("Peggy") and William K. Ford ("Bill"). At some point, three of the initial shareholders bought out the fourth, leaving William as the majority shareholder and president of the corporation.

In 1969, Bill began operating a golf cart business and a pro shop at the course as sole proprietorships. Both businesses were staffed by Riverview employees, who were paid by Riverview. Bill did not reimburse the corporation for either the employees' time or the rental value of the space occupied by his businesses.

When William died in 1995, Bill took over as president of Riverview. Shortly thereafter, Bill fired Peggy, who had worked at the golf course. Bill hired his wife and son as salaried employees, and both were elected to the corporation's board of directors.

Margaret and Peggy filed a suit in law and equity against Riverview in 1997, claiming Bill was using the corporation for his own benefit and not for the benefit of the minority shareholders or the corporation. The parties settled the case, executing a release dated July 19, 1998. Pursuant to the settlement, the corporation borrowed $200,000 to pay Margaret the balance of the notes to her as William's beneficiary.

Bill continued to own and operate the pro shop and cart business separately, but began paying Riverview $13,655 each year for the use of its assets, including paying only (i) $5.50 per hour for 500 hours per year for the use of corporate employees; (ii) $7.00 per square foot per year for 1,000 square feet of pro shop space; (iii) $3.00 per square foot per year for 1,200 square feet of cart barn space; (iv) $30.00 per month for grass cutting; and (v) $20.00 per month for water.

In 2002, Bill lent approximately $400,000 to the corporation: $200,000 for improvements to the clubhouse and course and $200,000 for repayment of the bank note taken to pay Margaret for the 1998 settlement. These debts to Bill are the only debts of the corporation.

Believing that they continued to be treated unfairly, in 1999 Margaret and Peggy again filed a complaint against Bill and Riverview in equity and at law. They claimed that Bill continued to manage the corporation for his own benefit while oppressing the minority shareholders and asked the court to appoint a custodian.

A non-jury trial was held before the court on April 15 and 16, 2003. Upon consideration of the evidence offered at trial, the court made findings of fact and conclusions of law, stating in essence that Bill had financially benefited himself, his wife, and his son to the detriment of the minority shareholders of the corporation. The court found Bill's conduct "oppressive" under 15 Pa. C.S.A. § 1767(a)(2), warranting the appointment of a custodian.

Pay Reasonable Dividends to Inactive Shareholders When Cash Flow Permits

One of the major areas of dispute with minority shareholders, particularly inactive ones, is the failure of the family business to pay reasonable cash dividends if and to the extent paying them is consistent with its current and future needs. There have been numerous litigations over this issue, particularly for family members who are not on the payroll of the business. It is not unusual for family members whose employment has been terminated to seek to compel the board of directors of the business to pay dividends.[7]

> **Best Practice**
>
> Although many small family businesses cannot afford to pay cash dividends to shareholders, at such time as the business has sufficient cash flow to cover both its current and future needs, reasonable dividends should be paid to minority shareholders.

For example, when Gottfried Baking Corporation, a family business engaged in the manufacturing and sale of bakery products, terminated the employment of minority stockholders Charles and Harold Gottfried, they sued the board of directors seeking to compel the payment of dividends. The plaintiffs alleged that the corporate surplus was unnecessarily large and that the controlling family stockholders had acted in bad faith and were attempting to coerce the plaintiffs into selling their stock at a grossly inadequate price by withholding dividends. The plaintiffs also alleged that the controlling shareholders were paying themselves excessive salaries and bonuses and were making corporate loans to themselves. The court ultimately denied the relief on the ground that the plaintiffs had failed to prove that the family surplus was unnecessarily large or that personal reasons had motivated the board's refusal to declare dividends.[8]

Family businesses may prefer to plow their earnings back into the business in order to increase their size and market penetration. For tax reasons, directors and officers of family businesses may prefer to receive their return in the form of compensation rather than in the form of dividends from their shareholders. Even in the case of Subchapter S corporations or limited liability companies, where the enterprise earnings pass through to the shareholders for federal income tax purposes, the controlling shareholders may have a similar temptation to use only salary as their return.

Legally, it is difficult for minority shareholders to compel the declaration of dividends so long as the board has acted in good faith in determining that the funds are necessary for the operation or expansion of the business.[9] A classic case in which the court compelled a dividend involved a suit by the Dodge boys against Ford Motor Company in 1916. At the time of the law suit, Ford was a close corporation with a surplus of $112 million, yearly profits of $60 million, and cash on hand and municipal bonds valued at $54 million. It had planned an expansion that would cost approximately $24 million. The Dodge boys, who were minority shareholders and beginning to produce their own brand of automobile, brought suit to force Ford Motor Company to declare a dividend. The court held that the directors had to distribute a substantial part of the surplus earnings but declined to interfere with the company's expansion plans.[10]

Regardless of the law, both ethically and as a matter of best practice, it is better to provide a reasonable dividend to minority shareholders consistent with the needs of the business. In any event, the board of directors must act in good faith in establishing what are the needs of the business.

Make Business Opportunities Available to Inactive Shareholders

Nothing is more troublesome to an inactive family shareholder than to be deprived of business opportunities that are made available to the active shareholders by reason of their employment in the company.

Best Practice

Active family shareholders should be careful to make available to inactive shareholders business opportunities created by their activity in the business.

Here are the facts of an actual court case which reached the Supreme Court of Massachusetts:[11] Gerald, Robert, and Virgil Aiello and their sister, Joy Hyland, each owned 25 percent of DeLuca's, a Massachusetts corporation. They also constituted DeLuca's board of directors. Since at least 1966, DeLuca's had operated a neighborhood grocery store on Charles Street in Boston. Their uncle owned the property from which the store operated until his death in November 1977. After Joy moved to Florida in 1984, Gerald, Robert, and Virgil took day-to-day responsibility for the operations of the store and the corporation.

Both before and after Joy moved to Florida, the three brothers started other business ventures. Joy was not consulted about these other ventures nor was she offered an opportunity to participate in them.

In March, 1994, Joy confronted Robert and Virgil about the disparity between her compensation and their own—a disparity extending back as far as 1981. Joy was told that the pay difference was a result of the brothers' involvement in the day-to-day full-time operation of the store after she had moved to Florida. Unsatisfied, Joy hired an accountant to investigate the disparities in the compensation of officers, payments to directors, and amounts received by shareholders. Throughout 1995, Virgil, Robert, and Gerald provided Joy with financial documents belonging to DeLuca's, including its tax returns.

Around this time, Joy also became aware of the brothers' other business ventures. These ventures and assorted related real estate transactions were the subject of discussion at a DeLuca's board meeting attended by Joy in 1996. Discussions among the four board members concerning these ventures and other "fairness" issues continued through 1997.

After their uncle died in 1997, everything fell apart. In 2000, the litigation frolic began. In the course of the litigation, Joy brought claims alleging breach of fiduciary duty, including the diversion of corporate opportunities and self-dealing. The trial judge dissolved the corporation and appointed a receiver to wind up its affairs and recommend the fair disbursement of corporate assets.

Our next chapter discusses various methods of eliminating minority shareholders.

CHAPTER 8

Eliminating Minority Shareholders[1]

I t may be necessary from time to time for family businesses to repurchase equity from minority shareholders. The motivations for eliminating minority shareholders include the following:

- Some minority shareholders may wish to obtain liquidity through the voluntary sale of their shares back to the company or to other shareholders.
- Family businesses are sometimes started with funding from persons outside the family who receive equity in the business, which the family business would like to eliminate.
- Family businesses sometimes give equity to shareholders who do not contribute to the business or are obstructive.

This chapter will discuss both voluntary sales, whether initiated by the minority equityholder or by the company, as well as involuntary sales by minority equityholders.

Voluntary Sales Initiated by Minority Equityholders

Family businesses are occasionally approached voluntarily by minority equityholders who wish to obtain liquidity through the sale of their shares or other equity back to the company or other equityholders. These minority equityholders may have a sale price in mind that, when finally negotiated, is acceptable to the business. If the sale price is deemed unacceptable, an independent appraisal can be helpful in negotiating the final price, as discussed later in this chapter.

> ### Best Practice
>
> Make full disclosure in writing to the minority equityholder of any favorable facts or trends that would be material to a selling minority equityholder before the minority equityholder becomes legally obligated to complete the sale. This is not only a best practice, but may be legally required by federal and state securities laws, as well as by fiduciary-duty standards, whether or not the sale is initiated by the minority equityholder.

Many owners of family businesses are not aware that federal and state securities laws apply to the repurchase of stock or other equity from minority equityholders, even in situations in which the equityholder initiates the sale. Federal and state securities laws apply not only to publicly held companies but also to closely held family businesses that are organized as corporations, limited liability companies, or limited partnerships. The stock or other equity of these businesses is considered a "security" under federal and state securities laws as interpreted by the courts.

The practical result is that if the purchasing business does not disclose material facts that could change the selling price to the selling minority equityholders, the selling minority equityholder will have the right to either rescind the sale in the future or obtain damages. The damages would be measured by the excess of what the minority equity was worth at the time of sale over the actual purchase price paid by the family business.

By not disclosing favorable material facts to the minority equityholder prior to the time that the equityholder is legally obligated to complete the sale, the family business has inadvertently granted a free legal right to that equityholder to obtain rescission of the sale in the future if it benefits the minority equityholder. If the value of the family business goes up, the minority equityholder can rescind (i.e., undo) the sale and obtain back his or her minority shares, subject to complying with any applicable statute of limitations. On the other hand, if the value of the family business stays stable or declines, the minority equityholder would not exercise the rescission right.

Aside from violating federal and state securities laws, failing to disclose favorable material facts to the selling minority equityholder may also breach fiduciary duties owed by the directors, officers, or majority equityholders to the selling minority equityholder.

Redeeming Stock in Contemplation of the Sale of the Family Business

The following case involved a suit by former minority shareholders of a closely held family business who claimed that their father and uncle breached their fiduciary duty to them in repurchasing their stock for $200 per share while negotiating a sale to a third party for a much higher price[2] The case illustrates the legal principles described above.

Nyman Manufacturing Company was a closely held family corporation that manufactured paper and plastic dinnerware. Nyman's articles of incorporation authorized the issuance of up to 13,500 shares of Class A non-voting stock and 1,500 shares of Class B voting stock. Nyman was managed by brothers Robert C. and Kenneth J. Nyman.

In the late 1980s, Robert and Kenneth owned all of the Class B stock and nearly half of the Class A stock then issued and outstanding. The other outstanding Class B shares were owned by their children; their sisters Judith A. Lawton and Beverly Kiepler; Judith's husband and children; a testamentary trust established by their father, Walfred Nyman; and the estate of Magda Burt, Walfred's sister. Judith, her husband, seven of their eight children, and Robert's son Jeffrey were the plaintiffs in these two consolidated cases.

In August 1994, Nyman was on the verge of bankruptcy. Robert and Kenneth hired Keith Johnson, an able and experienced manager, to try to turn the company around. After Johnson's arrival, business began improving and, in April 1995, Johnson was granted options to purchase 1,000 shares of Nyman's Class A shares.

Shortly thereafter, the company embarked on a program to repurchase the outstanding Class A shares not owned by Robert or Kenneth. As shares were redeemed, Johnson and the Nyman brothers were awarded options to purchase them.

On May 10, 1996, the children, the sisters, and related parties agreed to sell their 952 shares of Class A stock back to the company for $200 per share, which constituted an implicit valuation for the whole business of a little over $2 million.

On June 25, 1997, Van Leer Corporation, one of Nyman's competitors, signed a letter of intent offering to purchase all of Nyman's outstanding stock for roughly $30 million. The subsequent purchase agreement provided that the aggregate price for all of Nyman's stock and options was fixed at $28,164,735.

The lower court found for the plaintiff children, siblings, and related parties. On appeal, the U.S. Court of Appeals for the First Circuit upheld the lower court on liability but remanded the case for further proceedings on damages. The court found that Robert and Kenneth had breached their fiduciary duty by not disclosing to the children, siblings, and other related parties who sold their shares back to Nyman that they had "a realistic expectation that the company soon might be sold for much more than $200 per share."

The Mistake: It would have been very simple for Robert and Kenneth to have disclosed the possibility that the business might be sold in the future in connection with the repurchase of the stock by Nyman. Presumably, they did not do so either because they were unaware that they had any such fiduciary duty or did not want to have Nyman pay more than it had to.

Had they disclosed the possibility of the future sale of the family business, it is likely that the sellers would have requested a "look-back" clause that would have given the sellers the benefit of any sale at a higher price within a certain time period, typically one or two years. Had they negotiated this clause with the sellers, the brothers could have easily waited until the look-back period was over before selling the business.

Of course, advising the sellers of the possibility of a future sale of the family business could have resulted in the refusal to sell at all. That would have meant less money for the owners when the sale ultimately occurred. However, that is a risk that arguably should have been taken to preserve family harmony.

Worst Practice

Have the family business repurchase stock from family members without making full disclosure of all favorable facts and trends.

Voluntary Sales by Minority Equityholders Initiated by the Family Business

There are occasions in which the family business believes that it is important to eliminate undesirable minority equityholders, initially, at least, on a voluntary basis, and approaches the minority equityholder for the purpose of a negotiated sale. Note that the federal and state securities laws as well as fiduciary duty require full disclosure before any such sale.

Since these minority equityholders have not initiated the sale process, they will typically be suspicious of any price offered by the family business or its controlling equityholder. Therefore, it is preferable to obtain an independent appraisal before making an offer in order to determine a fair value for the minority interest. Of course, this assumes that there have been no other analogous sales of minority equity in the recent past that can be used to guide an arm's-length valuation. Any independent appraisal will take a discount typically of up to one-third for a minority equity interest.

If an offer is made without an independent appraisal, minority shareholders will typically reject it under the assumption that they are being underpaid for their own equity. Therefore, it is preferable for the majority owner of the business to start the negotiation with an independent appraisal performed by someone everyone trusts, such as the company's independent accounting firm or an independent appraisal firm. The independent appraisal should not be shown to the minority shareholder until such time as it is necessary to convince the shareholder to accept the offer as fair.

If litigation is a reasonable possibility, it is preferable to have the attorney for the company or its controlling shareholder obtain the appraisal in order to protect its results from discovery. The attorney can arguably prevent the appraisal from being discovered by invoking the attorney-client privilege or the work-product doctrine.

Mediation

If it is not possible to negotiate a fair price with the minority equityholder, nonbinding mediation should be suggested to the minority equityholder. A mutually agreeable mediator would then be selected by both the company and the minority shareholder to determine a fair price.

Note that mediation is not effective if the minority equityholder is not interested in selling for any price. Mediation is only helpful if the minority equityholder wants to sell, but there is a dispute as to the selling price.

Involuntary Sales: What Happens if the Minority Equityholder Will Not Sell?

There are many situations in which the minority equityholder will not sell under any circumstances or will only sell if the sale price is outrageously high. Under these circumstances, the business has several choices, including the following:

- Do nothing and live with the situation.
- Dilute the equity interest of the minority equityholder if it is consistent with the fiduciary duties of the board of directors or the managers of the company.
- Effectuate a reverse stock split to fractionize the shares of the minority shareholder if it is consistent with the fiduciary duties of the board of directors and managers of the company.
- Effectuate a merger with a new company formed by the remaining shareholders where the minority shareholder is cashed out, provided that the merger is consistent with the fiduciary duties of the board of directors and managers of the company.

The most common tactic by the company in this situation is a reverse stock split, which is discussed below.

Reverse Stock Split

In a reverse stock split, shareholders of a corporation receive one new share of stock for each "block" of old stock they turn in. For example, a shareholder may receive one share of stock for every 10, 100, or 1,000 shares of old stock he or she turns in. If a shareholder owns less than the number of old shares required to be converted into a new share, he or she generally receives cash rather than a fractional share in the corporation.[3] Reverse stock splits do not easily work for limited liability companies or limited partnerships.

The best way to explain a reverse stock split is to discuss an actual court case in which one was used successfully.[4] The case involved Arp and Hammond Hardware Company (the "Company"), a family business formed in 1950. Over the years, ownership of the Company had been passed to the various descendants of one of its founders. By the year 2000, the Company was owned by a cousin consortium consisting of four cousins.

- Francis Read
- Doran Lummis
- Catharine Holmes
- Elizabeth Arp Stoddard

The first three named cousins each owned approximately 20 percent of the business' stock and the fourth-named cousin owned approximately 40 percent. Doran Lummis was interested in buying the stock of the business. Francis Read (approximately 20 percent ownership) and Elizabeth Arp Stoddard (approximately 40 percent ownership) were prepared to sell their shares to an entity formed by Doran Lummis called Lummis Livestock Company, LLC ("LLC").

However, Catharine Holmes was unwilling to sell her company shares to the LLC. Instead, she transferred her shares to her daughter, Suzanne Brown, as successor trustee of two trusts. By June 12, 2003, Doran Lummis' LLC had acquired 2,123 shares of the Company, which constituted approximately 80 percent of the outstanding shares. The remaining 594 shares were owned by Suzanne Brown as trustee.

In order to eliminate the 594 shares owned by Suzanne Brown, the Company gave notice on June 13, 2003 of its intention to amend its articles of incorporation to cause a reverse stock split. The amendment proposed a reduction in the number of shares at a rate of 2,123 to 1 and required the Company to acquire all factional shares for cash. The reverse stock split was approved on September 25, 2003 by the majority of the outstanding shares then owned by the LLC.

The effect of the reverse stock split was to give the LLC one whole share of the Company and to fractionalize the shares owned by Suzanne Brown as trustee, which would then be acquired for cash by the Company. The reverse stock split permitted the Company to rid itself of a minority shareholder against her will.[5]

The litigation that followed, which was settled by the Supreme Court of Wyoming, related to the valuation of the fractional shares. Suzanne Brown exercised dissenters' rights of appraisal from the reverse stock split, as permitted by Wyoming corporate statute. The issue was whether or not a minority discount should apply to the valuation of her shares.

Fiduciary Duty

Any reverse stock split recommendation by a corporation's board of directors can be legally challenged on the ground that it is a breach of their fiduciary duties. Therefore, it is important to have a full discussion at the board level as to why it is appropriate and in the interest of the corporation to eliminate a minority shareholder. Business reasons for eliminating minority shareholders might include, for example, avoiding substantial legal expense caused by a litigious minority shareholder that was harming the business. Another reason might be a desire to eliminate any shareholdings by an employee whose employment has been terminated for good reason.

The laws of various states differ as to what is a good business purpose as well as whether or not a business purpose is required to effectuate a reverse stock split. For example, one Ohio court[6] has interpreted Ohio law to prohibit a reverse stock split that would eliminate a potential competitor who was a minority shareholder of a corporation on the ground that there was no evidence of actual competition in the marketplace between the corporation and the potential competitor. This was true even though the minority shareholder competed for similar customers and sold similar products throughout the United States. The court stated: "There was no evidence before the trial court that indicated that the two corporations have done battle in the market place."[7] The court believed that while the two businesses shared similar customers in the marketplace, both seem to be established in their own particular niche, vis-à-vis each other and the other competitors in the market.

Not every state law is clear as to whether a reverse stock split can be effectuated to eliminate a minority shareholder without any good business reason related to the corporation. Therefore, caution is important in this area.

Other techniques discussed above to dilute or eliminate the equity interest of a minority shareholder are also subject to a fiduciary duty challenge. For example, if the intention is to dilute the minority shareholder by selling more shares, an offer should be made to all shareholders to permit them to maintain their proportionate equity interest. This technique is unlikely to work legally if the minority shareholder is willing to pay for the additional shares in order to maintain his or her percentage of equity, since it is arguably deemed a breach of fiduciary duty to refuse to sell the additional equity to the minority shareholder. Of course, if the minority shareholder does not have the funds to invest in the corporation and the corporation clearly needs the additional capital for business reasons, the technique of equity dilution would probably be legally upheld.

Our next chapter deals with best and worst practices for family businesses which are in financial distress.

CHAPTER 9

Family Businesses in Financial Distress[1]

F amily businesses sometimes have financial troubles. There is no doubt that a family business has many characteristics that provide it with a competitive edge, such as paternalism, which is extended to family members and sometimes to non-family members and promotes a sense of trust, stability, and commitment to the firm among all the employees.[2] However, these same characteristics can backfire when the business is under financial distress, since they may make it difficult for the owner to take needed cost-cutting measures, such as layoffs.

Moreover, a family business is likely to limit top management positions to family members, rather than hire more qualified or capable outsiders who have experience in financial-distress situations. Such businesses are also prone to redistributing their benefits through excessive compensation or special dividends that can adversely affect the business in times of stress. Top management of family businesses may not be capable of making the difficult decisions needed to bring the business back to health.

Consult a Business Lawyer Specializing in Restructuring and Bankruptcy

Owners of family businesses typically do not have the expertise to understand how to prepare for a financial crisis, which may necessitate severe cost cutting, restructuring, composition with creditors, or ultimately, bankruptcy filing.

> **Best Practice**
>
> Consult with a business lawyer specializing in restructurings and bankruptcies at the earliest possible time.

A business lawyer who specializes in restructuring and bankruptcies should be consulted as early as possible in order to provide a road map for the owner of the family business as to possible alternatives and future steps. These steps may include a strategy for accumulating cash and possibly protecting assets from creditors. However, when the business is under financial pressure, it is usually too late to protect the assets from creditors since any transfers at that point may be viewed as fraudulent transfers or conveyances under state law or the federal bankruptcy statute. The time to consider asset protection from creditors is well before the business has any financial problems (see Chapter 3).

Think Twice Before Investing More Cash in the Family Business

The owners of a family business should not automatically invest or lend new money to the business in order to save it. There have been a number of situations in which money an owner has invested or lent money to a business only to have it dissipated because of negative cash flow. If the company is ultimately forced into a bankruptcy, the loan made by its owner may be subordinated to the rights of other creditors and never repaid. Likewise, the additional equity contribution to the business by the owner will likely also be wiped out. In effect, the owner may be "throwing good money after bad."

> **Worst Practice**
>
> Fail to seek legal advice before investing or lending any new money to the family business that is in financial distress.

Before investing new cash in a family business in financial distress, the owner should seek legal advice from a lawyer specializing in bankruptcy. The attorney may suggest that the family business consider either a composition with creditors or filing a Chapter 11 bankruptcy, as discussed below. If a Chapter 11 bankruptcy filing is necessary, the owner can, with court approval, lend the new money to the bankrupt company as debtor-in-possession financing that is superior to that of other creditors; use the new money to fund the purchase of the business out of bankruptcy in a Section 363 sale; or use the new money to fund a reorganization plan.

Consider Hiring a Turnaround Specialist

In times of financial distress, deep cost cutting is required, including laying off or furloughing employees or severely cutting their compensation. The head of the family may have difficulty making these decisions, particularly when they involve family members.

Owners who have not in the past experienced severe financial downturns tend to take a Pollyannaish view of the future of their businesses, falsely hoping that if they only wait a little longer the business will recover. As a result, they tend to take insufficient cost-cutting measures rather than the severe cost cutting that may be necessary to save the business. Waiting too long for Draconian cost cutting can be deadly for the survival of the family business.

> **Best Practice**
>
> Consider hiring a turnaround specialist or chief restructuring officer to assist in cutting costs and layoffs or furloughs of employees.

At a minimum, owners of family businesses that are experiencing financial difficulty should consider consulting with a management-turnaround specialist, especially if they do not have either the objectivity or the expertise necessary to make the hard cost cutting decisions. Employing a turnaround specialist is contrary to the secretive culture of most family businesses, and therefore a business should require a confidentiality agreement from any turnaround specialist. The specialist may also assist family members fill in the "credibility gap" with creditors, who may have more confidence in the specialist than in management.

However, while a turnaround specialist who advises the owner may be sufficient for smaller family businesses, larger family businesses may require a chief restructuring officer to actually operate the business until it once again begins to prosper. The terms and conditions of the employment of the chief restructuring officer must be carefully negotiated with the help of a business lawyer specializing in workouts and bankruptcy.

Banks are often the major lenders to the family business. Using a turnaround specialist or a chief restructuring officer will assist the family business in their relationships with the banks. In fact, many banks will recommend such individuals to family businesses in financial trouble and may actually insist upon a chief restructuring officer in connection with any workout agreements. However, the bank's recommendation should not automatically be accepted. Anyone the bank recommends should be carefully checked with other businesses that have in the past hired either the turnaround specialist or the chief restructuring officer.

Prior to hiring any turnaround specialist or chief restructuring officer, the owner of the family business should consult with independent members on the board of directors who have had similar experiences. If that competency does not exist within the company's board of directors (or if there is no independent board of directors), a business lawyer specializing in turnarounds and bankruptcy should be consulted. Many business lawyers who specialize in this area have had prior experience with turnaround firms that can be helpful in selecting the right turnaround specialist.

Consider a Composition with Creditors

> **Best Practice**
>
> If severe cost cutting is insufficient to save the family business, consider a composition with creditors.

If cost-cutting measures are not sufficient to save the family business, a composition with creditors should be considered as an alternative to a bankruptcy filing. The threat of a bankruptcy filing can induce creditors to agree to postpone payment of their debts or to accept a small percentage on the dollar of their debts.

However, to effectuate a composition with creditors, the family business must have sufficient cash resources. Cash must be accumulated to effectuate a composition, since creditors will undoubtedly insist upon cash as part of the composition agreement. This cash accumulation may require the stretching out of accounts payable and the vigorous collection of accounts receivable.

Many family businesses have a bank or other financial institution as a secured creditor. If possible, it is important to initially negotiate a moratorium with the secured creditors and revise repayment terms. The willingness of the secured creditors to negotiate a moratorium, revise repayment terms, or both is helpful in subsequently convincing unsecured creditors to accept a composition. If the owners of the family business have personally guaranteed the bank debt, they should also negotiate a moratorium on the enforcement of their guarantee or possibly seek to purchase the bank's position at a discount if available.

Family businesses tend to underestimate their negotiating strength with their secured lender bank. Banks typically do not wish to foreclose their liens on a family business since such foreclosures usually result in major losses to the bank. Banks may be comfortable with the family continuing to run the business if they have enjoyed a good track record, coordinate closely with the bank, and create what appears to be a viable recovery plan.

A composition with creditors is only effective if all of the substantial creditors join in. It is typical to initially negotiate the composition with the major creditors and hope that the smaller creditors are willing to accept the same terms as the larger creditors.

If major creditors refuse to join and proceed to effect collection, bankruptcy may be the only alternative, subject to two possible exceptions. First, if the assets of the family business are subject to a blanket lien in favor of a bank or other financial institution and the indebtedness secured by the lien equals or exceeds the value of the assets, then the bank may be willing to arrange a friendly foreclosure sale under Section 9-610 of the Uniform Commercial Code to a new entity controlled by the family as an alternative to a bankruptcy filing. Second, some states have statutes that permit an assignment of all assets of the family business for the benefit of creditors, and these statutes should be carefully examined before filing in bankruptcy.

Even if the composition with creditors fails because significant creditors refuse to join, the effort may be worthwhile since it will help identify cooperating creditors for a bankruptcy filing and may permit a prepackaged bankruptcy filing.

A Bankruptcy Filing Should Normally Be the Last Alternative

Bankruptcy should normally be the owner's last option since it carries many disadvantages. However, there are times when it is the only viable alternative, and it may even be preferred if the owner is going to invest or lend new money to the business, as discussed above. A business may be forced to file a bankruptcy petition in order to obtain the benefit of an automatic stay, which prevents creditors from foreclosing on business assets and from filing or continuing law suits against the business as well as to protect new money that the owner wishes to invest in or lend to the business.

A bankruptcy filing by a family business does not typically safeguard the owner from the effect of personal guarantees of indebtedness to banks and other financial institutions unless he or she also personally files. Therefore, the bankruptcy option may not be practical if the owner's personal assets are susceptible to the lenders' claims to the business. However, if the owner/guarantor utilizes some of the his or her personal assets in the bankruptcy, some bankruptcy courts have extended the automatic stay to cover the owner/guarantor without requiring that he or she file a separate personal bankruptcy.

> **Best Practice**
>
> Bankruptcy should normally be the owner's last option to save the family business unless it is part of a strategy to protect any new money that has been invested in or lent to the business by the owner.

A typical family business would file under Chapter 11 of the Bankruptcy Code to reorganize the company. This is a very expensive process that carries hefty attorney fees. A Chapter 11 grants the company the benefit of an automatic stay and permits the business to continue to be operated. However, many Chapter 11 filings are not successful and are ultimately converted to Chapter 7 liquidations, particularly if the business is not cash positive during the bankruptcy and is unable to obtain debtor-in-possession financing.

Chapter 11 permits the current management of the family business (unless it is a "small business debtor")[3] the exclusive right to propose a plan of reorganization, typically for a 120-day period after the filing that can be extended at the discretion of the bankruptcy judge to a maximum of 18 months. After the exclusivity period terminates, outsiders can file their own plan of reorganization, which can ultimately result in an auction of the family business. The plan may involve selling the business to an entity formed by family members that will continue it with new funding.

Unlike a composition with creditors, a Chapter 11 reorganization plan does not require all significant creditors or interest holders to agree. For example, a class of creditors has accepted a plan if at least two-thirds in amount and more than one-half in number of the allowed claims of the class that are voted are cast in favor of the plan. The two-thirds and one-half requirements are computed based on a denominator that equals the amount or number of claims that have actually been voted for or against the plan, rather than the actual total number and amount of claims in the class.[4] This means that there can be a significant number of unsecured creditors who may object to the plan but may nevertheless be forced to accept it.

Sometimes the only alternative for a business under distress is to find a buyer, which may include other members of the family. Some buyers may insist that the company file in bankruptcy in order to permit the buyer to purchase its assets in what is called a Section 363 sale. A sale pursuant to Section 363 of the Bankruptcy Code, which is approved by a final and nonappealable order of the bankruptcy court, permits the buyer to acquire title to the assets free of liabilities other than those that the buyer has specifically agreed to assume. It also prevents creditors of the family business whose debts are not assumed by the buyer from reaching the assets that are in the hands of the buyer. A sale to a new entity controlled by family members pursuant to Section 363 can, in many cases, be a faster procedure for removing the family business from the bankruptcy proceeding than a traditional reorganization plan.

The Boscov case, discussed below, involved a reorganization plan that provided for a sale pursuant to Section 363 to the Boscov family.

The Story of the Boscov's Chapter 11 Bankruptcy

Boscov's is a family-owned department-store business founded in 1911 by Solomon "Sol" Boscov, a Russian Jew who had emigrated to Reading, Pennsylvania, that same year. He had $1.37 in cash on arrival in the United States and worked as a traveling salesman with an initial $8 worth of merchandise. Because he spoke Yiddish, he was able to converse with those people in Berks County who spoke Pennsylvania Dutch.[5]

The first Boscov's was founded in downtown Reading as the Economy Shoe Store and Dry Goods Annex. Boscov's began opening satellite stores in the Reading suburbs in the 1960s. As early as 1968, Boscov's had five stores, 2,200 workers, and annual sales exceeding $50 million. Solomon Boscov retired and was succeeded by his son, Albert, as head of the company in 1968. Boscov's began opening stores in nearby counties, starting in 1972 with a store in Lebanon, Pennsylvania. Ultimately, there were 39 additional stores spread throughout the Mid-Atlantic states: Pennsylvania, New Jersey, Maryland, New York, and Delaware.

Upon retiring in 2006, Albert Boscov and his brother-in-law, Ed Lakin, cashed out $180 million of their holdings. Under the subsequent leadership of Ed's son, Ken, the company embarked on a

ten-store expansion. However, as the economy worsened in 2007, customers reduced their retail expenditures and by 2008 these newer
stores were draining the chain's cash flow.

On August 4, 2008, Boscov's filed for bankruptcy protection, saying it was reorganizing and that its bankruptcy was precipitated by
slowing sales and a nationwide credit crunch. The company announced
that it was closing ten underperforming stores. On October 15, 2008,
retired chairman and CEO Albert Boscov submitted the winning bid
to reacquire the company in partnership Ed Lakin. Ed Rendell, the
governor of Pennsylvania, offered a $35 million state loan to Boscov's,
funded by the United States Department of Housing and Urban
Development, on November 27, 2008. In December 2008, Albert
Boscov, Ed Lakin, and other businessmen took over the company,
officially exiting Chapter 11 bankruptcy.

The following article appeared in the September 18, 2009 issue of
The Philadelphia Inquirer:

> It was a rubber-stamp hearing, the kind of thing less-sentimental
> businessmen have their attorneys take care of. But that's not how Al
> Boscov rolls. No, the 79-year-old savior of his family's department
> store chain just had to be here yesterday.
>
> He had a primal urge to see and hear from U.S. Bankruptcy Judge
> Kevin Gross. He had to personally thank every lawyer. But most of
> all, Boscov had to witness for himself the end of an ordeal that had
> broken his heart, almost left thousands unemployed, and nearly
> ruined the business his once-penniless immigrant father had started a
> century ago in Reading.
>
> A sentimental man would have cried. Boscov, who turns 80 next
> week, did.
>
> Moments after Gross approved the company's exit form Chapter 11
> bankruptcy and adjourned the hearing, Boscov was asked why he had
> driven all the way from Reading fro a 30-minute technical proceeding
> in a virtually empty courtroom.
>
> 'I wanted to,' the notoriously jocular bundle of energy said as his
> vocal chords seized and his eyes watered.
>
> 'You know why,' Boscov said, 'Because we're alive.'

There are occasions when it is necessary to sell a family business.
Our next chapter reviews some of the best and worst practices in
a sale.

CHAPTER 10

Selling a Family Owned Business

The decision to sell a family business is gut wrenching for many families. Families tend to personally identify with the business and view its loss similarly to how they might view the death of a close relative. The emotional value of owning a family business cannot be overestimated.[1] As in so many other aspects of owning a family business, frank and open meetings are essential to maintaining family harmony in anticipation of a sale.

This chapter will discuss advanced planning to sell a family business either to other family members (including management buyouts, leverage buyouts, and cash flow acquisitions), an employee stock ownership plan (ESOP), or an unrelated third-party financial or strategic buyer in an auction. This chapter does not cover other methods of selling a business such as selling in a tax-free reorganization, typically to a public company. Some portions of this chapter are taken from the author's book entitled *Valuing Your Business: Strategies to Maximize the Sale Price* (John Wiley & Sons, Inc. 2005) which contains a much more comprehensive discussion of this subject, including advanced planning techniques.

Anticipate Potential Threats to the Family Business

The sale of a family business may be plagued by any one of the following problems that can reduce, if not destroy, its value:

- Key employees leave when the owner announces his or her decision to sell, taking important customers with them.
- The business is overpriced so that it takes so long to find a buyer that new well-financed competitors have time to establish

themselves before the sale, thereby lowering the value of the family business.

- Customers find out about the pending sale and seek out its competitors.
- Competitors find out about the pending sale and use this information to win away existing and potential customers from the family business.
- Suppliers who are important to the family business start to sell to its competitors after realizing that the business will be sold.
- The owner and his or her top executives spend so much time involved with the sale process that the family business itself begins to run downhill.
- The owner is the trustee of family trusts that own shares in the company, and the owner's children, who are the beneficiaries, hire their own lawyers in an effort to maximize their share of the sale price.
- The owner's spouse, anticipating the sale proceeds, decides to divorce him or her and hires the most aggressive lawyer in town to maximize the spouse's share.

These problems occur more frequently when selling to the unrelated third party than when selling within the family. However, even in-family sales can generate these potential risks.

> **Best Practice**
>
> Prepare for the sale of the family business by anticipating and attempting to ameliorate the possible threats to the business. Retain a team of professionals to assist in anticipating and countering these possible threats.

Each of these potential threats can be minimized by taking appropriate action well before the sale target date. For example, the threat of key employees (family or not) leaving and taking customers with them when the sale is announced can be avoided by using any of the following methods (among others) before the sale is announced:

- Enforcing any employee agreement that is already in place to prevent customer solicitation (see Chapter 2).
- Executing an agreement with key employees that offers them a small percentage of the sale proceeds if they remain with the company for a period of time after the sale closes.

- Awarding the key employee a phantom equity right accompanied by an agreement not to solicit customers for a period of time in consideration of the award.

The key to countering these threats is to hire a team of consultants to advise the family business before the sale process begins. The team should consist of a merger and acquisition lawyer, an accountant, and possibly a family business advisor and an investment banker.

Understand the Motivation for the Sale

Many times family business owners suffer from "seller's remorse" after the sale is completed. They regret having made the sale and feel guilty about separating the family from the business. This is particularly true if the business had been handed down from generation to generation.

> **Best Practice**
>
> Selling a family business requires an understanding of the motivation for the sale that should include careful and candid discussions with family members involved in the business.

The key to avoiding "seller's remorse" is a proper understanding of the motivations that justify the sale of the business. This requires both advance planning and communication with other family members involved in the business well before the target date for the sale.

The founder or owner of a business typically wants to cash out for a variety of personal reasons. He or she

- is tired of working so hard, ready to retire, and has no children who are interested in taking over the business;
- has competitors moving into the business area and does not have the capital with which to fight them;
- would like to have enough money in the bank to be able to support a comfortable lifestyle;
- needs more capital resources than he or she can acquire to grow the business;
- has a business that is going downhill, and would prefer to sell it before it reaches the bottom; or
- has just died and did not maintain enough life insurance to pay estate and inheritance taxes.

The motivations for the sale should be discussed, to the extent appropriate, with other family members involved in the business.

One reason not to sell is if a long-term financial projection of the family business, even with only a modest growth rate, shows that its owners could be collectively wealthier by a substantial margin if they did not sell.[2] Therefore, any sale decision should begin with a long-term financial analysis that takes into account the income taxes generated from the sale.

Selling to Family Employees

It is not unusual during the sale process to receive an expression of interest from a group of key employees, including family members. Indeed, the owner may, through feelings of family loyalty and camaraderie, prefer that his or her key employees, particularly other family members, are the buyer, even when they are not necessarily the highest bidder.

The primary difficulty in selling to key employees (whether family or not) is that they usually lack the capital and require the owner to finance them. Moreover, once the owner's key employees become active bidders, they will not necessarily be as cooperative with other potential buyers who are willing to pay a higher price and do not need the owner to finance them.

There are three major problems in selling the business to other family members.

- Agreeing upon a fair purchase price.
- Financing the payment of that purchase price if the other family member does not have cash.
- Negotiating what warranties and representations, if any, will be made by the seller.

Best Practice

To the extent the sale to a family member requires the seller to finance the purchase price by accepting a purchase price note from the family purchaser, the seller should obtain the same protections as would a bank that was lending that same amount to the purchaser.

It is typical for the buying family members to want financing from the selling family members if they do not have sufficient cash to close the transaction. In dealing with a request for financing, typically in the form of a purchaser's note, the selling family members should obtain the same protections they would receive if they were providing financing to a non-family member. These protections include the following:

- Collateral for the purchase price note, which should preferably include, at a minimum, any stock or other equity that is sold and preferably a lien on the business assets that is possibly subordinate to any bank financing.
- Personal guarantees by the purchaser and its equityholders and their spouses.

It is also important that the collateral not be released until the seller has been completely released from all personal guarantees with respect to the business that the seller has given before the sale closing.

These safeguards are important to protect the seller from any subsequent failure by the family member buyer to pay the purchase price note and any failure to have the seller released from any personal guarantees that were given with respect to the business.

Management Buyouts and Leveraged Buyouts

If the family business has sufficient cash flow or assets to support a leveraged recapitalization, the owner's key employees can probably find institutional financing for a management buyout (MBO) or a leveraged buyout (LBO). The only practical difference between the two is that in an MBO the management receives much more equity and generally leads the transaction. Even in an LBO it is not unusual for management to obtain at least 5 percent to 10 percent of the equity. An equity position of 30 percent or more is not unheard of in an MBO.

For family employees to locate institutional financing for an MBO or LBO, the business must be large enough to attract institutional lenders and investors. Typically, these institutional lenders and investors will not want to structure a transaction involving less than a minimum of $10 million in senior debt and would expect a valuation for the business that is north of $20 million. Senior debt is unsubordinated debt that may or may not be collateralized.

Changes to federal income tax law adopted in 1991 have made MBOs and LBOs requiring annual interest payments of more than

$5 million (subject to reduction) less attractive by denying interest deductions for these excess interest payments. These MBOs and LBOs usually involve purchase prices of at least $50 million in order to create an annual interest payment of approximately $5 million.

The senior institutional lenders will generally lend on an asset or cash-flow basis to the family business to permit the repurchase of its stock with the proceeds of the loan. If the family business has excellent growth prospects but does not have the assets or cash flow to satisfy senior institutional lenders, mezzanine lenders (typically unsecured lenders and subordinated lenders) or investors and possibly equity funds might be interested in financing the MBO or LBO.

Make sure that the family business has enough cash after the repurchase of the owner's stock to pay its debts in the ordinary course of business and that it is adequately capitalized. If not, in the event of a subsequent bankruptcy the trustee in bankruptcy or trade creditors will challenge the transaction as a fraudulent transfer.

If the owner's key employees are able to obtain institutional financing for an MBO or LBO, this probably means that the owner will be able to obtain institutional financing for a leveraged recapitalization. In a leveraged recapitalization the owner retains control of his or her company and receives some cash for some of his or her stock from the money supplied by the institutional lenders and investors. Of course, thereafter the owner must work in a highly leveraged environment and with significant restrictions on his or her operations.

If the owner is not willing to work under these conditions, an MBO or LBO with key employees would be a reasonable choice, since unlike in a leveraged recapitalization, the owner could receive cash for 100 percent of his or her stock.

On some MBOs and LBOs, the senior lenders and investors may require the owner to accept a portion of the purchase price for his or her equity in deferred payments, with the balance paid in cash at the closing. Typically, these deferred payments are evidenced by a note that is specifically subordinated to the senior lender's debt. Consequently, in the event of a default on the senior debt, the owner may never be paid his or her note.

The usual reason for requiring the owner to accept a subordinated note for a portion of the purchase price is that otherwise there will not be enough money left in the business to satisfy the senior lender.

To protect themselves under these circumstances, owners may try to negotiate the following:

- A right to resume control of the company in the event of a default until any defaults are cured
- A right of first refusal on any sale of the company by the senior lenders
- A lien on all assets and stock or other equity subordinate only to the senior lenders

Internal Cash-Flow Acquisitions

If the owner wants to sell to key family employees who cannot obtain outside financing, he or she may structure a sale that permits them to use internally generated cash flow to pay the purchase price.

The owner could sell his or her stock to the family business in exchange for deferred installments of the purchase price. The owner's employees would be given the right to purchase small amounts of stock with their own funds, through payroll deductions, or both. The owner has to protect him or herself against default through liens on the stock he or she sold and on the assets of the business.

If the owner's company is an S corporation and has never been a C corporation, the owner can sell his or her stock back to the company slowly until the key employees' stock constitutes the majority of the outstanding stock. The price paid to the owner would be treated as long-term capital gains (assuming that the owner held the stock for more than one year).

However, if the owner's company is or was previously a C corporation, a slow sale of his or her stock may produce ordinary income to the owner equal to the earnings and profits of the C corporation. To avoid this and obtain long-term capital gain, the owner may have to immediately sell all of his or her stock back to the company or at least create a "substantially disproportionate redemption."

To create a substantially disproportionate redemption, the owner must, after the redemption, own less than 50 percent of the combined voting power of all classes of stock entitled to vote, and the ratio of this voting stock to all voting stock after the redemption must be less than 80 percent of the same ratio before the redemption. Thus, if before the redemption the owner owned 100 percent of all voting stock, he or she must own not more than 49 percent afterwards. If the owner owns 60 percent before the redemption, he or she must own less than 48 percent afterwards. In computing these percentages, the owner is deemed to constructively own the stock of other related persons and entities, including his or her spouse and children.

Selling to the owner's key employees (whether family or not) who use internally generated cash flow to pay the purchase price is a dangerous method of selling the family business. The owner still retains the risks of the business prior to receiving his or her full purchase price. Such a sale should only be attempted if the owner has no ability to sell to outsiders or feels such loyalty to the business' key employees that he or she is willing to assume these risks.

Selling to an Employee Stock Ownership Plan

If the family business has a large annual payroll, an ESOP might be used to purchase the owner's stock. An ESOP is a type of qualified retirement plan that invests primarily in the stock of the business.

There are many consultants who develop and promote ESOP sales as an exit strategy for a family business. It is important that the owner understand both the advantages and disadvantages of an ESOP before pursuing this strategy. The author has seen situations where the owners of family businesses fail to fully understand the problems of administering an ESOP and rush too quickly to establish one as an exit strategy. Before pursuing this option, it is important the owner consider the yearly administrative costs, the cost of appraisals, and the necessity of buying back stock from retired employees.

Worst Practice

Establishing an ESOP as an exit strategy without fully understanding the pitfalls and disadvantages.

From the owner's viewpoint, the primary advantage of an ESOP is that a qualifying sale is free of any federal income tax and the owner can roll the cash he or she receives into a diversified portfolio of investments. Here is how it works:

- The owner sells anywhere from 30 percent to 100 percent of all outstanding stock to the ESOP (including any shares previously owned by the ESOP).
- The family business must not be publicly traded and must be a C corporation.

- If the owner held his or her stock for three or more years prior to the sale, there is no federal income tax on the owner's gain if the cash is used to purchase securities of most U.S. corporations.

For example, the owner can use the cash from the ESOP sale to purchase a diversified portfolio of blue-chip corporate debt securities, preferred stock, or common stock. Thus, the owner can acquire debt securities of AT&T, preferred stock of Exxon, and common stock of Microsoft—all without paying any federal income tax on the sale and rollover into the diversified portfolio.

The only limitation on the owner's portfolio is that all investments must be in U.S. corporations that derive not more than 25 percent of their gross receipts from passive investment income (e.g., a mutual fund) and use more than 50 percent of their assets in the active conduct of a trade or business. Most blue-chip companies will qualify under this standard.

A qualified cash sale to an ESOP is thus far more advantageous to the owner than a cash sale to an unaffiliated buyer for the same price or even a tax-free merger. For example, in a tax-free merger the owner receives the stock of only one company—all of the owner's eggs are in that one basket. In order to diversify, the owner must sell that stock, pay a tax, and then reinvest the after-tax money into a diversified portfolio.

By contrast, the qualified ESOP sale permits the owner to achieve a diversified portfolio without ever paying federal income tax.

If the family business is a Subchapter S corporation (which does not qualify for a tax-free rollover), or elects Subchapter S status after a tax-free rollover, the ESOP has other advantages. The ESOP does not pay federal income taxes on the income earned as a shareholder of a Subchapter S corporation. This means that the ESOP could borrow money from a bank to purchase the owner's stock and repay the bank loan with the federal income tax savings. Thus, instead of using the dividends from the family business to the ESOP to pay federal income taxes, the ESOP could use the dividends to repay its indebtedness to the bank.

It should be noted, however, that special rules apply to S corporation-sponsored ESOPs where the corporation stock is not widely held. Specifically, if through the application of constructive ownership rules certain "disqualified persons" (i.e., certain individuals and their families treated as directly or indirectly owning certain threshold percentages of stock in the S corporation) own in the aggregate at least 50 percent of the outstanding S corporation stock for a particular plan year, then:

1. a significant excise tax may be imposed upon the S Corporation and;
2. income of the S Corporation attributable to shares allocated to disqualified persons may be treated as having been distributed by the ESOP and will become taxable in the hands of the disqualified persons.

In general, the company's contribution to an ESOP is deductible for federal income taxes, but the deduction is limited to 25 percent of the owner's annual payroll (including other qualified plans and assuming all employees are plan participants) plus interest on the ESOP loan. Thus, if the family business' annual payroll is $10 million and has no other qualified plans, the business can contribute $2.5 million a year to the ESOP (plus any interest on ESOP loans).

This means that the principal amortization on the bank loan to the ESOP loan can equal as much as $2.5 million per year. If the ESOP repurchased the owner's stock for $12.5 million, it could finance the purchase with a five-year level principal amortizing loan requiring principal paydown of $2.5 million per year. This assumes, of course, that the family business has the cash flow to make contributions to the ESOP sufficient to permit the ESOP to pay annual principal debt service of $2.5 million plus interest. Since the contributions to the ESOP are deductible by the family business for federal income tax purposes, including the amount used to pay the principal of the ESOP loan, the cash flow of the business is increased by the benefit of these tax deductions.

The only limit on the duration of the ESOP loan is what lenders are willing to provide (assuming stock collateral is released from the loan in proportion to principal and interest payments). If the owner could obtain a ten-year level principal amortizing loan in the above example, the ESOP could repurchase his or her stock for $25 million, provided it was worth that much.

If the family business pays dividends on its stock, the dividend paid to the ESOP on the stock it holds may be tax deductible for federal income tax purposes if certain conditions are met.

From the owner's viewpoint, an ESOP sale is ideal if

- the owner sells 100 percent of his or her stock;
- the sale is all cash;

- The ESOP sale price is the same price that an unaffiliated buyer would pay.

If none of the above is true, the advantages of selling to the ESOP must be balanced against the disadvantages.

For example, if the owner sells only 30 percent of his or her stock to the ESOP rather than 100 percent, he or she may wind up someday with minority shareholders. Generally, when the company's employees retire they have the absolute right to receive their portion of the ESOP's stock ownership in the family business. They also have the right to "put" the stock to the family business or the ESOP, thereby forcing either to repurchase it for cash. But neither the family business nor the ESOP may be able to afford to do so, particularly if a large group of employees retire at the same time and put all of their stock.

Most employees who retire will not want to keep the stock of the family business. The business will be required to purchase the stock from these retiring employees if they exercise their "put" right. Those employees who do keep the stock can be prevented from selling the stock to outsiders without giving the business a right of first refusal. The family business can also adopt a bylaw preventing nonemployees from holding stock.

If the owner does not receive all cash from the ESOP upon the sale of his or her stock and instead takes a note, the owner is still at the risk of the business. The ESOP funding to pay the note depends upon the cash flow of the company. Moreover, unlike a note that the owner receives from an unaffiliated buyer, the owner will probably not be able to obtain a guarantee of repayment from anyone other than his or her own company. The stock the owner sold to the ESOP can also serve as collateral for the note.

An ESOP can also be costly to maintain because of the bookkeeping and the necessity for yearly, or at least frequent, appraisals. Typically, an ESOP appraisal can be obtained for $5,000 a year if the owner is not too picky about the appraiser. The administrative costs can easily run another $5,000 to $10,000 per year.

Even if the owner does not sell 100 percent of his or her stock to the ESOP, the ESOP can still be used by an unaffiliated buyer to sweeten the owner's after-tax cash flow. For example, an unaffiliated buyer might purchase 70 percent of the owner's stock and have the owner sell the remaining 30 percent to an ESOP with a tax-free rollover.

Selling to an Unrelated Third Party in an Auction

Once the owner decides that selling the business to other family members is not feasible, he or she should try to maximize the sale price for the business to unrelated third party buyers. These third party buyers can be categorized as either financial buyers or strategic buyers. A financial buyer is typically a private equity fund motivated solely by financial considerations in acquiring the business and may or may not be engaged in the business through portfolio companies. In contrast, a strategic buyer is looking for synergies between the owner's business and the buyer's existing business.

Many family business owners tend to negotiate with only one potential buyer who happens to approach them, in many cases on an unsolicited basis. These owners tend not to widely market their businesses. They may be flattered that they have received an unsolicited offer for their businesses and, as a result, fail to search for other potential buyers. Negotiating with only one potential buyer severely limits the negotiating power of the owner. Because of this decreased bargaining power, negotiations are unlikely to result in the best price and the best terms.

> **Worst Practice**
>
> Failing to market the business widely and negotiating solely with the first potential buyer who happens to present an offer.

It is generally agreed that an auction produces the highest price for a family business. Generally, the owner needs two or more bidders to conduct an auction. However, an auction can be conducted with only one bidder if it is a closed auction (i.e., no one knows who else is bidding).

To induce potential buyers to bid at an auction of the family business, the owner must assure them that the business will be in fact sold to the highest bidder and that the auction will be conducted fairly.

If the owner has not really decided whether or not to sell, the auction will not be held effectively. Likewise, if the owner favors one bidder over another and wants to give that favored bidder the last bid, it is unlikely that the owner will be able to induce other potential buyers to participate in the auction.

The most suitable businesses for an auction are those with good financial results and a strategic market position. If neither of these characteristics is present, the auction may not be as successful, but should still be considered if there are competing buyers.

The auction must be conducted by a person in whom bidders have confidence and pursuant to written rules and procedures that are uniformly applied to all bidders. The owner's investment banker or attorney can fulfill this role.

Bidders are generally turned off by open auctions (i.e., auctions where their bids are publicly disclosed) and by auctions with innumerable rounds of bidding.

Auctions can also be classified as "controlled" and "uncontrolled" auctions. In a controlled auction, the company initiates contact only with selected buyers, whereas in an uncontrolled auction (also sometimes called an "open auction"), there is no limit on the number of potential bidders. Uncontrolled auctions potentially attract the largest number of buyers, but may be highly disruptive to the company and its employees. Many companies prefer a controlled auction because it is less disruptive.

To induce bidders to participate in the owner's auction, bids should be submitted in writing and maintained in confidence. Cutoff dates for bids should be advertised and adhered to.

It is preferable from the seller's point of view to have at least two rounds of bidding, with the second round confined to the highest two bidders. If there are more than four bidders, the owner may wish to conduct a third round of bidding.

It is essential that the owner provide all bidders with the same agreement of sale form, which will be prepared by the owner's counsel. Each bidder should be requested to state any changes in the agreement of sale form when submitting a bid. In determining who is the highest bidder, the legal terms must be considered along with the price.

For example, suppose one bidder bids $15 million and a second bidder bids $14.5 million. If the $14.5 million bidder is willing to cut off any indemnification rights against the owner after the closing, but the $15 million bidder is unwilling to do so, the owner may consider the $14.5 million bid to be higher. The important question is how much the owner will be left with after the sale is completed and any indemnification rights of the buyer have terminated.

To make the bids meaningful, the agreement of sale should provide for a forfeitable deposit on signing and eliminate any due diligence out. Otherwise, the high bidder could use the auction as a vehicle to postpone making a final purchasing decision to the prejudice of the seller, who has lost the other bidders.

The agreement of sale form should contemplate a quick closing after the signing. If the sale to the high bidder does not close quickly, the other bidders will have lost interest by the time the seller realizes the sale to the high bidder will not be consummated.

We next discuss how to preserve and transfer family wealth while minimizing taxes.

CHAPTER 11

Preserving and Transferring Family Wealth[1]

In previous chapters we have discussed methods of protecting and preserving family wealth from the following risks:

- Divorce (see Chapter 2 on prenuptial agreements, postnuptial agreements, irrevocable spendthrift trusts and conditional gifts.)
- Conflicts within the family (see Chapters 1 and 3 on use of impartial tiebreakers and procedural due process.)

We have also discussed (in Chapter 1) the desirability of mentoring succeeding generations in both the family business and in other businesses that they may wish to start.

This chapter discusses preserving and transferring family wealth by minimizing the effect of federal and state income, gift, estate, and inheritance taxes on transfers of family wealth to succeeding generations, including using asset protection devices.

Many family business owners wait too long before attempting to transfer wealth to other family members. The ability to minimize gift, estate, and inheritance taxes is maximized when the valuation of the business is at its lowest point. As the business grows in value, the opportunity to minimize these taxes is much more limited.

> **Worst Practice**
>
> Waiting until the family business has a substantial value before transferring wealth to the next generation.

TAX PLANNING AND ASSET PROTECTION

There are several common estate planning techniques used by family businesses to reduce the impact of inheritance taxes on the transfer of wealth, namely, family limited partnerships, grantor retained annuity trusts, and intentionally defective trusts. We will also discuss the annual gift-tax exclusion.

This chapter assumes that estate and gift-tax laws are not changed from those that were in effect on December 31, 2009. Since it is likely that these tax laws will be changed, readers are cautioned to review any tax planning with their tax attorney.

Take Advantage of Annual Gift-Tax Exclusion

To minimize gift, estate, and inheritance taxes, stock or other equity of the family business should be gifted to children and grandchildren to take advantage of the annual gift-tax exclusion. The gift should be of non-voting stock so as to not compromise the control of the business' owner. Non-voting stock has the other advantage of having a slightly lower value than voting stock. Subchapter S corporations can have two classes of stock if the only difference between them is the ability to vote. Gifts can also be made of non-voting equity of limited liability companies.

Best Practice

Take advantage of the annual gift-tax exclusion by creating gifts of non-voting stock of the family business through irrevocable spendthrift trusts.

The annual federal gift-tax exclusion is the amount that can be given each year to any individual without it being subject to the federal gift tax. The annual federal gift-tax exclusion is indexed for inflation. For 2010, this amount is $13,000 per donee. A married couple will be able to give up to $26,000 to each donee without incurring any federal gift tax in 2010. Only Connecticut, North Carolina, and Tennessee impose a state gift tax; the Connecticut and North Carolina annual exclusion is the same as the federal exclusion.

Outright gifts to grandchildren of the annual exclusion amount will also be exempt from the generation-skipping transfer tax (GST). Gifts in trust for grandchildren that qualify for the gift-tax annual exclusion can also qualify for exclusion from the GST if the trust is properly structured. Transfers in the form of tuition payments, if paid directly to the educational institution, and payments of medical expenses, if paid directly to the provider of the services, are also not considered taxable gifts and are not subject to GST.

Gifts should be made through irrevocable spendthrift trusts rather than outright. Irrevocable spendthrift trusts not only protect the gift from the creditors of the donee, but also assist in limiting spousal rights in the event of a divorce, as discussed in Chapter 2.

The inability of creditors of beneficiaries of irrevocable spendthrift trusts to seize the trust's assets is only effective if the assets to be protected were not transferred to the trust in a transaction that is subject to state or federal fraudulent transfer or conveyance laws.

Consider Establishing a Family Limited Partnerships

Family limited partnerships (frequently called "FLPs") are commonly used to move wealth from one generation to another. Partners are either general partners or limited partners. One or more general partners is responsible for managing the FLP and its assets. Limited partners have an economic interest in the FLP but typically lack the two noteworthy rights of control and marketability. Limited partners have no ability to control, direct, or otherwise influence the operations of the FLP. They also substantially lack the ability to sell their interest, with the one possible exception being transfers to immediate family members (spouse, siblings, and direct lineal descendants and ascendants). FLPs are partnerships limited to family members, hence the name.

> **Best Practice**
>
> Consider forming a family limited partnership that could include stock of the family business, assuming that the family business is not an S corporation.

FLPS have several benefits. They allow family members with aligned interests to pool resources, thus lowering legal, accounting, and investing costs. They allow one family member, typically the general partner, to move assets to other family members (often children who are limited partners) while still retaining control over the assets. Because the limited partners have no rights of control, they cannot liquidate their partnership interest. The timing and amount of distribution is the sole and exclusive prerogative of the general partner, though distributions must be made to all partners according to their percentage interests. That is, a distribution cannot be made to one partner (general or limited) unless all partners receive their pro rata portion of any disbursements.

FLPs can be very powerful estate planning mechanisms that have the effect of reducing income, estate, and gift taxes if properly structured and maintained. FLPs can also serve as asset-protection mechanisms if properly structured and maintained. The asset protection results from the inability of the creditors of limited partners (typically the children of the owner) to reach assets of the FLP that are indirectly owned by the limited partners. Thus, a creditor of a limited partner will typically not be able to reach the assets of the FLP and will only be permitted, depending upon state law, to obtain any distributions made to the limited partner. If there are no distributions made to the limited partner by the FLP, a creditor of a limited partner will receive nothing, even if the creditor has a so-called charging order under state law.

The inability of creditors of limited partners to seize assets of the FLP is only effective if the assets to be protected were not transferred to the FLP in a transaction subject to state or federal fraudulent transfer or conveyance laws. FLPs do not necessarily protect general partner assets in the FLP from the creditors of the general partner.

Use Care in Structuring and Administering
Family Limited Partnerships

FLPs are subject to challenge by the Internal Revenue Service, state taxing authorities, and creditors of the partners of the FLP. Once the FLP has been formed and assets properly transferred to it, it is important to respect the FLP formalities and administrative requirements. Before gifts of limited partnership interests are made, written confirmation should be obtained that all assets have been properly contributed to the FLP.

Best Practice

Since FLPs are only effective as an estate planning and asset protection mechanism if properly structured and maintained, it is important for the family to pay close attention to both the original structuring and administration of the FLP.

If the operating agreement for the FLP requires that annual financial statements be provided to all partners, this must be strictly followed. If there is a requirement to hold partnership meetings to review investment performance and make investment decisions, prepare and maintain minutes documenting these meetings and memorializing the discussions.

The FLP should maintain its own stationery and all partnership decisions should be documented. The FLP should not make distributions that are not pro rata to all partners. Family members should not be permitted to treat FLP assets as if they personally belong to them. There should be no comingling of FLP assets with the assets of individual partners. All transactions between the partners and the FLP should be arm's-length.

Consider Establishing a Grantor Retained Annuity Trusts

A grantor retained annuity trust (GRAT) is a gift and estate planning technique for transferring wealth that uses IRS-approved discount factors to make gifts that "leverage" the owner's $1,000,000 lifetime gift-tax exemption ($2,000,000, combined with a spouse). A GRAT is a trust that the owner creates for a specified term of years (the "Term"). During that Term, the owner will receive from the GRAT an annual (or more frequent) annuity payment expressed as either a fixed dollar amount or a fixed percentage of the initial fair market value of the property transferred to the trust. The GRAT can pay the owner the annuity either in cash or in kind, based on the value of the trust property at the time of each payment. At the end of the Term, any remaining principal of the trust will be distributed to, or held in further trust for, those beneficiaries the owner has specified in the GRAT.

> **Best Practice**
>
> Consider the use of a grantor retained annuity trust to contribute non-voting stock of the family business in order to minimize gift, estate, and inheritance taxes.

The owner's gift to a GRAT is a federally taxable gift that will utilize some portion of his or her remaining lifetime gift-tax exemption. The amount of the gift is equal to the fair market value of the property transferred to the GRAT and less the actuarial value of the annuity payments that owner receives from the GRAT. The actuarial value of the annuity payments is based upon several factors, including the IRS interest rate for the month in which the GRAT is funded, the length of the Term, and the size of the annuity payments as a percentage of the initial fair market value of the GRAT's assets (the "Payout Rate"). A very short Term (usually 2–3 years) and a high Payout Rate can actually result in a remainder interest valued at close to zero dollars. In appropriate circumstances, such a GRAT (a "Zeroed-Out GRAT") can result in the transfer of significant value without incurring any gift tax. The valuation formula assumes that the GRAT's assets will grow at an annual rate equal to the IRS interest rate. Therefore, to the extent that the investment performance of the GRAT's assets exceed the IRS rate, the excess value will eventually pass to the remainder beneficiaries free of gift tax. On the other hand, if the GRAT's investments underperform the IRS rate, this benefit will not be realized.

The value of the reportable gift made upon funding a GRAT can be reduced by either increasing the Payout Rate or increasing the Term. However, for federal estate tax purposes, should the owner die before the end of the GRAT's term, all or a substantially all of the then value of the GRAT will be subject to federal estate taxation. On the other hand, if the owner survives the Term, the remaining assets of the GRAT will pass to the remainder beneficiaries free of any further gift or estate tax. Therefore, it is generally advisable to structure a GRAT with a Term that is significantly shorter than the owner's anticipated life expectancy.

During the Term, the owner will be required to report on his or her personal federal income tax return all of the taxable income (both ordinary income and capital gains) of the GRAT. This tax payment will inure to the benefit of the GRAT beneficiaries but is not considered an additional gift for federal gift tax purposes. It is even possible to structure the GRAT so that the owner will continue to pay federal

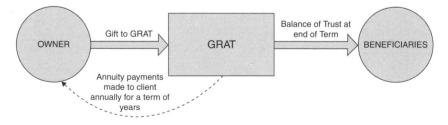

Figure 11.1 Grantor Retained Annuity Trust (GRAT)

income tax on the income of the GRAT after the Term. These rules do not necessarily apply for state income tax purposes. For example, Pennsylvania requires a GRAT to file its own income tax return and pay its own tax.

If a GRAT is to be used to hold the stock of the family business, the stock should be non-voting stock in order to avoid compromising the control of the owner of the family business, as discussed above. If the family business is a Subchapter S corporation, care must be taken to make sure the GRAT will not disqualify the Subchapter S election.

Consider Installment Sales to Intentionally Defective Grantor Trusts

An installment sale to an Intentionally Defective Grantor Trust (IDGT) is a gift and estate planning technique for transferring wealth. It involves the sale of appreciated or appreciating assets to a trust established by the owner that is structured so that its assets are excluded from the owner's estate for federal estate tax purposes but considered to be owned by the owner for federal income tax purposes. The trust is considered a "grantor trust" for federal income taxes. As such, the trust is disregarded as a separate taxable entity and the owner will be required to report on his or her personal federal income tax return all of the taxable income (both ordinary income and capital gains) of the IDGT. This tax payment will inure to the beneficiaries of the trust but is not considered an additional gift for federal gift-tax purposes. Note, however, that the same rule does not necessarily apply for state income tax purposes. For example, Pennsylvania requires an IDGT to file its own income tax return and pay its own tax.

> **Best Practice**
>
> Consider the use of an Intentionally Defective Grantor Trust as an alternative to a GRAT and contribute non-voting stock of the family business in order to minimize gift, estate and inheritance taxes.

The technique is structured as a combination of a gift and a sale to the IDGT. In a typical arrangement, the owner would first provide "seed" money to the IDGT, by making a gift, usually cash, to the trust. This cash can be used to make the down payment referred to below. Next, the owner would sell one or more appreciated assets to the IDGT in exchange for a promissory note ("Note") in the amount of the purchase price. The Note may provide for installment payments over a period of time with interest at the minimum required IRS interest rate, or annual "interest only" payments with a "balloon" payment of principal at the end of the term. Often, the IDGT makes a down payment of 10 percent to 15 percent of the purchase price, using the "seed" money referred to above. Typically, the property sold to the IDGT secures the Note. In addition, where possible, it is recommended that the beneficiaries of the IDGT personally guarantee the payment of the Note.

Since the IDGT is disregarded for federal income tax purposes, the sale transaction between the owner and the trust has no federal income tax consequences. No gain or loss is recognized on the owner's sale of the assets to the IDGT; the owner is not required to report the sale on his or her federal income tax return; the owner is not taxed separately on the interest payments that he or she receives from the IDGT; and the owner will continue to be taxed individually on all income generated by the IDGT as if it did not exist.

This technique is economically similar to the GRAT technique. However, while there are some advantages over the GRAT technique, there are also disadvantages.

One advantage of the IDGT is that it uses a lower interest rate as compared to a GRAT. The required interest rate used to value a GRAT is 120 percent of the federal midterm rate in effect on the date of the gift. (The midterm rate is used for loans of over three but less than nine years). For a sale to an IDGT, the minimum required interest rate is only 100 percent of the applicable federal interest rate, which varies based on the term of the Note. The IDGT interest rate is lower than the GRAT interest rate. As a result of the reduced interest rate, the IDGT technique produces estate and gift-tax savings at a lower total net return as compared to a GRAT.

Second, if the grantor dies during the term of the Note, the assets of the IDGT will not be subject to federal estate taxation (although the Note will be part of the estate). However, with a GRAT, all or substantially all of its value as of the date of death will be subject to federal estate taxation.

A major disadvantage of the IDGT as compared to a GRAT is that the IDGT technique is based only upon tax practitioners' interpretations of various provisions of the Internal Revenue Code, reported cases, and rulings. It is not specifically sanctioned under the law. As

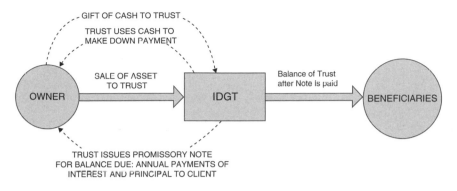

Figure 11.2 Intentionally Defective Grantor Trust

a result, there is some degree of legal uncertainty about the IDGT technique. On the other hand, the GRAT technique is statutorily approved in the Internal Revenue Code and in regulations, reported cases, and rulings.

A second disadvantage of a sale to an IDGT is that if the owner dies during the term of the Note, the "grantor trust" status of the IDGT will terminate and the owner or his or her estate may have to recognize the deferred gain attributable to the unpaid portion of the principal of the Note.

A sale to a third party of the stock of the family business will result in taxation of the gain to the owner (grantor) of the family business who has established the IDGT. This can be a serious disadvantage if the owner does not have sufficient assets to pay the tax and has not required the IDGT to pay the tax. However, there is also an advantage in that the tax depletes the owner's estate, thereby reducing estate and inheritance taxes upon the owner's death.

If stock of the family business is contributed to the IDGT, it should be non-voting stock in order to avoid compromising the control of the owner of the business. If the business is a Subchapter S corporation, care must be taken to make sure the IDGT will not disqualify the Subchapter S election.

Our final chapter discusses the considerations in having a family business go public, through an initial public offering or otherwise.

CHAPTER 12

Family Businesses Going Public

Larger family businesses may for various reasons elect to have a public offering of their stock. The decision to convert a family business into a public company typically involves a complete change in corporate culture.[1] Family businesses are usually secretive and do not share information except with those who need to know. Public companies, on the other hand, live in glass houses. They are legally required by federal securities laws to have open communication with investors and tend to have much more open communication with employees. This change in culture is sometimes very difficult for a family business.

One academic study has found that family firms constituted over 35 percent of the Standard and Poor's 500 (S&P 500) and that founding families on average owned almost 18 percent of their equity.[2] To identify a "family firm," the study used equity ownership on the part of the founding family or the presence of family members on the board of directors. A more recent study has confirmed these initial findings.[3]

The following are only a few examples of major public companies that are considered to be family affiliated or family influenced public companies:

Table 12.1 Public Companies Family Affiliated

Name of Company	Name of Family
Wal-Mart Stores, Inc.	Walton
Ford Motor Company	Ford
Hyatt Hotels Corporation	Pritzker
Comcast Corporation	Roberts
News Corporation	Murdoch

Academic research has shown that major, publicly traded family-controlled businesses actually outperform other types of businesses.[4] One study[5] has concluded that the most successful family-controlled large public companies have one or more of the following characteristics:

- The family's voting control was accompanied by significant family ownership.
- There was a strong family CEO without complete voting control who was accountable to independent directors.
- Multiple family members serve as managers.
- The family intends to keep the business for generations.

Motivation

There are a number of important reasons why family firms consider an initial public offering (IPO), including the following:

- To infuse a significant amount of investment capital into the firm.[6] Many family businesses fail because of insufficient capital and heavy debt loads.[7] Moreover, the additional capital can be used to expand the business through both internal growth and acquisitions.[8]
- Succession issues. As generations go by and fragmentation of ownership increases, family shareholders want or need liquidity beyond what can be provided by the business.[9]
- Better ability to attract professional managers who can be compensated with equity of the public company.[10]

Two Classes of Stock

Once a family business has an IPO, it subjects itself to the risk of the loss of control by the family. However, this loss of control may not occur immediately after the IPO so long as the family is unified and retains more than 50 percent of the post-IPO stock voting power.

One advantage of having a publicly traded stock is the ability to raise additional capital and to use the stock as a form of consideration for acquisitions and mergers. As new stock is issued for these purposes, the family's voting control will decrease below 50 percent and ultimately become a relatively small percentage of the voting power of all stock. At this point, the public company is vulnerable to hedge funds and other activist shareholders. Hostile action by activist shareholders has more than tripled the number of proxy contests in 2009 from the number of proxy contests five years earlier in 2004.[11]

Even when the family retains more than 50 percent of the voting power, activist shareholders may be successful in obtaining the support of disaffected family members, thereby breaking the family's control of the public company.

Best Practice

Consider establishing two classes of stock and sell the lower voting stock in the IPO, retaining the higher voting stock for the family.

Some family businesses that have gone public have used two classes of common stock, with the lower voting class sold to the public in the IPO. For example, the stock sold to the public may have one vote per share, whereas the higher voting class may have ten votes per share. The higher voting class of common stock is typically retained by the family and used to control the membership of the board of directors.

For example, Comcast Corporation, currently an S&P 500 company, had its IPO in 1972. It issued lower voting stock to the public in the IPO while retaining the higher voting stock for the founding Roberts family.

Outside of the United States, dual-class structures of family-controlled public companies are very common. For example, within a sample representing 95 percent of publicly traded Swedish firms, 75 percent have dual class share structures and 58.8 percent are controlled by family owned shares carrying at least 25 percent of voting power.[12] Of a sample of Australian-listed companies through the end of 1988, 45 percent had a blockholder controlling 25 percent or more of the company's equity and 72 percent had a blockholder controlling 10 percent or more of the company's equity; family accounted for 70 percent of the 10+ percent blocks.[13] Of the 246 publicly traded firms among the top 500 Canadian firms (by sales) in 1988, 44 had a controlling shareholder who was an heir of the firm's founder.[14]

It is likely that lower voting stock will have to be sold to the public at a discount to shares that have full or multiple voting rights. Two classes of stock may make it harder to market the IPO. Therefore, if the company elects to use two classes of stock, it may have to be very careful in selecting an underwriter.

Once the company has completed the IPO with the lower voting stock, any further equity financings or acquisitions are completed with the publicly traded stock that has a much lower dilutive effect on the family's control. Likewise, stock options and other equity incentives are given to employees with the lower voting stock.

To maintain family voting block unity, the founder or owner should attempt to establish voting agreements and voting trusts during his or her lifetime and provide for the continuation of such agreements or trusts in the founder's or owner's succession planning. In this respect, the succession planning discussed in Chapter 1 for private companies also applies to family-controlled blocks in public companies.

Advanced Planning

Some private family businesses think that they can easily go public once there is a hot IPO market. The reality is that most private businesses have no idea as to how much effort and advanced planning is required to have a successful IPO.

It is not unusual for the IPO window to open and close quickly. The author represented a family business in mid-1999 that was planning an IPO. By the time they straightened out their accounting to satisfy the requirements of the Securities and Exchange Commission and performed their corporate housekeeping, it was April 2000 and the IPO window had closed.

Best Practice

A successful IPO for a family business requires advanced planning for a significant period of time before the IPO target date in order to take advantage of IPO windows.

The key to a successful IPO for a family business is careful advanced planning well before the IPO target date. Advanced IPO planning permits the family business to take advantage of short IPO windows. As discussed more fully in the author's book *International and U.S. IPO Planning: A Business Strategy* (John Wiley & Sons, Inc. 2009) advanced planning steps include the following:

- Developing an impressive management team and using equity incentives to attract and retain key executives

- Growing the business to make the company more attractive for an IPO, including "roll-ups"
- Making sure auditing or auditable financial statements are available
- Changing questionable business practices well before an IPO
- Avoiding a hostile takeover by inserting provisions into the charter of the public company
- Implementing corporate governance mechanisms, including the formation of an audit committee consisting of independent directors, the development of good internal controls, and a whistleblower policy
- Creating insider bailout opportunities so that insiders can directly or indirectly receive some of the proceeds from the IPO
- Taking advantage of IPO windows and fads

Many of the advanced planning items described above take time to effectuate. Planning must start well before the intended IPO. For example, creating insider bailout opportunities may take several years before the IPO target date to be effectuated.

Any family business thinking about an IPO in the future must be aware of the necessity of obtaining audited or auditable financial statements that use IPO-acceptable accounting principles. This is true whether the IPO will be in the United States or overseas.

The most common reason why IPOs are delayed is because the financial statements are not and cannot be audited or, even if audited, do not use IPO-acceptable accounting principles. The author has experienced numerous situations where the IPO was delayed because of the inability of the family business to provided audited financial statements. However, even if the financial statements are audited by one of the so-called Big Four accounting firms, that is no assurance that they contain IPO-acceptable accounting principles. The author has experienced situations where, because of the failure to apply acceptable accounting principles, the SEC delayed an IPO for so long that the IPO window closed and the business was unable to raise capital.

The SEC normally requires audited income statements for three years in order to go public if the family business or a predecessor has been in business that long. It may not be possible, on the eve of the IPO, to retroactively obtain audited financial statements. This is particularly true if sales of inventory account for a significant portion of the company's revenues, and no auditor has ever observed the company's inventory.

Therefore, it is preferable to obtain either currently audited financial statements or "auditable" financial statements (i.e., financial statements that are capable of being audited retroactively at the time of the company's IPO). Waiting until the eve of the company's IPO to obtain audited financial statements can delay the IPO and cause the company to lose an IPO window. Therefore, the company should start its audit at least six months before the proposed IPO filing date.

Advanced IPO Estate and Equity Incentive Planning

To maximize the advantages of an IPO, the owner should be transferring wealth well before the IPO target date, as discussed in Chapter 11. If this planning is postponed until shortly before or after the IPO, the valuation of the equity of the family business will have dramatically risen, thereby minimizing gift, estate, and inheritance tax planning opportunities, as discussed in Chapter 11.

Likewise, if the strategic plan of the family business contemplates an IPO, and if no equity incentive is given to key employees to encourage them to realize its objective, one of the great benefits of the IPO has been lost.

Best Practice

Years prior to the target date for an IPO or a merger into a public shell, the owners of a family business should engage in estate planning and create equity incentives for both family and non-family key employees that will vest upon going public.

Many years prior to any contemplated IPO (or merger into a public shell), there should be significant estate planning by the owner to minimize gift, estate, and inheritance taxes. During this same period, equity incentives should be created for key employees, both family members and non-family members.

These equity incentives typically should vest only upon the completion of the IPO (or the public shell merger) and preferably should not vest until at least one year afterwards. The purpose of delaying vesting until at least one year after the IPO is to continue to motivate key employees until the family members can sell their own stock in a secondary offering. Underwriters generally do not want personal family stock sold in the IPO.

ADVANTAGES AND DISADVANTAGES OF AN IPO

Family business owners should think carefully about the advantages and disadvantages of going public. Some owners become so enamored with advantages of going public that they do not carefully consider its downsides. The failure of a family business to understand the disadvantages and risks of an IPO can result in a failed IPO or "IPO remorse."

> **Worst Practice**
>
> Proceeding with an IPO before carefully considering its disadvantages and risks in addition to its advantages.

The Advantages

The major advantages of being public are as follows:

1. *Lower cost of capital.* A public company has more alternatives for raising capital than a private company. A private company, once it has exhausted its bank lines, generally raises additional equity and subordinated debt capital from individual and institutional investors in so-called private placements. These investors, particularly venture capital funds, insurance companies, and others usually require very stiff terms, including significant operational restrictions.

In contrast, a public company has the alternative of going to the public marketplace. The public marketplace typically does not demand the same strict terms of individual investors. This results in less dilution to the existing shareholders if equity capital is raised. If debt securities are publicly sold, the marketplace tends to be much more liberal in imposing operational restrictions.

Two identical companies, one private and the other public, are valued quite differently by investors. Investors in the private company discount the value of its equity securities by reason of their "illiquidity" (that is, the inability to readily sell them for cash).

The availability of the public capital alternative also permits the public company greater leverage in its negotiations with individual and institutional investors. Most institutional investors prefer investing in public companies since they have a built-in "exit" (that is, they can sell their stock in the public market).

Suppose the market price of the company's stock never rises above the IPO price (a so-called broken IPO). Even in this disaster scenario, the IPO permits the owner to raise what is probably the cheapest form of equity capital, even if the owner has not achieved his or her other IPO objectives.

2. *Personal wealth.* A public offering can enhance the owner's personal net worth. Stories abound of the many millionaires and multimillionaires created through public offerings. Even if the owner didn't realize immediate profits by selling a portion of his or her existing stock during the initial offering, the owner can use publicly traded stock as collateral to secure loans.

In as little as three months after the owner's IPO, he or she may be able to have another registered underwritten public offering in which the owner sells a significant percentage of his or her personal holdings. These secondary or follow-on offerings are only possible if the company's earnings have grown and the market price had risen significantly since the owner's IPO.

These secondary or follow-on offerings permit the owner to diversify his or her personal wealth without selling or otherwise losing control of the company. The owner can have his or her cake and eat it too!

For approximately six months after the IPO (the "lock-up period"), the underwriter will restrict the owner from selling his or her personal stock except in a secondary or follow-on offering authorized by the underwriter. Thereafter, the owner can sell stock under Rule 144. Rule 144 permits the owner to personally sell up to 1 percent of the company's total outstanding stock every three months or one week's average trading volume, whichever is higher. The sales have to be in unsolicited brokerage transactions or transactions with brokerage firms that make a market in the owner's stock. The owner also has to publicly report these sales. Thus, it may not be desirable for the owner to utilize Rule 144 too frequently for fear of giving the investment community the impression that he or she is bailing out.

3. *Competitive position.* Many businesses use the capital from the IPO to enhance their competitive position. The additional capital resources permit greater market penetration. A 2009 academic study has shown that competitors of the company with the IPO suffer significant deterioration in their competitive position.[15]

Some businesses have only a short window of opportunity to grow the business and dominate their competitors. For example, a technology-based company can use the IPO proceeds to achieve a dominant position in the marketplace well before its underfinanced competitors.

Customers like to deal with well-financed businesses. A strong balance sheet is a good marketing tool.

4. *Prestige.* The owner and his or her cofounders gain an enormous amount of personal prestige from being associated with a company that goes public. Such prestige can be very helpful in recruiting key employees and in marketing the company's products and services. For example, the publicity surrounding the Internet IPOs, like eBay's, significantly increased the visitors to their Web sites.

5. *Ability to take advantage of market price fluctuations.* The market price of public companies' stock can fluctuate greatly. These fluctuations may relate to overall stock market trends and have nothing to do with the company's performance. The stock market from time to time tends to unreasonably overprice the company's stock or severely underprice it. So-called momentum investing, caused primarily by day traders, can occasionally cause wild price gyrations.

During a period when the company's stock is severely underpriced, the company has the ability to repurchase its stock on the stock market at these depressed prices provided the company has been wise enough to retain a cash reserve. Likewise, during periods when the company's stock is unreasonably overpriced, the owner can sell stock on very favorable terms. None of these opportunities are available to a private company.

6. *Enhanced ability to grow through acquisitions.* The cash proceeds from the IPO can be used to make acquisitions to help the company grow faster. Indeed, underwriters prefer companies that can use the IPO proceeds to grow the business. A publicly traded company also may grow by using its own stock to make acquisitions. This option is generally not available to a private company that is forced to use cash or notes for acquisitions. Private company stock is not an attractive form of consideration to a seller since it lacks liquidity.

The company's ability to use stock instead of cash as an acquisition currency will permit greater growth opportunities than are available to competing private companies.

7. *Enhanced ability to borrow; no personal guarantees.* When the company sells stock, it increases its net worth and improves its debt-to-equity ratio. This should allow the company to borrow money on more favorable terms in the future.

The principals of private companies are often required to personally guarantee bank loans made to their companies. Once the company is public, banks and other financial institutions are less likely to require any personal guarantees.

8. *Enhanced ability to raise equity.* If the company continues to grow, the owner will eventually need additional equity financing. If the stock performs well in the stock market, the company will be able to sell additional stock on favorable terms.

The company may be able to raise equity quickly if the volume of the company's stock trading permits it to attract equity in so-called PIPE (private investment, public equity) transactions. In a PIPE transaction, the company sells equity to hedge funds and other institutional equity investors on a private placement basis at a discount below its then-market price together with investor registration rights, permitting the investor to resell the stock in the public marketplace.

However, if the company's stock is not heavily traded or is not followed by securities analysts because the company is too small, it is likely to fall below the IPO price and make it more difficult to raise additional equity in either PIPE or other transactions. Many smaller companies today are not followed by securities analysts and, as a result, their prices have drifted below the IPO price.

9. *Attracting and retaining key employees.* Stock options offered by emerging public companies have much appeal and can help the company to recruit or retain well-qualified executives and motivate the company's employee-shareholders. Although the accounting for such options will require the expensing of such options, the benefit of using stock options to attract and retain key employees remains.

10. *Liquidity and valuation.* Once the company goes public, a market is established for the stock and the owner will have an effective way of valuing that stock. Subject to Rule 144, the owner can sell whenever the need arises.

The owner's stock prices can easily be followed. Prices are quoted daily and are printed in many newspapers.

11. *Estate planning.* Many private companies have to be sold upon the death of their founders in order to pay inheritance taxes. This may prevent an owner from passing the ownership of a private company onto his or her family or to key employees.

Founders of private companies sometimes fund inheritance taxes by maintaining large life insurance policies. However, the premiums on these policies can be a significant drain on the business. These premiums are not deductible for federal income tax purposes.

If the company's stock is publicly traded, the owner's estate will have a liquid asset with which to pay inheritance taxes.

The Disadvantages

The major disadvantages of going public are as follows:

1. *Expense.* The cost of going public is substantial, both initially and on an ongoing basis. As for the initial costs, the underwriters' discount or commission average is approximately 7 percent of the total offering proceeds in the United States.

In addition, the owner can incur out-of-pocket expenses of $2 million or more for even a small offering of $50 million of the company's securities. If as a private company the owner did not have audited financial statements from a large accounting firm, the IPO accounting bill can substantially balloon the $2 million figure. If the offering is complicated or there is significant corporate restructuring involved, the owner's costs can also skyrocket. The approximately $900 million IPO of Hyatt Hotels Corporation in November 2009 cost close to $8 million (excluding underwriters' discounts). If the IPO is cancelled at the last minute, the owner is liable for substantial costs. However, it is typical to discount professional fees and printing costs in the event of a failed IPO.

On an ongoing basis, regulatory reporting requirements, stockholder meetings, investor relations, and other expenses of being public can run substantially more than $2 million annually, even for a small public company (see, however, the discussion below for methods of minimizing costs). Such expenses are actually even higher for most public companies. Included in this figure are additional auditing costs (including the evaluation of internal controls) that will undoubtedly rise when the owner converts from a private to a public company because of the significant additional time required to comply with SEC financial disclosure requirements and the requirements of the Public Company Accounting Oversight Board established under the Sarbanes-Oxley Act of 2002. Printing and distributing annual and quarterly reports, proxy statements, and stock certificates can be extremely costly if the owner chooses to use expensive glossy and colorful printing processes and first class mail. These costs are in addition to the owner's management time, which can be considerable.

The owner will need independent directors (typically three) to satisfy the listing requirements for NASDAQ or the New York Stock

Exchange, although he or she will have up to one year after the IPO to find a third director. The owner should expect to spend more than $100,000 per year on these three directors collectively.

In addition, there is a significant amount of initial time and effort required to establish and maintain disclosure controls and procedures and internal control over the financial reporting sufficient to satisfy the requirements of the federal securities laws as amended by the Sarbanes-Oxley Act of 2002. The initial establishment of these disclosure and internal controls can be very expensive even for a small public company, although this should be a one-time expense.

The owner may need to hire additional financial and accounting personnel to help prepare the company's financial disclosures. Likewise, he or she may be required to hire a shareholder relations employee and upgrade the quality of existing financial and accounting employees. These are all additional hidden costs of going public.

A number of smaller public companies have developed methods of minimizing the ongoing costs of being public. The author is aware of companies in which the ongoing costs are less than $400,000 per year (exclusive of director and officer liability insurance). These methods include the judicious use of outside professionals, sending bare-bones annual and quarterly reports to shareholders, using inexpensive techniques to reproduce and mail these shareholder reports (such as third class mail), avoiding expensive shareholder meetings, and so on. Minimizing such expenses can help reduce the owner's ongoing costs, exclusive of director and officer liability insurance.

Director and officer liability insurance is a must for public companies. Enron and other corporate corruption scandals have significantly increased the cost of this insurance. A $10 million policy with a $500,000 retention can cost over $300,000 per year.

2. *Pressure to maintain growth pattern.* The owner will be subject to considerable pressure to maintain the growth rate he or she has established, particularly from analysts who follow the company's stock. If the owner's sales or earnings deviate from an upward trend, analysts may recommend that the owner's stock be sold and investors may become apprehensive and sell their stock, driving down its price. These price declines can be severe as investors flee *en masse*. The owner may not have the capital to buy back the stock at these depressed prices. As a result, the owner will have unhappy stockholders.

The owner must report operating results quarterly. People will thus evaluate the company on a quarterly basis rather than annually. This intensifies pressure and shortens the owner's planning and operating horizons significantly. The pressure may tempt the owner to make short-term decisions that could have a harmful long-term impact on the company.

In an interview with Leonard Lavin, founder of the public company Alberto-Culver Corporation, he claimed that his company would be three to four times bigger if it were not public. He stated that the need to increase sales and profits every quarter led them to avoid investments that would have been profitable in the long term but that would have shown a downturn in revenue in the short term.[16]

3. *Orphan public companies.* Analysts do not follow many smaller public companies since they prefer companies with market capitalizations above $250 million. If after the IPO the company is unable to attract the attention of analysts, it is likely that the owner's stock price will fall below the IPO price and the owner will have unhappy shareholders. The owner may even have difficulty attracting market makers to the stock. Such public companies are sometimes called "orphan" public companies.

If the company becomes an orphan, it will be difficult to raise additional equity or use the stock as an acquisition currency without significantly diluting existing shareholders. Thus, although the company will enjoy the benefits of the additional equity capital from the IPO, many of the other advantages of the IPO would be lost. The owner may ultimately have to consider a sale of the company or take it private in a management buy-out.

4. *Disclosure of information.* The company's operations and financial situation are open to public scrutiny. Information concerning the company, officers, directors, and certain shareholders—information not ordinarily disclosed by privately held companies—will now be available to competitors, customers, employees, and others. Such information as the company's sales, profits, the owner's competitive edge, material contracts with major customers, and the salaries and perquisites of the CEO and certain highly paid executive officers must be disclosed not only when the owner initially goes public, but also on a continuing basis thereafter.

The SEC staff has a procedure to authorize confidential treatment for the documents the company files. However, the company must apply to the SEC early in the IPO registration process to avoid holding up the IPO. Very sensitive information can typically be excluded from public scrutiny.

The SEC-mandated disclosures should not be a major concern to most family businesses. The competitors of the business may already possess a lot more information about the company than the owner realizes. This information may have been revealed by customers, suppliers, and former employees. Many family businesses already provide some financial information to business credit agencies. Although public companies disclose much more financial information than private ones, the additional information is not necessarily a competitive disadvantage.

In general, public companies are only required to disclose information that is material to investors. Information about specific customers for the owner's products do not have to be disclosed unless the customer's purchases are such a high percentage of the owner's total sales as to be material to investors. Likewise, the exact profitability of specific products does not normally have to be disclosed, provided the product lines do not constitute a separate industry segment for financial reporting purposes. Management is given reasonable discretion in determining whether its business includes separately reportable industry segments. Accordingly, it is usually possible to avoid disclosure of the exact profitability of separate product lines.

5. *Loss of control.* If a sufficiently large proportion of the company's shares is sold to the public, the owner of the family business may be threatened with the loss of control of the company. Once the company is publicly held, the potential exists for further dilution of the owner's control through subsequent public offerings and acquisitions. Likewise, the company may be subject to a hostile tender offer.

This disadvantage can be alleviated by the careful insertion of anti-takeover provisions in the company's charter or by creating two classes of stock with disproportionate voting rights. Although there are few, if any, anti-takeover defenses that are completely, legally foolproof, some defenses can in practice be very effective against raiders. Defenses that deprive the raiders of voting power or that otherwise penalize them are particularly effective.

Many underwriters, particularly prestigious ones, object to anti-takeover defenses in the charter of IPO companies. Such defenses may make it more difficult to attract certain institutional investors. This may result in the IPO selling at a discount ranging from 5 to 20 percent, or not selling at all. The few underwriters who do not primarily sell to institutional investors are usually more relaxed about these clauses.

What is a "normal" anti-takeover defense and what is "unusual" are typically matters of negotiation with the underwriter. For example, some underwriters object to the staggering of the terms of the board of directors' members. Others will not. In general, anti-takeover provisions, which are part of state law and require special shareholder action to opt out of, will usually be accepted by underwriters.

Even if anti-takeover defenses cannot be inserted into the company's charter prior to its IPO, the owner can usually amend the charter after its IPO to insert these defenses. However, in today's environment, it is likely that the owner will have shareholder opposition. This should be accomplished before the owner's personal stock ownership falls below 50 percent of the outstanding stock.

6. *Shareholder lawsuits.* Public companies and their directors, officers, and control persons are susceptible to being sued by their shareholders in lawsuits.

Shareholder class action lawsuits typically follow a significant drop in the market price of their company's stock, caused by adverse news about the company. The theory of these lawsuits is that the company knew or should have known of the adverse news and had a duty to publicize it at an earlier date than when the news actually became public. The lawsuit will allege that failure to publicize the information earlier constitutes "fraud on the market."

Overly optimistic or exaggerated statements contained in the company's reports to shareholders or in press releases are usually cited in these lawsuits to support their allegations. These statements are typically the result of misguided attempts to generate interest in the company.

Public companies can prevent such lawsuits, or at least win them, only by a careful program that promptly discloses adverse news to the trading markets and by avoiding overly optimistic or exaggerated comments in shareholder and press releases. This requires that the company be sensitive to the need for such disclosures.

Since everyone makes a mistake occasionally, it is a good idea to obtain sufficient director and officer liability insurance to cover this risk. Some private companies already maintain this insurance, but usually at lower cost. Thus, only the extra insurance premium costs of being public should be considered the real disadvantage of an IPO.

7. *Estate tax disadvantage.* One of the advantages of an IPO is to create sufficient liquidity to pay inheritance taxes. However, there is

a concomitant disadvantage: it is more difficult to obtain a low estate tax valuation for a publicly traded stock than for the stock of a private company. This is true because the public market tends to value stocks on a multiple of earnings basis rather than a book value basis.

Worst Practice—Benihana and the New Wife

> **Worst Practice**
>
> Have the family business go public, reserving voting control through a separate higher voting class of stock, and then give the board of directors that the owner does not control the legal authority to issue additional voting stock to dilute family control.

Rocky Aoki founded Benihana of Tokyo, Inc. ("BOT") and its subsidiary, Benihana, Inc. ("Benihana"), which own and operate Benihana restaurants in the United States and other countries. Aoki owned 100 percent of BOT until 1998, when he pled guilty to insider trading charges. In order to avoid licensing problems created by his status as a convicted felon, Aoki transferred his stock to the Benihana Protective Trust ("Trust"). The trustees of the Trust were Aoki's three children (Kana Aoki Nootenboom, Kyle Aoki, and Kevin Aoki) and Darwin Dornbush (who was then the family's attorney, a Benihana director, and effectively the company's general counsel).

Benihana, a Delaware corporation and a publicly traded company, has two classes of common stock. There are approximately 6 million shares of Class A common stock outstanding. Each share has 1/10 vote and the holders of Class A common are entitled to elect 25 percent of the directors. There are approximately 3 million shares of common stock outstanding. Each share of common has one vote and the holders of common stock are entitled to elect the remaining 75 percent of Benihana's directors. Before the transaction at issue, BOT owned 50.9 percent of the common stock and 2 percent of the Class A stock.

The nine member board of directors of Benihana was classified and the directors served three-year terms. In addition, the certificate of incorporation of Benihana gave the board of directors full authority to issue, without shareholder approval, preferred stock containing "the voting powers, if any, designations, preferences and relative, participating, optional or other special rights, and the qualifications, limitations or restrictions of such series to the full extent now or hereafter permitted by the law of the State of Delaware."[17]

In 2003, shortly after Aoki married Keiko Aoki, conflicts arose between Aoki and his children. In August, the children were upset to learn that their father had changed his Will to give Keiko control over BOT. Joel Schwartz, Benihana's president and CEO, also was concerned about this change in control. He discussed the situation with Dornbush and they briefly considered various options, including the issuance of sufficient Class A stock to trigger a provision in the certificate of incorporation that would allow the common and Class A stock to vote together for 75 percent of the directors.

The Aoki family's turmoil came at a time when Benihana also was facing challenges. Many of its restaurants were old and outmoded. Benihana hired WD Partners to evaluate its facilities and plan and design appropriate renovations. The resulting Construction and Renovation Plan anticipated that the project would take at least five years and cost $56 million on more. Wachovia Bank (Wachovia) offered to provide Benihana a $60 million line of credit for the plan, but the restrictions the bank imposed made it unlikely that Benihana would be able to borrow the full amount. Because the Wachovia line of credit did not assure that Benihana would have the capital it needed, the company retained Morgan Joseph & Co. to develop other financing options.

On January 9, 2004, after evaluating Benihana's financial situation and needs, Fred Joseph of Morgan Joseph, met with Schwartz, Dornbush, and John E. Abdo, the board's executive committee. Joseph expressed concern that Benihana would not have sufficient available capital to complete the Construction and Renovation Plan and pursue appropriate acquisitions. Benihana was conservatively leveraged, and Joseph discussed various financing alternatives, including bank debt, high yield debt, convertible debt or preferred stock, equity and sale/leaseback options.

The full board met with Joseph on January 29, 2004. He reviewed all the financing alternatives that he had discussed with the executive committee, and recommended that Benihana issue convertible preferred stock. Joseph explained that the preferred stock would provide the funds needed for the Construction and Renovation Plan and also put the company in a better negotiating position if it sought additional financing from Wachovia. Unfortunately for Rocky Aoki, the preferred stock was convertible into the common stock that had the higher voting right than the publicly traded stock.

Rocky Aoki, through BOT, challenged the issuance of the preferred stock and lost.[18]

The Mistake: Reading between the lines, when Rocky Aoki announced that, upon his death his new wife would control Benihana, he upset his family as well as the board of directors and management of Benihana. His first mistake was to announce who his successor would be, thereby uniting the family, the board of directors, and management against him. The second mistake was to give the board of directors the legal authority in the certificate of incorporation to issue convertible preferred stock or any other kind of voting stock that could dilute his voting control without legally requiring the approval of the common stock that he controlled.

APPENDIX 1

Selected Portions of a Speech by Philip Clemens, Chairman/CEO, Clemens Family Corporation October, 2008

A FAMILY BUSINESS OR A BUSINESS FAMILY?

What is the difference between a family business and a business family? Aren't they the same thing? Are we just twisting words to confuse us—or is there a real difference between a business family and a family business?

I contend that there is a real difference between the two. They are as different as night and day, and yet many people fail to see the difference. Today I want to help you see why being a business family will allow business to continue for many years into the future and not become a statistic like so many other businesses.

Today in the US, the majority of the businesses are small businesses and most of them are family owned. Current statistics show that between 80 to 90% of businesses in the US are family owned. But they aren't all small business. 37% of the Fortune 500 companies are family owned. The average family business last 25 years; only 40% of the businesses go to the next generation; only 12% go beyond the second generation; only 3% go to the fourth generation; and very few family businesses leave a legacy for others to follow.

So, why did you invite an individual here to speak to you today about this topic? As advisors, our business just happens to be in the center of your sweet spot.

Do you know what a sweet spot is? Two different sports will give you a great understanding. Golf! A few years ago, drivers started to grow in size. One reason, so many people were taking up the sport, but many had a real problem hitting the ball well on their first shot. They had a good driver—maybe even a great driver, but you had to hit the ball perfectly to have it go where you wanted it to go and how far you wanted it to go. The average duffer had real problems with this. They could swing with all their might, but if they were only a small amount to the left or right they either hooked or sliced the ball.

Along came the clubs with bigger heads. One that had a much larger sweet spot that more people could drive like the pros. The same happened in tennis, and tennis racquets grew larger for a bigger sweet spot.

As a result, many more people took up golf and tennis because they could be much better and not be an embarrassment at a sport they like to do. It is my hope that as I share about our business that you may be able to enlarge your sweet spot and be much better at helping others.

Let me share briefly about our business and why working with families in business is a real passion for me.

Our family business began much like many family businesses do. It never began as a business or was intended to grow to what it is today. It was a hobby that became a business.

My Grandfather started our family business at age 16 on his father's farm. His Dad gave him 1 hog a week to butcher. He took the meat from that 1 hog and loaded in his wagon and went 30 miles to Philadelphia to sell his products. He would then go to the wharf in Philadelphia and get fish to bring back to the country folk to sell. His slogan—"Never an empty wagon".

At the turn of the twentieth century you didn't have refrigeration, so you only processed pork in the winter time or until the ice that you stored would no longer keep the meat fresh. So he began supplementing his meat with produce, poultry, dairy products and other items. His business was often referred to as a "huckster business." He would take his farm goods to the city and sell them to the "city folk."

His business continued to grow and he began supplying meat to local stores and in some, he set up the meat counter to serve the customers. He quickly developed two types of businesses—production and retail. Slowly he narrowed his product lines down to the meat business and retail.

Along the way, he married at age 20 and he and his wife bought their own farm, after running his business out of his father's farm for about eight years. My grandparents also began raising a family. They had 14 children; 4 of those children died between birth and their first birthday; but they raised 10 children—5 boys and 5 girls.

Family businesses generally begin with the parents starting the business and then putting their children to work in the business. If needed, they hire a few key people to help run the business. As I said earlier, rarely do they intentionally start as a business, but as the work load increases, they become a family business.

I find it a bit humorous as you look at the early beginnings of many family businesses. Often times the male has the idea to get a business started, but it takes a CEO to get it going right. The CEO most always is the wife of the entrepreneur—the Chief Emotional Officer, who steadies the ship in the early days of the business. Then it takes cheap or free employees—the kids to really make it cash flow. It is a real family affair.

Each family business has events that mark significant milestones that forge who they become as a business. In our case there were many of these events. The first major event was when the family home burned to the ground in 1921. My grandparents were forced to place their children in different homes around the community until the home could be rebuilt. The home was right next to the business and the business had to take priority to keep running.

The next major event happened in 1933. My Grandmother went to Philadelphia for routine gall bladder surgery and died. It changed everything.

My Grandfather decided his priorities had to change. He sold the retail business to two of his sons. When you have 10 children, it is difficult to divide the business up and give it to the family, so he sold the business. He continued to operate the meat business along with the rest of the family and the employees they had hired. He also remarried a few years later—but things were different.

... [You] should realize that untimely events often force families to make decisions they have not prepared for. However, you also need to realize that parents often don't want to make a decision of forcing the family business on their family members and that choosing to sell the business to some of the family—including their own children, will be the only option that they want to consider. Especially if they have gotten signals from some or all of their family that they have no interest in the business.

So, in 1941, my Grandfather decided it was time to retire. So he sold the meat business to two sons. Again, sold the business—did not give it to the family. In 1946, that business burned to the ground and the family lost everything, except their spirit of doing business.

The two brothers asked two other brothers to join with them as investors and they approached a neighboring competitor to see if they would sell them their business. The original answer was no. So they attempted to rebuild. However, since this was just after World War II, steel was rationed and could not be purchased to rebuild the plant.

So the brothers approached the competitor again and they decided to sell the business. The business had not been doing very well because meat was still rationed from the War and the three owners were not getting along real well due to business pressure. So within three months of the fire the family was back in business at a new location. Within one week of purchasing the business, all war rationing was dropped and the business took off like a rocket. Good luck never hurts!

Today our business has grown to annual revenues of $575 million, employing 2,300 people and producing products and services in many different areas. The Clemens Family Corporation has two main divisions—Clemens Food Group and Clemens Development.

Clemens Food Group consists of both branded products companies and manufacturing and service companies. Our brands include Hatfield, Nick's Sausage, Hatfield's Phillies Franks, Prima Porta, Wild Bill's Foods and Creta Farms. Our services include Country View Family Farms, our hog raising operation; PV Transport, our trucking company; and CFC Logistics, a public refrigerated warehouse business.

Clemens Development is a real estate business that owns warehouse buildings, a shopping center, and other land and buildings for development.

The Clemens Family Corporation is owned by 229 Clemens family members that span nearly a century (from less than one year old to 93 years old—from the second to the sixth generation). We have 23 family members working in the business today, ranging from the thrid to the fifth generation. Our family shareholder base is very unique, but having this number is also both very rewarding and challenging.

However, we are not a family business, we are a business family.

What are the major differences between a family business and a business family? The biggest difference is how you see the business. A family business exists for the family. It is there to give them jobs and have the business revolve around the family. A business family is a family that just happens to own a business or businesses. The businesses exist for the owners. Owners are free to become employees if they are qualified and are hired by the business. The business is there to give a return to the owners and to operate independently from ownership. The two models are exact opposites of each other.

I call this a mirror principle. When you look into a mirror, do you see an exact reflection of who you are? No, you see just the opposite. It looks almost exactly like the image, but it is exactly backward. So it is with a business family and a family business.

A family business has family as the owners—so does a business family. A family business often has family running the business —as does a business family. But, the main difference is understanding how the family sees themselves in the business. I often refer this to "knowing what hat you are wearing".

In a family business, family members always wear their family hat. It is the most prominent hat they wear. A family hat takes precedent over all other hats. In a business that is owned by a business family, the family hat is not appropriate to wear. When owners are employed in the business, they only wear the employee hat. All other hats are irrelevant.

Earlier I said that only 40% of family businesses last until the second generation, 12% to the third and 3% to the fourth. Why don't family business last very long? One main reason, how family is treated in the business—a critical factor.

Family business is often known for giving preferential treatment—which could be better or worse—to family members—after all they wear the "family hat." Family members often do not have job descriptions, are rarely given performance appraisals, and generally operate under different rules than all other employees. This spells disaster for a harmonious working environment.

Family members in family businesses often hold all the key leadership positions and many times they do not allow non-family members into key leadership positions. Family members are almost guaranteed any job they want, because family is the most important thing in a family business. Family power has the ability to hold a business back from achieving its real potential even though the family sees it quite differently.

One final killer of family business is the lack of profits to continue to run the business. The key to keeping a family business healthy is family harmony, not profits. Family harmony becomes paramount to profits, yet without profits, there will not be family harmony. It can become a vicious circle.

If a family is to have a long-term legacy, they must move from being a family business to become a business family. This doesn't mean that family isn't important—in fact family might even be more important.

Business families make sure their business is run in a way that rewards ownership for the way the business is operated. This means they do several things.

First the business is operated by the most qualified people. If these people happen to be family—great; if non-family that's OK also, it is always the most qualified person. This means that all jobs are open to the most qualified persons and the family role only comes into play if two candidates have equal qualification.

Second, all employees are held to the same standard. No one gets preferential treatment because of who they are. Employees know what each of the job requirements are and what standards they will be measured against. No one gets favoritism.

Third, the business is there to help the family owners, not the family is there to help the business. If anyone prevents the business from meeting the set objectives, the person is separated from the business—whether family or not. Everyone is pulling for the same results.

Finally, the business is run like a business and profits are respected. When a business operates profitability, it can pass financial rewards to the owners through dividends or sharing of profits. If the business exists for the benefit of the family, profits are often the last thing that is looked at. Profitability is only an extra, not an essential.

So why do many families continue down the family business path and not choose to be a business family? It is difficult to say, but I believe one of the main reasons is that they like the family hat so much that it means more than anything to them—even the family business.

Choosing to be a business family is critical if you are going to have long-term staying power. Many successful family businesses we see today are looked at as a family business, when in reality they are a business that just happens to be owned by a business family.

It is the mirror principle. You think you are looking at a family business—when in reality you are looking at a business family. They look alike, but operate very differently.

Our family has successfully operated as a business family for many years. It is tough to break out of the mold of being a family business.

Being a family business is very comfortable and a fun thing. However, you rarely see the end coming and when it eventually comes—it gets very ugly.

One area that has greatly helped us to keep focused as a business family is our trust triangle. Businesses that are owned by families need to be earning trust each day in everyway possible. Trust is hard to earn and can be easily lost, so you must learn to work hard at both earning and keeping it. This is especially true when new employees come into the business or when things aren't going so well in the business, whether financially or managerially.

How do we earn trust? Through our Trust Triangle. We have established an Owners' Advisory Council. This Council is there to speak as one voice for all of our 229 family shareholders. They are the ones responsible to interview candidates to serve on our independent Board of Directors. They also set up annual expectations for the business. Having this group, speaking with one voice about what the business should accomplish is a very critical step.

Our owners' expectations follow a balanced scorecard approach. Each year the owners decide on the metrics that are needed to drive the results that they desire. These expectations fall into four different categories:

1. *Financial metrics.* These metrics may be RONA (return on net assets), cash flow; NIBT (net income before tax) or other financial metrics as the Council thinks the company needs to be directed in.
2. *Shareholder satisfaction.* This metric is based on how much the value of the business has grown, and not the share price. Our stock is valued twice a year by and outside professional firm. We want to see how management has used assets to grow the real value of the business.
3. *Risk management.* The Council sets how much risk the owners are willing to give management. They want to see that the risk is bringing the expected return. Some of our risk range is set by our lending institutions, but the owners also want to have their own limits.
4. *Stewardship.* This clearly goes to our values. The Council is interested in seeing how well we have been regarding the sustainability, employee turnover, philanthropy efforts or other such measures.

Today, too many managers never know what their owners really want from what they own. When managers struggle to meet either unknown, unspoken or unrealistic expectations, trouble will come and no one will trust anyone. When owners clearly state their expectations with management and through negotiations, management agrees, trust can start to be earned. These expectations are agreed upon before we begin the fiscal year and help build a win/win philosophy.

The next step is to have the Independent Board of Directors review the expectations. The Directors need to evaluate if the owners are being too lenient or too strict on management. When the Directors come to agreement with the owners on expectations, the Directors can then hold management accountable for their results. Thus, a trust triangle is formed and all sides know what the rules of the game are.

This is especially critical for non-family managers so they and family employees that have made a decision to be an employee in the business know what is expected of them. Having known expectations allows everyone to trust each other. Its critical to not only know expectations but then to know the rewards of achieving expectations. Both sides know what is expected and they can strive to reach a common goal. Each of these things helps build trust.

When trust is the foundation in any business things can move forward and long-term relationships and results can be achieved. It is a win for everyone.

Having an independent board is very critical. We have some very stringent requirements to keep our board independent. First, no employee is permitted to be on the board except for the current CEO. The only exception is the known replacement for the current CEO can serve within 18 months of retirement of the CEO.

All board members must meet the following criteria:

1. Currently a senior management individual (or recently retired) from a successful business. We prefer the individual to be the president or CEO.
2. Strong financial background and clearly understands the need and value of business metrics
3. Unquestionable ethics and integrity
4. Embraces the vision, values and culture of the corporation
5. Does not have a conflict of interest with any of the CFC businesses

Our philosophy is to have a board consist of a majority of outside individuals. Both outside and inside directors (inside being defined as either they or their spouse own stock in the Corporation) must meet the same criteria. Board members are elected for a one-year term with no limitations. We generally prefer that board members agree to serve a minimum of a three years and prefer that the service does not exceed 10 years.

Earning trust is critical if you are going to embrace a business family model. It takes a great deal of effort to earn trust each day—but only one mistake to lose trust. Our Trust Triangle has its checks and balances to make sure that we are balancing the trust load as wide as possible to make it effective.

So, is the business family model a sustainable model in the twenty-first century? I believe it absolutely is. Again, as I stated earlier, I do not believe the family business model is—except in very rare occasions.

So, what are we doing at the Clemens Family Corporation to have the next generations both catch this vision and keep developing our legacy?

In addition to all of the above, the critical factor is to keep your owners both informed and engaged. Owners need to understand what the expectations are for what they own. One thing that happens in family businesses that are at least in the 3rd generation—very few shareholders have ever invested a dime of their personal money into the business. You must educate them that they do have an investment and should be seeking the right return.

I believe it is critical for shareholders to have known expectations. They all have expectations, whether they know it or not. However, if you try to meet unknown or unachievable expectations—you will have trouble, you just don't know what trouble or when it will occur.

The most important thing you can do to have the next generation carry on the legacy is to communicate. The key to keeping your shareholders engaged is communications and involvement. Many of them may want to be involved in the day-to-day business—even if they don't work there. That is not good! You want them to be involved in the proper way and one that will build harmony and not distrust and interruption. Let people know what you are doing, why you are doing it and make them a part. Owners often need to be educated in the role of ownership—especially if they have only been given their stock and not really put any of their own capital in the business. This is a very tricky area.

We try to do this in multiple ways and don't believe there is only one way to do it. First, on a monthly basis we send out our "Shareholder Information" to our shareholders. This newsletter lets them know what is happening around the Corporation. We also share how current events or news will impact the businesses and their investment. In addition, we share what is happening in the industry.

We also hold shareholder information meetings. Sometimes these meetings are to share information, other times to gather information from shareholders. We believe telling the story from multi-generational sources is critical. People need to both hear and understand the things that really make us tick. We need to tell both the good and the bad.

At least one informational meeting per year is to review the financial results of the business. We do this in a fun and entertaining way. The presentations are geared toward a 16-year-old audience. We invite all shareholders over age 14 to attend. Any question can be asked and all and any figures are available for shareholders. Participation by the audience is both encouraged and welcomed.

We also want as many of our shareholders that are willing to participate in community events that we have throughout the year. Some of our annual events are a Christmas dinner at a local Salvation Army Shelter where we feed the families and pass out gifts. We encourage our shareholders to bring their children to help with the gifts, play with younger residents of the shelter and help those who need help in getting their food.

We also have an event where we rent the Philadelphia Zoo for an evening to allow children with leukemia from the Philadelphia area to bring their families and their health care providers for a free night at the zoo, with lots of food. We do this in conjunction with an organization that works with the Philadelphia Eagles.

We also have an annual shareholders' meeting. This is very different from most shareholder meetings. We do not discuss finances at this meeting. However, we do honor employees that have given significantly to the corporation. In addition, we mix our management, owners, board, and others to encourage communication.

This past year we had some of our fourth and fifth generation family members share how they are intentionally communicating to the next generations. One family shared about their experience at the Salvation Army and the zoo and how their children are impacted by these events. Another shareholder shared how they use the monthly shareholder information sheet to teach their children about what the business is all about. Another shared how they got involved in a philanthropic project and how the Corporate Philanthropic group helped them see how we help others.

We also have weekend retreats for those owners that chose to be employees of the business and to help them understand the difference between being an employee and being an owner and how these are very separate issues.

But, the main thing to keep this legacy going to the next generation is to communicate. You can hardly communicate too much. You must be very creative and just do it.

One thing I have also done over the past several years is to create a theme for the year. I want the communication to have a central theme. This year was focus. I gave out compasses each time we communicated to different groups. A compass is a great tool to help you know what direction you are going. However, a compass can never set a destination for you. However, once you know your destination, a compass can help you determine the course you need to take to reach your destination.

Last years theme was keep sharp. Since many of our businesses require sharp knives to do their work right—a knife sharpener was a great illustration gift. However, we wanted to remind them as shareholders, managers and board members they also needed to keep sharp. We reminded them of the sharpening tools that were available to keep them sharp.

If you want the business to go to the next generations you must be creative and keep it in front of them all of the time—both in good and bad times. It is easy to do it in good times, but in bad times you can't stop communicating. Keep them informed of why these are bad times and what you are doing to get back to their expectations. Tell the story.

You must work hard at making the business successful. In addition, I run several mentoring programs with family members in the business to help with our succession planning. It is our family's goal to always have the CEO be a qualified family member. I would like to have five qualified individuals to take my place. It is then up to our independent board to choose the next CEO—not the family. Again, we don't want this to be political—we want the most qualified person.

Being a business family leaves a great legacy for the next generations. It allows you to focus on the right things. However, here is where the mirror principal comes in to play one more time. The more successful you are as a business family, the more people see you as a family business. It's not a bad thing—in fact it can often work in your favor from a marketing viewpoint. However, you look into the mirror and you see a business family—others look at you and see you as a family business.

Finally, one of the best thing business families can do is to get competent professionals to help them think through what they are doing.

One challenge we have as a family is how do we creatively have an organization that permits the maximum amount of family members and still remain private. Also, how do we maintain the best tax structure that is best for everyone?

APPENDIX 2

Prenuptial Agreement*

AGREEMENT made this day of _____, 20____, by and between
_____, residing at _____,
New York _____ and _____, residing at
_____, New York _____.

<u>W I T N E S S E T H:</u>

WHEREAS:

The parties to this Agreement intend to be married to each other.

Each party desires and has expressed a willingness to enter into this Agreement, believing that such an agreement will enhance and encourage a harmonious marital relationship between them and will enable them to avoid conflict or controversy in the future arising out of any separation or dissolution of the marriage.

The parties agree that this Agreement, which is entered into after due and considered deliberation, shall be and constitute an agreement pursuant to New York Domestic Relations Law Section 236, Part B(3), with respect to all assets and properties, both real and personal, tangible and intangible, wherever situated, now owned by the parties or either of them, or standing in their respective names, or that may hereafter be acquired by either of the parties.

NOW, THEREFORE, with full knowledge and understanding of the laws governing their relationship and in consideration of these premises and of the marriage between them about to be solemnized, _____ and _____ intending to be legally bound, do hereby agree as FOLLOWS:

---

* Prepared by Norman S. Heller, Esq., Blank Rome LLP, New York, NY.

ARTICLE I

EFFECTIVE DATE AND RECITALS

This Agreement is made in consideration of and is conditioned upon _____ and _____ entering into a valid marriage with each other, and shall become effective only upon _____ and _____ entering into a valid marriage with each other (the "Effective Date"). The recitals in the Whereas clauses are true and correct and are incorporated herein by reference.

ARTICLE II

INDEPENDENT LEGAL ADVICE; FINANCIAL DISCLOSURE; ACKNOWLEDGMENTS

1. Each of the parties acknowledges and represents that they have had separate legal counsel advise him or her fully with respect to his or her rights (in the absence of this Agreement) in and to the present and future property and income of the other and the nature and extent of the valuable property rights that he or she is relinquishing by signing this Agreement and that they each understand and are satisfied with such advice.

2. Each party has freely, without coercion of any kind and at his or her own expense, sought and obtained independent legal advice from counsel of his or her own selection. _____ has been represented by_____, of _____, _____, New York, New York _____, and _____ by _____, of _____, New York, New York _____.

3. _____ and _____ have given due consideration to all facts and circumstances likely to influence her or his judgment with respect to matters embodied in this Agreement. She and he, as well as their respective separate legal counsel, have received satisfactory answers to any questions they have asked with respect thereto.

4. _____ and _____ further acknowledge that the terms and provisions contained in this Agreement are fair and reasonable.

5. _____ and _____ have not made or received any promise or representation from the other (or from any third person or entity) not contained in this Agreement as to financial or other support from the other or as to any right to future earnings, profits or revenue of the other.

6. Exhibits A and B annexed hereto contain a summary statement of each party's financial condition. _____ and _____ each represent that they have described to the best of their knowledge their respective assets, liabilities, beneficial interests in trusts, and income on Exhibits A and B.

7. _____ acknowledges his understanding that _____'s present interest in the assets listed on Exhibit A and her net worth may actually exceed or be less than the values listed on Exhibit A._____ further acknowledges that the purpose of Exhibit A is to identify the assets that _____ owned at the time of the marriage for the purposes of this Agreement and to generally inform him of the approximate extent of her net worth and that Exhibit A is not consistent with Generally Accepted Accounting Principles.

8. _____ acknowledges her understanding that _____'s present interest in the assets listed on Exhibit B and his net worth today may actually exceed or be less than the values listed on Exhibit B._____ further acknowledges that the purpose of Exhibit B is to identify the assets that _____ owned at the time of the marriage for the purposes of this Agreement and to generally inform her of the approximate extent of his net worth and that Exhibit B is not consistent with Generally Accepted Accounting Principles.

9. _____ and _____ each acknowledges and recognizes that the property and estate of the other may be increased by reason of gifts, inheritances, distributions from trusts and other such additions, and each acknowledges that this Agreement is being entered into freely, irrespective of the value or amount of such additions.

10. _____ and _____ and each of their attorneys have had the opportunity to make inquiries relating to details of the other party's income and net worth and other relevant financial information, have made inquiries and are satisfied with the financial information provided by the other party and waive any rights to further disclosure. Each party further acknowledges that she or he (i) believes Exhibit A and Exhibit B are sufficient for the purposes of this Agreement and each party's evaluation of the terms hereof, (ii) understands the nature and extent of the income, property and future financial prospects of the other party, and (iii) fully understands the contents of such financial disclosure. Each party confirms that she or he desires no further financial disclosure from the other and, accordingly, each party has expressly and knowingly directed counsel not to seek further financial information from the other party.

11. Each of _____ and _____ acknowledges that this Agreement and the Exhibits annexed hereto contain confidential information and represents that she or he as the case may be has taken, and agrees to continue to take, precautions to maintain such confidentiality and prevent the disclosure of such information other than for purposes of obtaining family and professional advice in connection with such party's legal and financial affairs and in any proceeding to enforce this Agreement.

ARTICLE III

SEPARATE PROPERTY DEFINED

1. The parties agree that, notwithstanding any contrary provision of the laws of the State of New York or any other state or country which may assert jurisdiction over the parties or their marriage, the provisions of this Agreement will limit the rights, if any, that each party will have in the property of the other upon a divorce, legal separation, annulment, or other dissolution of the parties' marriage.

2. Except as specified herein, the following shall constitute and remain the Separate Property of each party:

(a)   The property listed on Exhibits A and B;

(b)   Any real, personal or mixed property or interests therein acquired by a party before the contemplated marriage;

(c)   Property and interests therein acquired at any time after the marriage by inter vivos gift from a third party;

(d)   Any bequest or inheritance from a third party by last will and testament, pursuant to the laws of intestacy, or testamentary substitute, including but not limited to life insurance proceeds or retirement benefits received from third parties;

(e)   Income and other distributions from any trust;

(f)   Any increase in the value of Separate Property, whether or not such increase is due in whole or in part to the contributions or efforts of either party to this Agreement;

(g)   Property acquired in exchange for Separate Property;

(h)   The dividends, interest, rents and other income from, other distributions upon, gains from and the proceeds of, the sale of Separate Property;

(i)   Compensation for personal injuries;

(j)   Any monies, investments, jewelry, furs, cars, objects of art, antiques, furniture, whether previously owned, now owned or hereafter owned by either party if purchased with Separate Property;

(k)   Income earned and property obtained by either party after the occurrence of an Operative Event;

(l)   Gifts of tangible personal property from one party to the other shall be the donee's Separate Property; and

(m)   "Retirement Assets" of a party, defined as all of such party's rights and interests in or under any retirement or pension plan including any defined benefit plan, defined contribution plan, money purchase plan, Keogh (H.R. 10) plan, profit sharing plan, individual retirement account, 401(k) plan or similar employee plan acquired before or after the date of marriage. Rights to stock awards, options, stock units, deferred compensation plans and the like derived from employment shall not be considered Retirement Assets pursuant to this Agreement.

3. No contributions by either party to the care, maintenance, improvement, custody or repair of the Separate Property of the other, whether such contributions be in the form of money, property or personal property or personal services rendered, shall in any way alter or convert any of such property, or any part or portion of said property to marital property.

4. For purposes of this Agreement, the change in form or appreciation in value, if any, in either party's Separate Property, including, without limitation, property deemed to be separate pursuant to this Article, which occurs during the parties' marriage, shall belong solely to the person entitled to such Separate Property, without regard to the reasons for or nature of the change in form or appreciation in value, and the other party shall make no claim to an interest in such property as it may have changed in form or appreciated in value, unless the parties specifically contract otherwise in writing, executed by both parties in the manner which would entitle a deed to be recorded in the State of New York.

5. (a)   Separate Property contributions by either party to the acquisition of any real estate obtained during the marriage shall be governed by Article VIII herein.

(b)   Should either party invest Separate Property into a business created during the marriage between the parties, the investing party shall be entitled to recoup such Separate Property upon an Event of Marital Dissolution. The income generated from any such business created during the marriage, however, shall be Marital Property to be divided pursuant to Article V contained herein.

6. Neither (a) the joint use of Separate Property, nor (b) either party permitting the other party to use his or her Separate Property

shall give rise to joint ownership of that property, unless the parties agree otherwise in a writing signed by each of them and executed in the manner which would entitle a deed to be recorded in the State of New York.

7. Without limiting the generality of the foregoing and as more specifically set forth in Article VIII, Separate Property shall also include any Separate Property which has been used for the purchase or capital improvement of real property otherwise considered in part or whole as marital property or which is invested in real property owned jointly by the parties (a "Separate Property Contribution"). Such Separate Property Contribution shall remain Separate Property and shall belong solely to the party who contributed it.

8. As to any Entity (the "Original Entity") in which a party has an interest that is Separate Property as defined in this Agreement, any successor interest into which such Separate Property was converted (voluntarily or involuntarily) shall be such party's Separate Property, and any interest such party has in another Entity that is the successor in interest (by sale, merger, reorganization, restructuring or otherwise) of the Original Entity shall be such party's Separate Property; and for purposes of this Agreement, the term "Entity" shall mean any corporation, limited liability company, limited or general partnership, joint venture, or other type of entity, domestic or foreign.

9. (a) The parties agree, furthermore, that neither will assert that the filing by them of joint income tax returns or the payment of capital gains or other income taxes due on the proceeds, interest or income from Separate Property with income earned through employment during the marriage or other marital income will have caused any otherwise Separate Property of either to have become marital property.

(b) Each party shall be solely responsible for any and all debts, obligations and liabilities incurred in connection with his or her Separate Property, whether incurred before or after execution of this Agreement and agrees to hold the other party harmless from and indemnified against all such liabilities, obligations and debts. Payments made with income earned during the marriage on account of such liabilities, obligations and debts shall not affect the Separate Property nature of the asset and shall not be a basis for reimbursement to the marital estate.

ARTICLE IV

WAIVER OF SEPARATE PROPERTY

Each party agrees that to the extent permitted by law now or hereafter in effect:

1. Upon marriage, _____ will continue to retain all right, title and interest of every kind and character in and to all Separate Property she may now own or hereafter acquire in any manner, separate and apart from _____ and free of any and all claims, liens, or rights, inchoate or otherwise, of _____. Without limiting the generality of the foregoing, _____ agrees that _____ may dispose of any part or all of such Separate Property, at any time and in any manner she may see fit, free from interference or claim of _____. In the event of separation or a dissolution of the marriage of the parties, it is acknowledged that all such Separate Property, income received from such Separate Property, the proceeds of sale and reinvestment of such Separate Property, all property acquired in exchange for such Separate Property, and any successive appreciation thereon and any income derived therefrom shall constitute Separate Property of _____, and none shall be considered Marital Property under the laws of the State of New York or under this Agreement or marital or community or quasi-community property under the laws of any other jurisdiction within or without the United States.

2. Upon marriage, _____ will continue to retain all right, title and interest of every kind and character in and to all Separate Property he may now own or hereafter acquire in any manner, separate and apart from _____ and free of any and all claims, liens or rights, inchoate or otherwise, of _____. Without limiting the generality of the foregoing, _____ agrees that _____ may dispose of any part of all or such Separate Property, at any time and in any manner he may see fit, free from interference or claim of _____. In the event of separation or a dissolution of the marriage of the parties, it is acknowledged that all such Separate Property, income received from such Separate Property, the proceeds of sale and reinvestment of such Separate Property, all property acquired in exchange for such Separate Property, and any successive appreciation thereon and any income derived therefrom shall constitute Separate Property of _____, and none shall be considered Marital Property under the laws of the State of New York or under this Agreement or marital or community or quasi-community property

under the laws of any other jurisdiction within or without the United States.

3. Neither party shall have any right, title, or claim in the value of the other party's Separate Property, inclusive of, but not limited to any right, title or claim in the difference between the increase in value of all or part of one party's Separate Property as compared to the increase in value of all or part of the other party's Separate Property, during the course of the parties' marriage or their cohabitation.

4. Each party waives all rights to any beneficial interest in trusts of the other party and all claims that such beneficial interests in trusts may be characterized as Marital Property. The waiver with respect to the other party's beneficial interest in trusts shall apply even if such other party has received regular distributions from any such trusts during the course of the marriage.

5. Each party shall cooperate in filing any joint income tax returns, if applicable, which cooperation shall include but not be limited to, assistance after a divorce, separation or annulment. Each party shall be responsible for any tax liabilities, deficiencies, and penalties with respect to his or her own Separate Property.

ARTICLE V

MARITAL PROPERTY

1. Except for property deemed to be either party's Separate Property in this Agreement, all other property obtained by either or both parties after the Effective Date and prior to the occurrence of an Operative Event, shall be Marital Property.

2. Notwithstanding the provisions of Articles III and IV of this Agreement, _____'s interest in any business, including but not limited to the increase in value of _____ above the value set forth in _____'s financial schedule attached to this Agreement, and the increase in value of any other such business interest occurring prior to the date of an Event of Marital Dissolution shall be marital property.

3. Upon the occurrence of an Event of Marital Dissolution, as defined herein, Marital Property shall be divided as agreed to by the parties in a validly executed Property Settlement Agreement or as determined by a court of competent jurisdiction at the time an application is made for such relief. In determining an appropriate division of Marital Property, the terms and provisions of Article VIII concerning the disposition of a marital residence, shall be fully enforceable and binding upon the parties.

ARTICLE VI

EVENT OF MARITAL DISSOLUTION

"Event of Marital Dissolution" is defined as the first to occur of the following events:

(a) the filing and service of a Summons with Notice or Summons and Complaint by either party in an action for divorce, annulment or separation, whether or not said action ultimately results in a divorce, annulment or separation;

(b) the execution of a separation or property settlement agreement;

(c) delivery of written notice by one party to the other of an intention to separate permanently and file for divorce, annulment or separation ("Termination Notice"). A Termination Notice may be retracted by the party having served it by giving written notice of reconciliation ("Notice of Retraction") within thirty (30) days of the service of the Termination Notice. The Event of Marital Dissolution derived from the delivery of such Termination Notice, shall, for the purposes of this Agreement, be deemed never to have occurred, upon the service and acceptance of such Notice of Retraction. The written notice may be served personally, by certified mail, return receipt requested, or by Federal Express or other similar mail delivery service, or by written acknowledgement of the receipt of the notice signed by the party to whom the notice is addressed.

ARTICLE VII

RESERVATION OF RIGHTS TO SPOUSAL MAINTENANCE

Upon the occurrence of an Event of Marital Dissolution, each party reserves all rights to seek an award of alimony, maintenance or support, temporary or permanent and it is expressly understood and agreed by the parties that the determination of whether or not such an award is appropriate and, if so, the duration and amount of such award, shall be made by further agreement of the parties or by a court of competent jurisdiction based upon the circumstances which exist at the time such an application is made.

ARTICLE VIII

FUTURE MARITAL RESIDENCE

Marital Residence In Joint Names

1. In the event, after the marriage of the parties, one or more residence(s) is (are) purchased in joint names or transferred into the

joint names of the parties for the purposes of the parties' use and occupancy and not for investment ("Residence(s)"), said Residence(s) shall be distributed pursuant to the terms and provisions of paragraphs 2 through 12 of this Article VIII.

2. At the time of the happening of an Event of Marital Dissolution, the party who made the largest Separate Property contribution to the Residence(s) (the "First Optionee") shall have the first option of purchasing and retaining sole ownership of the Residence by purchasing the other party's (the "Second Optionee") ownership interest at the then fair market value. The respective ownership interest shall be calculated as set forth in paragraphs 4 and 5 of this Article VIII. The parties shall attempt to agree on the then fair market value. If the parties cannot agree, the fair market value shall be determined by the methods set forth hereinafter in paragraph 9 of this Article VIII.

3. The First Optionee shall have ninety (90) days from the time that fair market value of the Residence has been determined either by agreement of the parties or by the valuation methodology set forth in paragraph 9 to advise the Second Optionee in writing by personal delivery or overnight courier mail, return receipt requested (the "Initial Option Period") whether or not she or he will purchase the other party's interest in the Residence. Closing with respect to such Residence shall take place not later than ninety (90) days from the date of delivery of such written notice to the other party exercising the aforesaid option. In the event that the First Optionee declines to exercise within the Initial Option Period, then the Second Optionee shall have the option to purchase the interest of the First Optionee by notifying the First Optionee within thirty (30) days after the expiration of the Initial Option period, on the same terms and conditions set forth herein. The Second Optionee shall advise the First Optionee in writing within thirty (30) days of the expiration of the Initial Option Period (or the sooner of the First Optionee declining to exercise his or her option) by fax and overnight courier mail, return receipt requested, as to whether or not he or she will purchase the other's interest, if any, in said premises. Said closing shall take place not later than ninety (90) days from the date of delivery of the Second Optionee's written notice to the First Optionee exercising his or her option to purchase. In the event one party buys out the other party's interest, the buying party shall be responsible for, and shall pay, all reasonable selling expenses, including but not limited to, recording and transfer tax expenses, mansion tax, flip tax and reasonable closing costs.

4. In the event that _____ has exercised his option to purchase _____'s ownership interest in the Residence, then at the time of the closing, _____ shall pay to _____ an amount equal to _____'s Separate Property Contributions, if any, towards the purchase of and capital improvements to the Residence and an additional sum equal to fifty percent (50%) of the excess of (i) the fair market value of the Residence on the occurrence of an Event of Marital Dissolution over (ii) the sum of (x) _____'s and _____'s Separate Property Contributions towards the purchase of and capital improvements to the Residence and (y) the principal amount of any mortgage indebtedness (including home equity debt) on the Residence on the date of closing.

5. In the event that _____ has exercised her option to purchase _____'s ownership interest in the Residence, then at the time of the closing, _____ shall pay to _____ an amount equal to _____'s Separate Property Contributions, if any, towards the purchase of and capital improvements to the Residence, and an additional sum equal to fifty percent (50%) of the excess of (i) the fair market value of the Residence on the occurrence of an Event of Marital Dissolution over (ii) the sum of (x) _____'s and _____'s Separate Property Contributions towards the purchase of and capital improvements to the Residence and (y) the principal amount of any mortgage indebtedness (including home equity debt) on the Residence on the date of closing.

6. Except as otherwise expressly agreed to by the parties, in the event that at the time that _____ purchases _____'s interest in such property, there is a mortgage or home equity debt on said property, then it shall be _____'s obligation within ninety (90) days of purchasing _____'s interest in the Residence to use his best efforts to refinance said mortgage in order to remove _____'s name from said encumbrance. If _____ fails to comply with this obligation, _____ has the right to force a sale of the Residence.

7. Except as otherwise expressly agreed to by the parties, in the event that at the time that _____ purchases _____'s interest in such property, there is a mortgage or home equity debt on said property, then it shall be _____'s obligation within ninety (90) days of purchasing _____'s interest in the Residence to use her best efforts to refinance said mortgage in order to remove _____'s name from said encumbrance. If _____ fails to comply with this obligation, _____ has the right to force a sale of the Residence.

8. If neither party elects to purchase the interest of the other in the aforesaid Residence as provided herein, then the Residence shall be immediately listed for sale with a broker mutually agreed upon by the parties. It shall be listed within ten (10) days of the expiration of both option periods, or sooner if the parties agree.

9. In the event that the parties are not able to agree as to the fair market value of the Residence, then, upon written notice by one party to the other, each party shall select a licensed real estate appraiser who will render a written appraisal of the fair market value of the residence. Should the appraisals be within ten percent (10%) of each other, the fair market value will be fixed at an amount equal to the average of the two prior appraisals rendered. If the two appraisals are not within ten percent (10%) of each other, the two appraisers shall jointly choose a third appraiser and the parties shall be bound by the fair market value determined by the third appraiser. Each party shall be responsible for paying one-half of the cost of said third appraiser and each party shall be responsible for paying the cost of the appraiser selected by said party.

10. If the Residence does not sell within a reasonable time after being placed on the market, the price at which the residence is being offered for sale shall be reduced from time to time until the Residence is sold. If the parties cannot mutually agree as to the timing or the amount of the price reduction, then the asking price for the Residence shall be reduced by 5% every three months until the sale of the Residence and the parties shall be obligated to accept any bona fide offer for the purchase of the Residence within 95% of the asking price.

11. The net proceeds derived from closing after the repayment to _____ and _____ of his/her Separate Property Contribution towards the purchase of and capital improvements to the Residence, if any, shall be divided equally between the parties after deducting and satisfying all outstanding mortgages and liens, real estate commissions, realty transfer taxes, legal fees in connection with the closing, and other normal and customary closing costs and fees. Each party shall be responsible to report on his or her income tax returns 50% of the capital gain in reference to said sale.

12. If _____ elects to purchase _____'s interest in the aforesaid Residence pursuant to paragraphs 3-9 of this Article VIII, then _____ shall have the right to remain in the Residence for a period not to exceed sixty (60) days from receipt of such notice, or until closing of title, whichever shall last occur, at which time

_____ must vacate the aforesaid Residence. If _____ elects to purchase _____'s interest in the aforesaid Residence pursuant to paragraphs 2-8 of this Article VIII, then _____ shall have the right to remain in the Residence for a period not to exceed sixty (60) days from receipt of such notice, or until closing of title, whichever shall last occur, at which time _____ must vacate the aforesaid Residence.

Marital Residence in the Name of One Party

13. In the event that the primary marital residence is titled in the name of one party and constitutes that party's Separate Property ("Separate Property Residence"), upon the death of the party holding title to such residence and provided that no Event of Marital Dissolution has occurred, the surviving spouse shall be permitted to continue to reside in the Separate Property Residence according to the following terms in this paragraph:

(a)   In the event there are no surviving children of the parties, the period of occupancy shall terminate one year after the deceased party's death.

(b)   In the event there are surviving children of the parties, the period of occupancy shall terminate upon the first to occur of the following:

(i)   The remarriage of the surviving party or such party's entering into a civil union, domestic partnership or similar legal relationship; or

(ii)   The cohabitation of the surviving party with another person for a period of six months in any twelve-month period; or

(iii)   The earliest date when the surviving party is no longer living in the Separate Property Residence on a continual basis as his or her primary residence; or

(iv)   The date that the surviving party gives written notice to the personal representative of the deceased party's estate that he or she intends to vacate the Separate Property Residence; or

(v)   Provided it does not impose an undue tax or financial burden on the estate of the deceased party, the date on which the youngest child of the parties attains the age of 18 years or graduates high school, but in no event beyond such child's 19th birthday.

(c)   During the period the surviving party is permitted to reside in such Separate Property Residence pursuant to this paragraph 13, the estate of the deceased party shall be responsible for and shall pay any monthly mortgage interest and principal payments, real estate taxes, homeowner's insurance and capital repairs (not ordinary repairs and maintenance). The surviving party shall be responsible for and shall pay all other expenses of such residence during the period of his or her occupancy including without limitation utilities, maintenance and ordinary repairs. The surviving spouse shall vacate the Separate Property Residence after the permissible period of his or her occupancy expires and thereafter shall have no further interest in, claim, or rights with respect to the Separate Property Residence, other than a right to be reimbursed for any expense that should properly have been paid by the deceased party's estate as provided in the first sentence of this subparagraph.

(d) Nothing herein shall be deemed to preclude the transfer of a Separate Property Residence from the deceased party's estate into a trust established by the deceased party (pursuant to his or her Last Will or otherwise), provided the terms of such trust comply with the preceding provisions of this paragraph 13 and provide the surviving party with all of the rights set forth above. Following such transfer, all references in this paragraph 13 to the deceased party's estate, or to the personal representatives of the deceased party's estate, as the case may be, shall be construed as references to the trustees of such trust.

Separate Property Residences

14. _____ shall vacate any residence which is the Separate Property of _____ within ninety (90) days after an Event of Marital Dissolution. _____ shall vacate any residence which is the Separate Property of _____ within ninety (90) days after an Event of Marital Dissolution.

ARTICLE IX

WAIVER OF ESTATE RIGHTS AT DEATH AS TO SEPARATE PROPERTY

1. _____ shall not have or acquire any right, title, interest or claim in and to _____'s Separate Property upon _____'s death.

2. Without limiting paragraph 1 of this Article IX in any way, _____, with respect to _____'s Separate Property does hereby waive, disclaim and renounce any and all rights accruing

under any section of the Estates, Powers and Trusts Law of the State of New York, or that may hereafter accrue under such Estates, Powers and Trusts Law or under any law of the State of New York or any state, territory or possession of the United States of America or under any law of any foreign nation and does particularly, but without limitation, waive, disclaim, and renounce any and all rights which have accrued or which may hereafter accrue to him in _____'s Separate Property by reason of any Last Will and Testament of _____, pursuant to Sections 5 1.1-A (right of election) and 4¬-1.1 (laws of intestacy) of the said Estates, Powers and Trusts Law of the State of New York or by any amendment thereto or extension thereof, or any other law conferring rights to or in the estate (or any part thereof) of a deceased spouse and _____ does hereby specifically waive any and all right or claim of election that he may at any time have to take any share of _____'s Separate Property with the same force and effect as though there had never been a marriage between the parties.

3. _____ hereby waives all statutory allowances of any kind related to _____'s Separate Property under Section 5 3.1 of the Estates, Powers and Trusts Law of the State of New York, as said Section now exists or may hereafter be amended, or any similar or subsequently enacted statute of the State of New York or of any other state or jurisdiction.

4. _____ shall permit any Last Will and Testament of _____, now or hereafter in existence, to be probated and/or allow Letters of Administration to Issue and _____ shall promptly execute and deliver any and all documents deemed necessary by the administrator or executor of _____'s estate from time to time to carry out the provisions of this Article.

5. _____ shall not have or acquire any right, title, interest or claim in and to _____'s Separate Property upon _____'s death.

6. Without limiting paragraph 5 of this Article IX in any way, _____, with respect to _____'s Separate Property does hereby waive, disclaim and renounce any and all rights accruing under any section of the Estates, Powers and Trusts Law of the State of New York, or that may hereafter accrue under such Estates, Powers and Trusts Law or under any law of the State of New York or any state, territory or possession of the United States of America or under any law of any foreign nation and does particularly, but without limitation, waive, disclaim, and renounce any and all rights which have

accrued or which may hereafter accrue to her in _____'s Separate Property by reason of any Last Will and Testament of _____, pursuant to Sections 5–1.1-A (right of election) and 4–1.1 (laws of intestacy) of the said Estates, Powers and Trusts Law of the State of New York or by any amendment thereto or extension thereof, or any other law conferring rights to or in the estate (or any part thereof) of a deceased spouse and _____ does hereby specifically waive any and all right or claim of election that she may at any time have to take any share of _____'s Separate Property with the same force and effect as though there had never been a marriage between the parties.

7. _____ hereby waives all statutory allowances of any kind related to _____'s Separate Property under Section 5–3.1 of the Estates, Powers and Trusts Law of the State of New York, as said Section now exists or may hereafter be amended, or any similar or subsequently enacted statute of the State of New York or of any other state or jurisdiction.

8. _____ shall permit any Last Will and Testament of _____, now or hereafter in existence, to be probated and/or allow Letters of Administration to issue and _____ shall promptly execute and deliver any and all documents deemed necessary by the administrator or executor of _____'s estate from time to time to carry out the provisions of this Article.

9. Without limiting paragraphs 1 through 8 of this Article, provided no Event of Marital Dissolution has occurred, each party shall be entitled to assert any and all rights accruing under any section of the Estates, Powers and Trusts Law of the State of New York, or that may hereafter accrue under such Estates, Powers and Trusts Law (whether such rights are by reason of Sections 5-1.1-A and 4-1.1 of the said Estates, Powers and Trusts Law or by any amendment thereto or extension thereof) or under any law of the State of New York or any state, territory of the United States of America or under any law of any foreign nation which may hereafter accrue to the other's estate which does not consist of either party's Separate Property.

10. Should an Event of Marital Dissolution occur prior to the death of the first to die of _____ or _____: (a) neither party shall have or acquire any right, title, interest or claim in and to the real, personal or other property of the deceased party upon the death of said party, (b) each party hereto shall have the right to

dispose of his or her property by Last Will and Testament ("Will") or otherwise, as each party sees fit, free from any claim, dominion, or cause of action of, or arising in favor of, the other party hereto, and (c) the estate of each party hereto, whether real and/or personal, shall descend to, vest in, and belong to the person or persons, legatees or devisees, prescribed in his or her Will, or as provided by the laws of the State of New York, or the laws of any other state or country with jurisdiction over the estate or its property, all as though no marriage had ever taken place between the parties and each of the parties will be deemed to have expressly revoked his or her Will insofar as the same makes any disposition (whether outright or in trust) therein to or for the benefit of the other and further will be deemed to have expressly revoked any nomination of the other party as an estate representative, including any rights to act as the administrator of the estate of the other, or as the executor, trustee or in any other representative or fiduciary capacity thereunder, it being the intention of the parties that all Wills made and executed by either of them prior to the occurrence of an Event of Marital Dissolution will be read and administered as if the other party had predeceased him or her for purposes of distribution of his or her respective estate or the property interests otherwise passing thereunder.

11. Death of a Party After an Event of Marital Dissolution. Should the death of a party occur after an Event of Marital Dissolution, but before either a divorce decree has been issued between the parties or a Settlement Agreement has been executed between them, the surviving spouse shall be entitled to his or her share of Marital Property as set forth in this Agreement, as if the parties were divorced as of the date of death of the deceased party.

12. Voluntary Transfers and Appointments. Should no Event of Marital Dissolution occur, nothing contained in this Agreement shall be construed to prevent or restrict either party from making a provision for the benefit of the other party by his or her Last Will and Testament or by gift or otherwise in excess of the amount required herein, or from nominating or appointing the other party to serve as a fiduciary under his or her Last Will and Testament or inter vivos trust instrument, or the right of the other party to receive or accept such benefit, gift, nomination or appointment; and no such gift, bequest, nomination or appointment shall be deemed a waiver of any of the provisions of this Agreement.

ARTICLE X

WAIVER OF PENSION AND OTHER EMPLOYEE BENEFIT RIGHTS

1. Each party hereby waives and releases any and all rights and claims that he or she may have in and to any participation or interest that the other party may have in any Retirement Assets. Accordingly, the following paragraphs in this Article shall apply to Retirement Assets.

2. Each party hereby consents to the election by the other party to waive a qualified joint and survivor annuity form of benefit and a qualified preretirement survivor annuity form of benefit under any plan of deferred compensation to which Section 401 (a)(11) of the Code, or Section 205(b)(1) of the Employee Retirement Income Security Act of 1974, as amended or replaced from time to time ("ERISA"), shall apply and in which the other party currently is or shall become a vested participant within the meaning of Section 417(f) (1) of the Code and Section 205(h)(1) of ERISA. Each party further consents to the other party's designation of any beneficiaries selected by such other party under any of such plans (and to any revocation or modification of such designations), including any of such plans referred to in Section 40l(a)(ii)(B) of the Code or Section 205(b)(1) of ERISA. Each party hereby acknowledges that he or she understands the effect of such elections by the other party and his or her consents thereto.

3. Nothing contained in this Agreement shall be construed to prevent or restrict either party from voluntarily i) providing the other party with an interest in, or ii) designating the other party as a survivor beneficiary to a Retirement Asset.

4. If, at any time, a party voluntarily i) provides the other party with an interest in, or ii) designates the other party as a survivor beneficiary to a Retirement Asset, then upon an Event of Marital Dissolution, the party so designated (in other words, the party who is not the plan participant) waives all rights and claims to such Retirement Asset and the provisions of paragraph 1 of this Article shall apply as if the plan participant had never designated the other party as a beneficiary. The party who is not the plan participant consents to the modification of beneficiary and related rights as provided for in paragraph 2 of this Article.

5. To the extent that the law requires any additional documentation to enforce the consents set forth herein, each party agrees to execute and deliver the same at the request of the other party or the personal representative of the other party.

ARTICLE XI

INDEMNIFICATION IN EVENT OF SUIT TO ENFORCE

1. If either party or the legal representatives of _____'s or _____'s estate (the "Defendant") shall interpose the terms, conditions and covenants of this Agreement as a defense to an action or other proceeding instituted by the other party (the "Plaintiff"), including, but not limited to an action to rescind all or part of this Agreement, and such defense shall result in a judgment, decree or order in favor of the Defendant, the Plaintiff shall pay to the Defendant the reasonable costs and expenses incurred by the Defendant, including reasonable attorneys' fees, or shall permit such costs, expenses and fees to be completely offset against any obligation due by the Defendant to the Plaintiff hereunder.

2. If either party or the legal representatives of his or her estate (the "Plaintiff") shall bring an action or proceeding to enforce the terms, conditions and covenants of this Agreement against the other party (the "Defendant") or to declare the Agreement or any of its terms valid and enforceable, and such action or proceeding is opposed or contested by the Defendant, if the action or proceeding results in a judgment, decree or order in favor of the Plaintiff, the Defendant shall pay to the Plaintiff the reasonable costs and expenses incurred by the Plaintiff, including reasonable attorneys' fees, or shall permit such costs, expenses and fees, to be completely offset against any obligation due from the Plaintiff to the Defendant hereunder.

ARTICLE XII

CONFIDENTIAL DOCUMENT

Much of the information contained in the exhibits to this Agreement is confidential. Each party agrees not to disclose any information contained in the exhibits relating to the other party without the other party's written consent except as necessary to enforce the provisions contained herein, or as necessary to obtain financial or legal advice or assistance. Additionally, each party agrees that should the exhibits or the information contained therein be relevant to a judicial proceeding, the parties will agree to seek a protective order protecting the confidentiality of such information and providing for its filing with the court under seal.

ARTICLE XIII

FURTHER DOCUMENTS

Each of the parties hereto shall, without cost or charge to the other party, upon request by the other party or his or her personal representatives, do all acts and execute, acknowledge and deliver all releases, deeds, or other instruments appropriate or necessary to carry out the purpose and intention of this Agreement.

ARTICLE XIV

INCORPORATION AND SURVIVAL (BUT NOT MERGER) OF AGREEMENT INTO JUDGMENT OR DECREE

1. This Agreement shall not be invalidated or otherwise affected by any judgment or decree made in any court in any action or proceeding between the parties.

2. Upon an Event of Marital Dissolution, the parties shall promptly execute a Separation Agreement incorporating all the substantive terms of this Agreement to the extent not already performed.

3. In any matrimonial action or other action or proceeding in which either party may seek an order, judgment or decree affecting the marital status of the parties, or their financial rights or obligations with respect to the other party, (i) no party shall seek or receive an order, judgment or decree granting relief that differs from or is inconsistent with this Agreement; (ii) this Agreement or the provisions thereof, and/or any written Separation Agreement between the parties incorporating same, shall be submitted to the court; and (iii) the provisions of this Agreement and the Separation Agreement shall be incorporated in said judgment, order or decree with such specificity as the court shall deem permissible and by reference as may be appropriate under law and under the rules of the court, however, notwithstanding said incorporation, the provisions of this Agreement and the Separation Agreement shall survive the decree, order or judgment and shall not merge therein, and this Agreement may be independently enforced. Notwithstanding incorporation, this Agreement shall be enforceable as a contract.

ARTICLE XV

GENERAL PROVISIONS

1. General Understanding: This Agreement contains the entire understanding of the parties hereto, and neither party has made any

representation, promises or warranties to the other to induce the execution of this Agreement or to induce continuation of the parties' financial and living arrangement, except as may be specifically set forth herein.

2. Severability: If any provision of this Agreement should be held to be contrary to or invalid under the law of any country, state or other jurisdiction, such illegality or invalidity shall not affect in any way any other provision of this Agreement, all of which shall continue, nevertheless, in full force and effect. Any provision which is held to be illegal or invalid in any country, state or other jurisdiction shall, nevertheless, remain in full force and effect in any country, state or jurisdiction in which the provision is legal and valid.

3. Third Party Amendments: The parties hereto may at any time jointly amend this Agreement without the consent of any other third person, and no other third person shall be deemed to have been given any interest or right hereunder. Any such amendment shall be by written instrument, acknowledged and witnessed in the same manner as this Agreement.

4. Waivers: No failure of either of the parties to exercise any right hereunder or to insist upon strict compliance by the other party with any obligation hereunder and no custom or practice of the parties at variance with the terms hereof shall constitute a waiver of either party's right to demand exact compliance with the terms hereof. Waiver by either party of any particular default by the other shall not be deemed a continuing waiver and shall not affect or impair the waiving party's right in respect of any subsequent default of the same or of a different nature, nor shall any delay or omission of either party to exercise any right arising from such a default affect or impair his or her rights as to such default or any subsequent default.

5. Binding on Parties' Estates: This Agreement and all the obligations and covenants set forth in this Agreement shall bind _____ and _____, their heirs, executors, administrators, legal representatives and assigns.

6. Counterparts: This Agreement may be executed in counterparts, which, taken together, shall be deemed an original and shall constitute one and the same instrument.

7. Interpretation of the Agreement: The parties agree that this Agreement, the validity and interpretation of this Agreement and the rights of the parties under this Agreement shall be governed and construed under the substantive laws of the State of New York applicable to agreements made in and wholly to be performed in the State of

New York (and not its choice of law provisions), and shall be binding in all respects even if the parties shall be or become residents of or domiciled in another state or country.

8. Modification: Neither this Agreement nor any provision of this Agreement shall be amended or modified except by a written instrument signed by the parties hereto and acknowledged in the same manner as this Agreement.

9. Notices: Any notice required to be given hereunder shall be provided by personal delivery or by mailing same in a sealed envelope, postage prepaid by overnight courier. Notices to _____ shall be mailed to him at his then current address or to such other address _____ shall give to _____. Notices to _____ shall be mailed to her then current address or to such other address _____ shall give to _____. All notices hereunder shall be deemed provided upon personal delivery or one day after deposit with overnight courier with next day delivery specified.

ARTICLE XVI

SIGNING AND ACKNOWLEDGMENT

1. Each of the parties has read this Agreement carefully and in its entirety prior to the signing thereof.

2. EACH PARTY TO THIS AGREEMENT FULLY UNDERSTANDS AND AGREES THAT HE OR SHE IS RELINQUISHING VALUABLE PROPERTY RIGHTS BY SIGNING THIS AGREEMENT.

IN WITNESS WHEREOF, the parties have executed this Agreement on the day and year first above written.

_____

_____

_____

_____

STATE OF NEW YORK   )

        : ss.:

COUNTY OF NEW YORK)

On the_____day of _____, in the year 20__ before me, the undersigned, a Notary Public in and for said state, personally appeared _____ _____, personally known to me or proved to me on the basis of satisfactory evidence to be the individual whose name is subscribed to the within instrument and acknowledged to me that she executed the same in her capacity, and that by her signature on the instrument, the individual or the person upon behalf of which the individual acted, executed the instrument.

                                        _____

                                        Notary Public

STATE OF NEW YORK)

        : ss.:

COUNTY OF NEW YORK)

On the_____day of _____, in the year 20__ before me, the undersigned, a Notary Public in and for said state, personally appeared _____ _____, personally known to me or proved to me on the basis of satisfactory evidence to be the individual whose name is subscribed to the within instrument and acknowledged to me that he executed the same in his capacity, and that by his signature on the instrument, the individual or the person upon behalf of which the individual acted, executed the instrument.

                                        _____

                                          Notary Public

APPENDIX 3

Irrevocable Spendthrift Trust**

THE JAMES SMITH, JR., TRUST

IRREVOCABLE AGREEMENT OF TRUST

Between

JOSEPH SMITH, SR.
(hereinafter called "Settlor")

and

JAMES SMITH, JR.

FRANK SMITH

and

ROBERT SMITH
(hereinafter called "Trustees")

DATED: December 31, 2009

EIN:

AGREEMENT OF TRUST made this 31st day of December, 2009, between JOSEPH SMITH, SR. (hereinafter called "SETTLOR"),

** Prepared by Leonard P. Nalencz, Esq., Blank Rome LLP, Philadelphia, PA.

and JAMES SMITH, JR., FRANK SMITH AND ROBERT SMITH (the initial Trustees, together with all additional and successor Trustees, hereinafter called "TRUSTEES").

The parties agree as follows:

1. Trust Property and Trust Name

(a)   Settlor has caused, or may cause, Trustees to be transferees of certain property or named beneficiaries of certain insurance policies (including, but not limited to, shares of stock of ABC Inc., subject to an existing shareholder agreement) of stock and direct that any sums payable to Trustees pursuant to such shares of stock or under such policies, together with any other property which may be added hereto by Settlor, or which Trustees may accept pursuant to Item 1(b) hereof, shall be held by Trustees, IN TRUST, subject to the terms and conditions of this Agreement.

(b)   Any person other than Settlor may, at any time, add to the property to be held hereunder, by Will, transfer, or otherwise, subject to acceptance by Trustees.

(c)   This trust shall be known as "THE JAMES SMITH, JR., TRUST."

2. Dispositive Provisions

(a)   Until the death of Settlor, all or any part of the net income of the trust may be accumulated, paid to or applied for the benefit of any one or more than one of the group consisting of Settlor's son, JAMES SMITH, JR. and his issue, at such times and in such proportions, equal or unequal, as Trustees, other than a Trustee who may be a beneficiary hereunder, shall in their discretion determine. In making such determination Trustees may, but need not, take into consideration other resources, including, but not limited to, governmental, private or public sources, available to Settlor's said son and his issue. Any undistributed income may from time to time be added to principal; provided, however, that a decision not to add undistributed income to principal shall not be construed to give any potential beneficiary an interest in such undistributed income.

(b)   (i)   Upon the death of Settlor, if Settlor's son, JAMES SMITH, JR., is then living, all or any part of the net income of the trust may be accumulated, paid to or applied for the benefit of Settlor's said son, at such times and in such amounts as Trustees, other than a Trustee who is the beneficiary hereunder, shall in their discretion determine. In making such determination, Trustees may, but need not, take into consideration other resources, including, but not limited to governmental, private or public sources, available to Settlor's said son. Any undistributed income may from time to time be added to principal; provided, however, that a decision not to add undistributed income to principal shall not be construed to give Settlor's said son an interest in such undistributed income.

(ii) Upon the death of Settlor's said son, or if Settlor's said son shall not survive Settlor, upon the death of Settlor:

A. The then principal of such trust, together with any undistributed income, shall be distributed to such organization or organizations described in Sections 170(c), 2055(a) and 2522(a) of the Internal Revenue Code and/or shall continue to be held in separate trusts for the benefit of, or distributed to, such person or persons other than Settlor's said son, his creditors, the estate of Settlor's said son or the creditors of the estate of Settlor's said son, in such proportions, equal or unequal, as Settlor's said son shall appoint by Will, making specific reference to this power.

B. Any unappointed property shall be subdivided, per stirpes, among the then living issue of Settlor's said son and shall be held as separate trusts, IN TRUST, for the benefit of such issue, upon the same terms and conditions as are set forth in Item 2(c) herein. If there be no such issue, distribution shall be to THE FRANK SMITH TRUST, of which Settlor is the Settlor, dated this day, for administration and distribution as a part of trust principal, and subject to the terms and provisions of said Agreement, including any alterations or amendments thereto.

(c) (i) During the lifetime of the beneficiary, the net income of the trust may be accumulated, paid or applied for the benefit of the beneficiary, at such times and in such proportions, equal or unequal, as Trustees, other than a Trustee who may be a beneficiary hereunder, shall in their discretion determine. In making such determination, Trustees may, but need not, take into consideration other resources, including, but not limited to, governmental, private or public sources, available to the beneficiary. Any undistributed income may from time to time be added to principal; provided, however, that a decision not to add undistributed income to principal shall not be construed to give any potential beneficiary an interest in such undistributed income.

(ii) Upon the death of the beneficiary:

A. The then principal of such trust, together with any undistributed income, shall be distributed to, or held in trust for the benefit of such organization or organizations described in Sections 170(c), 2055(a) and 2522(a) of the Internal Revenue Code and/or such person or persons other than such beneficiary, his or her estate, his or her creditors or the creditors of his or her estate, and upon such estates and conditions as such beneficiary shall appoint by Will, making specific reference to this power.

B. Any unappointed property shall be subdivided, per stirpes, among the then living issue of such beneficiary and shall be held as separate trusts, IN TRUST, for the benefit of such issue, upon the same terms and conditions as are set forth in this Item 2(c) herein. If there be no such issue, distribution shall be, per stirpes, among the separate trusts created hereunder for the then living issue of Settlor's son, JAMES SMITH, JR., and shall continue to be held in a separate trust for the benefit of each such issue upon the same terms and conditions as are set forth in this Item 2(c) herein. If there be no such issue, distribution shall be to THE FRANK SMITH TRUST, of which Settlor is the Settlor, dated this day, for administration and distribution as a part of trust principal, and subject to the terms and provisions of said Agreement, including any alterations or amendments thereto.

(d) If, upon the termination of an interest, there shall be no beneficiary or class of beneficiaries otherwise entitled to receive a portion of any trust property hereunder, Trustees shall distribute such property to the estate of the person eligible to receive income from such trust immediately prior to the termination of the interest.

(e) Anything is this Trust Agreement to the contrary notwithstanding, if any trust created hereunder owns stock in an S Corporation, as defined in the Internal Revenue Code ("S Stock"), either (X) at any time during Settlor's lifetime upon or after Trustees have renounced the powers granted to them in Item 2(f) of this Trust Agreement or (Y) after Settlor's death, Trustees shall hold the S Stock in separate trusts, each of which shall be administered and distributed as follows:

(i) During the lifetime of the beneficiary, Trustees shall distribute the entire net income of such trust to such beneficiary in such periodic installments as Trustees shall find convenient, but at least as often as annually.

(ii) Upon the death of the beneficiary, his or her trust shall be distributed as set forth in Item 2(c)(ii) herein and, if held in separate trusts, shall be administered upon the same terms and conditions as are set forth in this Item 2(e).

(f) (i) Notwithstanding the foregoing, or that additional taxes may result, or that the size of any amount distributable hereunder may be affected, until the death of Settlor, Trustees, other than a Trustee who may be a beneficiary hereunder, may in their discretion:

A. add as a beneficiary of the income and/or principal of any trust created hereunder any organization or organizations described in Sections 170(c), 2055(a) and 2522(a) of the Internal Revenue Code;

B. remove as a beneficiary of the income and/or principal of any trust created hereunder any such organization or organizations added pursuant to Item 2(f)(i) herein; and

C. renounce, at any time, the power granted to Trustees in Item 2(f)(i) herein.

(ii) During Settlor's lifetime and until Trustees renounce the power granted to them in Item 2(f)(i), Trustees may, in their sole discretion, make annual distributions to Settlor equal to all or any portion of the increase in Settlor's personal income tax liability resulting from the application of Subpart E of Subchapter J of the Internal Revenue Code with respect to this trust.

3. Invasion of Trust Principal

(a) If Trustees in their discretion determine that the amount from all sources, including, but not limited to, governmental, private or public sources, received by or available to any beneficiary then eligible to receive income from a trust established hereunder shall be insufficient to provide for the education, health, support or maintenance of such beneficiary and/or his or her issue, Trustees in their discretion may pay to, or use for the benefit of, such beneficiary and/or his or her issue, at any time and from time to time, any portion of the principal from which such beneficiary is then eligible to receive income for such purposes.

(b) Anything in this Trust Agreement to the contrary notwithstanding, no Trustee who is then eligible to receive income from a trust established hereunder shall take part in any decisions to invade trust principal for himself or herself.

4. Termination At Trustees' Discretion

(a) Whenever Trustees, in their discretion, determine that a trust, or any part thereof, should be terminated for any reason, Trustees, without any liability to any person whose interest may be affected, shall terminate such trust, or part thereof, and shall distribute the terminated portion of the trust to the individual or individuals at that time eligible to receive the income therefrom.

(b) Anything in this Trust Agreement to the contrary notwithstanding, no Trustee to whom part of a trust would be distributed pursuant to Item 4(a) hereof shall take part in any decisions to terminate such trust.

(c) The discretion granted Trustees pursuant to Item 4(a) hereof shall in no event be construed to give any potential beneficiary of a terminated trust the right to compel a termination in whole or in part of such trust.

5. Protective Provision

No beneficial interest under this Trust, whether in income or principal, shall voluntarily or involuntarily be subject to anticipation, assignment, pledge, sale or transfer in any manner. No beneficiary shall, voluntarily or involuntarily, anticipate, encumber or charge such interest, nor shall any such interest, while in the possession of Trustees, be liable for or subject to the debts, contracts, obligations, liabilities or torts of any beneficiary.

6. Disability of Beneficiary

(a) Anything in this Trust Agreement to the contrary notwithstanding, if any beneficiary under this Trust is under the age of Twenty-five (25) years, or is determined by Trustees in their discretion to be physically or mentally incapable of properly using any property or income which he or she otherwise would receive pursuant to this Trust, Trustees may:

(i) Pay such property or income to a parent, grandparent or guardian of the property or estate of such beneficiary, or to a person acting in a fiduciary capacity for the benefit of such beneficiary;

(ii) With respect to any beneficiary who has not attained the age of majority, deposit such property or income in a federally-insured, interest-bearing account in a bank or other savings institution of Trustees' choosing, payable to the beneficiary upon attaining the age of majority;

(iii) Distribute such property or income to a custodian for the beneficiary's benefit under the Uniform Transfers to Minors Act or any similar law, payable to such beneficiary upon attaining such age as shall be determined by Trustees but no later than the time the beneficiary attains the age of Twenty-five (25) years; or

(iv) Hold such property or income, IN TRUST, for such beneficiary and apply without the intervention of a guardian all or part of the income and/or principal thereof as in their opinion is necessary for the health, support, education and maintenance of such beneficiary, until the later to occur of such beneficiary attaining the age of Twenty-five (25) years or the determination by Trustees in their discretion that such beneficiary is physically and mentally capable of properly using such property or income. If the beneficiary for whom Trustees are holding such property shall die before the entire remaining balance of the trust created under this Article has been distributed to the beneficiary, distribution shall be to the estate of the beneficiary.

(b) Trustees shall be fully discharged from liability upon obtaining receipts from persons to whom distributions are made pursuant to this Item.

7. Survival Provision

In the event that any beneficiary of a trust created hereunder shall fail to survive Settlor by a period of at least Ninety (90) days, such beneficiary shall be deemed to have predeceased Settlor.

8. Insurance Policies

(a) Settlor authorizes Trustees to use trust income and/or principal to purchase all types of insurance on the lives of Settlor and members of Settlor's family and vest Trustees with all right, title and interest in and to the policies of insurance transferred hereto as the absolute owners thereof, and authorize and empower Trustees to assume any loans on such policies and to exercise and enjoy for the purposes of the Trust herein created, all of the options, benefits, rights and privileges under such policies, including, but not limited to, the right to borrow upon such policies, to pledge the same for loan or loans and to pay interest on policy loans. Settlor relinquishes all his right, title, interest and powers in such policies of insurance and will upon written request by Trustees, execute all other instruments which may be required to effectuate this relinquishment.

(b) By accepting the within trust, Trustees assume no responsibility for the validity of any policy of insurance or any assignment or designation to or of the Trustees as owner or primary or contingent beneficiary. In addition, without intending to limit any protection afforded to Trustees by law, Trustees shall have no duty to (i) evaluate the financial strength or otherwise inquire into the status of the insurance company that issues any policy; (ii) compare the costs of policies of competing insurance companies; (iii) review periodically any insurance policy owned by the trust or determine whether the policy is or remains a proper trust investment; (iv) exercise any non-forfeiture provisions available under any policy; or (v) diversify any insurance policies. It is the intent of Settlor that Trustees be relieved of any liability for the failure of an insurance company to perform its obligations, or for the comparative costs and investment performance of any insurance policy.

(c)   Any life insurance company issuing a policy held hereunder is hereby authorized and directed to recognize Trustees as the absolute owners of such policy of insurance and as being fully entitled to all options, rights, privileges and interests under such policy. Any receipts, releases, and other instruments executed by Trustees in connection with such policy shall be binding and conclusive upon the insurance company and upon the persons interested in this Trust. No insurance company shall be responsible to see to the execution of this Trust.

(d)   Trustees may but shall be under no obligation to pay the premiums which may become due and payable under the provisions of any such policy of insurance, or to make certain that such premiums are paid by Settlor or others, or to notify any persons of the nonpayment of such premiums and Trustees shall be under no responsibility or liability of any kind in case such premiums are not paid.

(e)   Upon the death of any insured:

(i)   Trustees shall collect such sums of money as shall be due Trustees under the terms of any policies of life insurance; and

(ii)   To facilitate the collection of such sums of money, Trustees shall have the power to execute and deliver receipts and other instruments, to compromise or adjust disputed claims and to take other necessary steps for collection thereof. If payment on any policy is contested, Trustees shall not be obligated to take any action for collection unless and until indemnified to Trustees' satisfaction against any loss, liability or expense, including attorneys' fees; provided that Trustees are authorized to use any funds, whether principal or income, to pay the costs and expenses, including attorneys' fees, of bringing an action for such collection, and may reimburse themselves for any advances made for such purposes.

(f)   Upon payment to Trustees of the amounts due under any policies of insurance, the insurance companies issuing such policies shall be relieved of all further liability and shall have no responsibility to see to the performance of this Agreement.

(g)   Trustees at any time may assign any life insurance policy owned by Trustees to another Trust for adequate consideration and may rely on the insurance company which issued the policy to determine the fair market value of such policy at the time of the assignment.

(h)   Any one of the Trustees acting alone may sign any documents required in connection with the acquisition of a policy of life insurance.

9. Powers of Trustees

Subject to specific direction in this Trust Agreement and in addition to the powers vested in them by law and other provisions of this

Trust Agreement, all of the Trustees serving hereunder at any time in administering all trusts created hereunder shall have the following powers, exercisable in their discretion without court approval and effective until actual distribution of all property.

(a) <u>Property Retention and Investments</u>. To retain any or all property; to invest in all types of investments permissible by law; to purchase assets from and to make loans to Settlor's estate, or any other person, including any Trustee or beneficiary; and to invest any or all of the trust property in policies or contracts of life insurance, with or without cash value.

(b) <u>Use of Nominee</u>. To hold shares of stock or other securities, life insurance policies and any other assets in nominee registration form, including that of a clearing corporation or depository, or in book entry form or unregistered or in such other form as will pass by delivery.

(c) <u>Disposition of Property</u>. With regard to any property and for such prices and upon such terms as they determine: to exchange or sell at public or private sale; to lease for any period of time, even though the term may extend beyond the termination of any trust created hereunder; and to give options for any such sales, exchanges or leases.

(d) <u>Borrow Money and Pledge Property</u>. To borrow money from any person, including Settlor's Personal Representatives and any other fiduciary, and in connection therewith, to mortgage or pledge any property.

(e) <u>Compromise Claims</u>. To compromise any claim or controversy.

(f) <u>Distribution</u>. To distribute property, income or principal, in cash and/or in kind.

(g) <u>Employment of Others</u>. To engage attorneys, accountants, custodians, investment counsel and other persons as they deem advisable in the administration of any trust created hereunder and to make payment therefore as they determine.

(h) <u>Apportionments</u>.

(i) Notwithstanding that the size of the gift or interest passing to any beneficiary or trust may be affected, to allocate receipts, income, administration and other expenses and disbursements, to principal or income, or partly to each, as Trustees, at any time and from time to time, in their discretion may determine, or otherwise in accord with applicable law, and this power to allocate shall include, but not be limited to, stock, extraordinary and liquidating dividends, premiums and discounts on investments, compensation for professional and other personal services, and gain or loss on disposition of assets.

(ii)   To allocate depreciation and amortization expenses, including such expenses taken by a partnership owning depreciable assets, to income or principal, or partly to each, and to the extent such allocation is made to principal, Trustees are directed to establish and to fund a reserve equal to such principal allocation which shall be added to and made a part of principal.

(i)   Business and Investment Interests. With regard to any business or investment interests owned solely by Trustees, or with others, whether incorporated or not:

(i)   To conduct any such business, for whatever period of time they deem proper, with all powers of an owner with respect thereto, including without limitation, the power to borrow money and pledge trust property as security therefor, or to delegate such powers to partners, managers or employees.

(ii)   To dispose of any interest therein or any assets thereof, at public or private sale, upon such terms and conditions as they deem proper.

(iii)   To form partnerships or corporations to manage such business or investment interests and to transfer any trust property as capital thereof or as loans thereto.

(iv)   To employ, elect or permit to be retained any Trustee as a director, officer or employee of such entity.

(j)   "S" Corporation Stock. Notwithstanding that additional tax burdens may result, Trustees shall have the following powers, to be exercised in their discretion, and the following provisions shall apply with respect to stock of a corporation ("Stock") which is or becomes an asset of any trust ("Trust") created hereunder, if such corporation has elected to be an "S" corporation (hereafter "'S' Corporation") pursuant to Section 1362 of the Internal Revenue Code, or if such corporation desires to elect to be an S Corporation and Trustees in their discretion determine that such election should be made:

(i)   Electing Small Business Trust Election. If the Trust qualifies as an electing small business trust ("ESBT") as defined in Section 1361(e) of the Internal Revenue Code, Trustees may make the election under Section 1361(e)(3) of the Internal Revenue Code on behalf of the Trust ("ESBT Election"), and, if applicable, may consent, on behalf of the Trust, to the corporation's election to be an S Corporation;

(ii)   Qualified Subchapter S Trust Election. If the Trust does not qualify as an ESBT, or if the ESBT Election is not made by Trustees:

A. If the Trust does not otherwise qualify as a qualified Subchapter "S" trust ("QSST") as defined in Section 1361(d)(3) of the Internal Revenue Code, Trustees may divide such Trust into two separate trusts, one trust consisting of the Stock, and the other trust consisting of the remaining assets. Each such trust shall be held under the terms hereunder applicable to the trust so divided, except that with respect to the trust containing Stock, the trust shall be subdivided into as many parts as there shall be beneficiaries who are then eligible to receive income from such trust, in such manner as to maintain the same relative percentages among the shares. The provisions of each such subdivided trust shall have such terms as meet the requirements of a QSST; to the extent that a provision of such trust does not meet the requirements of a QSST, such provision shall have no force or effect and such trust shall be administered without regard to such provision, and in particular:

(I)   During the life of the Current Income Beneficiary within the meaning of Section 1361(d)(3)(A) of the Internal Revenue Code ("Current Income Beneficiary"), there shall be only one income beneficiary of the QSST.

(II)   During the life of the Current Income Beneficiary, distributions of income and permitted distributions of principal from the QSST shall be made only to the Current Income Beneficiary.

(III)   The income interest of the Current Income Beneficiary in the QSST will terminate on the earlier of the death of the Current Income Beneficiary or the termination of the QSST.

(IV)   If the QSST terminates during the life of the Current Income Beneficiary, the QSST shall distribute all of its assets, including any accumulated and undistributed income, to the Current Income Beneficiary.

(V)   All the QSST's income (within the meaning of Section 643(b) of the Internal Revenue Code) shall be distributed to the Current Income Beneficiary currently (within the meaning of Section 1361(d)(3)(B) of the Internal Revenue Code). Any income that is accrued, accumulated, or undistributed at the time of the death of the Current Income Beneficiary shall be distributed in a manner permitted by Section 1361(d)(3)(B) of the Internal Revenue Code.

(VI)　No distribution of income or corpus by the QSST shall be made in satisfaction of the legal obligation to support or maintain an income beneficiary.

B. If the beneficiary of any such separate trust has not attained the age of Twenty-one (21) years or is determined to be incapacitated pursuant to the provisions hereunder, Trustees are hereby appointed as the legal representative of such beneficiary for the purpose of making the QSST election on behalf of such beneficiary and, if applicable, consenting, on behalf of such beneficiary, to the corporation's election to be an S Corporation.

(k)　Combining Assets of Several Trusts.

(i)　To merge any trust created hereunder with any other trust held by Trustees who are then acting, however created, if the beneficiaries are the same and the Trustees determine that the terms thereof are substantially similar.

(ii)　For investment purposes, to pool the assets of any or all trusts created hereunder or created by Settlor under separate trusts, allocating to each trust an undivided interest in all assets so held.

(l)　Separation of Trusts. Except as otherwise provided herein, to divide a trust into separate trusts, allocating to each separate trust either a fractional share of each asset and each liability held by the original trust or assets having an appropriate aggregate fair market value and fairly representing the appreciation or depreciation in the assets of the original trust as a whole.

(m)　Additional Property. To accept any property transferred by Deed, Will or in any other manner for addition to the principal of any trust created hereunder.

(n)　Partnership and Limited Liability Company Interests. With regard to the interest in any partnership, limited liability company or limited liability partnership transferred to or acquired by Trustees, and not in limitation of the foregoing powers:

(i)　To continue Settlor's ownership interest in such business for such period of time as they shall in their discretion determine.

(ii)　To take an active part in the management and control of the internal affairs of any such business in such way and to such extent as they in their discretion deem advisable, and to take any action in respect to the management of said business which Settlor, as partner and/or member, could have taken, including, but not by way of limitation, to vary the nature of the business by reducing, expanding, limiting or otherwise changing the same, the type or merchandise used, product manufactured or service rendered by the business.

(iii)   To enter into any agreements with the surviving partner(s) or member(s), including agreements obligating part or all of Settlor's general estate to the debts of the business or permitting the business to be continued by the surviving partner(s) or member(s) or authorizing them to supervise the liquidation of the business.

(o)   Execution of Documents. To execute and deliver any and all documents and instruments which they in their discretion may deem advisable.

(p)   Generation Skipping Transfer Tax Provision. To divide any trust hereunder at any time into two (2) separate trusts in order that the Federal generation-skipping transfer tax inclusion ratio for each such trust will be either zero or one; provided, however, that each trust will receive assets representative of the net appreciation or depreciation in value of all the assets available to fund the trusts.

(q)   General Authority. To perform all acts, institute such proceedings and exercise all rights and privileges, although not herein specifically mentioned, with relation to any property, as if the absolute owners thereof.

(r)   Withdrawal Authority. Upon unanimous written agreement, Trustees may authorize any one or more than one of the Trustees to sign checks and other instruments to make withdrawals from any checking, savings, money market, brokerage or other account.

(s)   Change of Situs. Trustees shall have the power to change the situs of any trust created hereunder at such times and to such places as they shall, in their discretion, determine.

10. Limitation on Powers

Notwithstanding anything herein to the contrary:

(a)   No powers enumerated herein or accorded to Trustees generally pursuant to law shall be construed to enable Settlor, or Trustees, or any of them, or any other person to purchase, exchange, or otherwise deal with or dispose of all or any part of the corpus or income of the trusts for less than an adequate consideration in money or money's worth, or to enable Settlor to borrow all or any part of the corpus or income of the trusts, directly or indirectly, without adequate interest and security.

(b)   No person, other than Trustees, shall have or exercise the power to reacquire or exchange any property of the trusts by substituting other property of an equivalent value.

(c)   No Trustee shall take part in any discretionary decision to distribute income or principal of the trusts to or for the benefit of a beneficiary in satisfaction of any legal obligation of such Trustee to support such beneficiary.

   11. Trustees' Actions and Responsibility

   (a)   Waiver of Security and Accounting. Trustees shall not be required to give any bond or other security for the faithful performance of their duties as such, nor shall they be required to file an accounting with any court.

   (b)   Transactions with Related Parties. Trustees may engage or enter into any contract, transaction, dealing or matter whatsoever, with any partnership in which any one or more of them is a partner, or any corporation in which any one or more of them is a stockholder, director or officer.

   (c)   Trustees' Responsibility. No individual Trustee shall be liable for any act, matter, cause or thing whatsoever, except his or her own dishonesty, gross negligence or the wilful commission of an act known by him or her to be a breach of trust.

   12. Irrevocability

Settlor, having been advised of the effect of this paragraph, relinquish forever the right to alter, amend or revoke this Agreement in whole or in part.

   13. Decisions Concerning Investments.

Individual Trustees, by agreement in writing of a majority of such individual Trustees, shall have the right to relieve any corporate Trustee of investment authority and responsibility in any way incident or relating to any and all of the assets hereunder by delivering such written agreement to the corporate Trustee. Thereafter, the individual Trustees shall have sole authority to exercise all investment authority and responsibility with respect to investment or reinvestment of the assets subject to such written agreement and their decisions shall not be subject to question by any corporate Trustee. Furthermore, Settlor expressly exonerates the corporate Trustee from any liability or responsibility with regard to any act or omission to act of any individual Trustee with respect to investment or reinvestment of the assets subject to such written agreement. In the event the corporate Trustee is relieved of investment authority and responsibility, the terms, conditions and amount of its compensation shall be reduced as the individual Trustees and corporate Trustee may agree pursuant to Item 14(b)(iii) hereof. Moreover, individual Trustees, by agreement in writing of a majority of such individual Trustees, which is delivered to the corporate Trustee, shall have the right to reinstate the corporate Trustee's investment authority and responsibility. If at any time there are no individual Trustees serving hereunder, the corporate Trustee's investment authority and responsibility, if then relieved, shall be reinstated.

14. <u>Successor and Additional Trustees</u>

The following provisions shall apply separately to each trust created hereunder:

(a) (i) Until the death of Settlor, Settlor may in writing: (1) remove any Trustee then serving provided that such Trustee is replaced by Settlor, or replace any named successor Trustee not then serving, provided that each successor or replacement Trustee who may serve during Settlor's lifetime is not a related or subordinate party, as defined in Section 672(c) of the Internal Revenue Code, to Settlor, and (2) add additional Trustees and fill any vacancy in the office of Trustee.

(ii) Notwithstanding the foregoing, in no event shall Settlor become a Trustee hereunder.

(b) After the death of Settlor, unless Settlor has otherwise provided in accordance with paragraph (a):

(i) Should any individual Trustee fail to qualify or cease or be unable to act, he or she shall be replaced in said office by such individual as he or she may in writing designate, and in default of such designation, by such individual as may be designated by the remaining individual Trustee.

(ii) Individual Trustees, by unanimous agreement in writing, shall have the right to appoint one or more individuals to serve with them.

(III) Individual Trustees, by majority agreement in writing, may appoint a corporate fiduciary to serve with them as a Trustee hereunder, may remove any corporate fiduciary and may enter into an Agreement with any corporate fiduciary regarding the amount of its compensation.

(iv) With respect to any trust created hereunder from which Settlor's son, JAMES SMITH, JR., is at that time eligible to receive income, Settlor's said son, while serving as a Co-Trustee of the trust created for his benefit, may in writing remove any Trustee(s) then serving and may replace any named successor Trustee(s) not then serving, provided that Settlor's said son shall designate one or more successor or replacement Trustee(s) who are not related or subordinate parties to him, as defined in Section 672(c) of the Internal Revenue Code.

(v) A. If the only Trustee serving is a corporate fiduciary, a majority in interest of the trust beneficiaries, by written agreement, may remove the corporate fiduciary and shall appoint a successor corporate fiduciary.

B. If the only remaining Trustee shall cease or be unable to act, and if no provision is made for the appointment of a successor Trustee, a majority in interest of the trust beneficiaries, by written agreement, shall remove such Trustee and shall replace such Trustee with one or more Trustees, who are not related or subordinate parties to the individual or individuals at that time eligible to receive trust income, as defined in Section 672(c) of the Internal Revenue Code, to serve hereunder.

C. If there is no Trustee then serving and if no provision is made for the appointment of a successor Trustee, a majority in interest of the trust beneficiaries, by written agreement, shall appoint one or more Trustees, who are not related or subordinate parties to the individual or individuals at that time eligible to receive trust income, as defined in Section 672(c) of the Internal Revenue Code, to serve hereunder.

(c)   Only individual Trustees shall have the right to delegate investment and management functions in accordance with applicable state law.

(d)   Any Trustee serving hereunder shall have the right to resign from such office at any time.

14. Construction and Applicable Law

(a)   Construction. As used herein, wherever the context requires or permits, the gender and number of words shall be interchangeable; persons adopted while minors shall be treated as though they were natural born children of their adoptive parents; Trustees shall include all Trustees serving hereunder at any time; the word "discretion," unless otherwise expressly limited herein, shall mean the sole and absolute right, power and authority to make a determination which shall not be subject to question by any person and shall be conclusive and binding on all persons; and any reference to the Internal Revenue Code shall refer to the Internal Revenue Code of 1986, as amended, or any successor provisions thereto.

(b)   Generation Skipping Transfers. Anything herein to the contrary notwithstanding with regard to any transfer hereunder that otherwise will be subject to Federal Generation Skipping Transfer Tax at the death of an income beneficiary who is issue of the parents of Settlor (exclusive of a transfer that qualifies for an exemption from such tax), such income beneficiary is hereby given a testamentary Power of Appointment in favor of the creditors of his or her estate with respect to the property subject to such transfer. In no event shall it be construed that such income beneficiary has exercised such Power of Appointment unless there is a specific reference thereto in his or her Will. In default of the proper exercise of such Power of Appointment, the property subject thereto shall be distributed as if such Power did not exist. Settlor intends by this provision to avoid the imposition of the Federal Generation Skipping Transfer Tax on such transfer of property by making such transfer of property subject to the Federal Estate Tax at the death of such income beneficiary.

(c) <u>Representation</u>. During the administration of any trust under this Trust Agreement, the unanimous decision by the sui juris members of any class of beneficiaries shall represent the entire class for all purposes.

(d) <u>Duration of Trusts</u>. Anything in this Trust Agreement to the contrary notwithstanding, no trust created hereunder shall continue beyond the period permitted by any applicable rule against perpetuities or other law that limits the duration of trusts. Any property still held in trust at the expiration of such period shall be distributed to the individual or individuals at that time eligible to receive the income therefrom.

(e) <u>Situs</u>. This Agreement shall be construed and administered in accordance with the laws of the State of Pennsylvania, the validity of the trusts hereby created shall be determined in accordance with such laws, and the State of Pennsylvania shall be the initial situs of such trusts.

(f) <u>Charity</u>. No charitable entity or organization which is the beneficiary of a non-vested interest under this Trust Agreement, the value of which is not deductible under Section 2055 or Section 2522 of the Internal Revenue Code, shall have the right to contest or question any discretionary distribution by Trustees regarding any portion of any trust created hereunder, including, but not limited to, a decision to invade trust principal or to terminate any trust, or any part thereof.

(g) <u>Headings</u>. Any headings preceding the text of the several paragraphs are inserted solely for convenience of reference and shall not constitute a part of this Agreement, nor shall they affect its meaning, construction or effect.

IN WITNESS WHEREOF, Settlor and Trustees have set their hands and seals the day and year first above written.

WITNESS:

_____ (SEAL)

_____ JOSEPH SMITH, SR.
Settlor

_____ (SEAL)

_____ JOSEPH SMITH, JR.
Trustee

_____ (SEAL)

_____ FRANK SMITH
Trustee

_____ (SEAL)

_____ ROBERT SMITH
Trustee

APPENDIX 4

Phantom Unit Agreement
for Key Employees

This Phantom Unit Agreement For Key Employees (the "Agreement") entered into as of November 1, 2010, (the "Agreement Date"), by and between Family Business Corporation (the "Company"), a Delaware corporation, and John Doe (the "Participant"), a key employee of the Company or an Affiliate (as defined herein).

BACKGROUND

The purpose of this Agreement is to reflect the phantom unit ("Phantom Unit" or "Phantom Units", individually and collectively) compensation arrangements between the Company and the Participant. It is understood that a Phantom Unit represents a notional share of common stock of the Company, but a grant thereof does not make the Participant a stockholder of the Company or give the Participant any rights as a stockholder of the Company.

NOW, THEREFORE, the Company and the Participant, each intending to be legally bound hereby, agree as follows:

ARTICLE I

AWARD OF PHANTOM UNITS

1.1 <u>Grant of Phantom Units</u>. The Participant is hereby granted the following number of Phantom Units (also called "Unit" or "Units, individually and collectively), subject to the time and event vesting conditions set forth in Section 1.2 and Section 1.4 hereof, respectively, as well as the other provisions of this Agreement:

Table A 4.1   Award of Phantom Units

Date of Grant	November 1, 2010
Total Number of Phantom Units	50
Date of 100% Vesting	November 1, 2015
Partially Vested Units at Date of Grant	25
Employment Start Date	November 1, 2005
Number of Months From Employment Start Date Until 100% Vested	120

In the event of any change in the outstanding shares of the common stock of the Company by reason of a stock dividend, stock split, combination of shares, recapitalization, merger, consolidation, transfer of assets, reorganization, division, split-off, spin-off, or what the Company deems in its sole discretion to be similar circumstances, the number and kind of Phantom Units shall be appropriately adjusted in a manner to be determined in the sole discretion of the Company.

   1.2   Vesting Conditions.

      (a)   Summary. To be fully vested, Phantom Units must satisfy both an Event Vesting Condition set forth in Section 1.4 and the Time Vesting Condition set forth in Section 1.1 and this Section 1.2, except that the Time Vesting Condition shall not apply in the event of a Change in Control. The Time Vesting Condition shall be deemed satisfied as to all the Phantom Units if the Participant continues to be an employee of the Company or its Affiliates at all times from the Date of Grant until the Date of 100% Time Vesting set forth in Section 1.1 and, prior to such date, the number of Phantom Units which have satisfied the Time Vesting Condition is computed as provided in Section 1.2(c) hereof. All vesting of Phantom Units hereunder is subject to the forfeiture provisions of Section 1.5 hereof. The Phantom Units will be vested upon the following events which are described more fully in Section 1.4:

         (i)   Upon a Change in Control provided the Participant is then employed by the Company or an Affiliate as more fully set forth in Section 1.4(b); or

         (ii)   Upon an involuntary termination without Cause (as defined in Section 1.5(b)) of employment as more fully set forth in Section 1.4(c), but only to the extent of the number of Phantom Units which have satisfied the Time Vesting Condition on the date of employment termination; or

(iii) Upon an involuntary termination without Cause (as defined in Section 1.5(b)) of employment due to death or permanent disability of the Participant while employed by the Company or an Affiliate as more fully set forth in Section 1.4(d), but only to the extent of the number of Phantom Units which have satisfied the Time Vesting Condition on the date of employment termination.

(b) Definitions.

A "Change in Control" shall be deemed to have occurred upon the happening of any of the following events, provided that such event, in addition, unless an exemption is otherwise available, otherwise satisfies the requirements of Section 409A of the Internal Revenue Code of 1986 as amended ("Code") which are set forth in the Appendix to this Agreement:

(i) The closing of a sale of more than 50% of the outstanding voting stock of the Company to an unaffiliated third party;

(ii) The closing of a sale of substantially all of the assets of the Company to an unaffiliated third party; or

(iii) Any other event deemed by the Company in its sole discretion to constitute a "Change in Control" of the Company, provided such event satisfies the requirements of Section 409A of the Internal Revenue Code of 1986, as amended ("Code").

An "unaffiliated third party" does not include either (i) an entity which is directly or indirectly controlled by an individual member of the same family that controls the Company or (ii) an individual who is a member of the same family that controls the Company. An individual is considered a member of the same family that controls the Company if such individual is related to the same family that controls the Company by blood, marriage, adoption, not more remote than second cousin.

The term "Affiliate", as used herein, shall refer to an entity which is controlled by the Company, controls the Company, or under common control with the Company.

(c) Time Vesting.

The number of Phantom Units which have satisfied the Time Vesting Condition as of any given date is the total of the Number of Time Vested Phantom Units as of the Date of Grant as set forth in Section 1.1 plus the number of Phantom Units which have vested thereafter and prior to such given date as provided in this Section 1.2(c). Phantom Units will vest proportionately over the Number of Months From Employment Start Date Until 100% Time Vested as set forth in

Section 1.1. Phantom Units vest on the last day of each calendar month of employment by the Company or an Affiliate. Time Vested Phantom Units are forfeited in the event of the voluntary termination of employment of the Participant, or for Cause, as provided in Section 1.5 hereof. Time Vested Phantom Units are not forfeited in the event of an involuntary termination of the Participant's employment, including, but not limited to, an involuntary termination by reason of death or permanent disability, except for terminations for Cause, as provided in Section 1.5(b) hereof. Unvested units are forfeited in the event of the termination of the employment (whether voluntary or involuntary) of the Participant as provided in Section 1.5 hereof.

(d) Final Decision

All decisions as to whether Phantom Units have vested (including, but not limited to, decisions as to what constitutes "permanent disability" and whether the Time Vesting or Event Vesting Conditions have been satisfied or who is an "unaffiliated third party") shall be made by the Company and its decision shall be final, binding and conclusive in the absence of clear and convincing evidence that such decision was not made in good faith.

1.3 Phantom Unit Account. The Company shall maintain a Phantom Unit Account for the Participant to which shall be credited the total number of Phantom Units. Each Phantom Unit shall represent one notional share of common stock of the Company, but shall not entitle the Participant to any of the rights or privileges of an owner of common stock (regardless of class) of the Company. Fractions of a Phantom Unit shall be combined to the extent possible; any remaining fraction shall be rounded up.

1.4 Payment With Respect to Fully Vested Phantom Units.

(a) Event Vesting. No payment shall be made to the Participant from or with respect to the Participant's Phantom Unit Account except to the extent that both an Event Vesting Condition and the Time Vesting Condition have been satisfied, except that the Time Vesting Condition shall not be applicable in the event of the Change in Control. The Event Vesting Conditions are set forth in Sections 1.4(b), 1.4(c) and 1.4(d).

(b) Change in Control. Subject to Section 1.5 hereof, in the event of a Change in Control and provided the Participant is then employed by the Company or an Affiliate, the Company shall pay to the Participant with respect to the Participant's Phantom Unit Account an amount equal to the following percentage of the consideration (whether cash, notes, securities, delayed payments, earn-out payments or otherwise) to be received by the common stockholders of the Company upon the Change in Control: divide (a) the number of the Phantom Units owned by the Participant at the time of the Change in Control by (b) the number of outstanding shares of common stock of the Company (of all classes) at the time of the Change in Control computed on a fully diluted basis, i.e. inclusive of Common Stock of the Company which may be issued pursuant to options, warrants, convertible securities, phantom units (inclusive of the Participant's Phantom Units) or other rights, whether or not similar to the foregoing. All payments to the Participant shall be made in the same form (whether cash, notes, securities, delayed payments, earn-out payments or otherwise), at the same time or times, and in the same percentage as the consideration to be received by the common stockholders of the Company upon the Change in Control. The Company shall have the right, at its option, to substitute cash for any non-cash form of consideration, but not vice versa.

(c) <u>Employment Termination</u>. Subject to Section 1.5 hereof, in the event of the involuntary termination without Cause (as defined in Section 1.5(b)) of the employment of the Participant with the Company or an Affiliate, the Company shall purchase such numbers of Phantom Units of the Participant as have satisfied the Time Vesting Condition on the date of such termination. The purchase price for the Phantom Units which have satisfied the Time Vesting Condition shall be determined as set forth in the Formula Value contained in Exhibit I hereto, which Formula Value shall be computed as of the date of termination. The purchase price shall be paid in thirty-six (36) equal consecutive monthly installments, the first monthly installment to be due and payable sixty (60) days after the date of employment termination and all subsequent monthly installments to be due and payable on the same day of subsequent calendar months . Any amounts owed by the Participant to the Company or an Affiliate shall be deducted from the purchase price. The aggregate purchase price, less any indebtedness owed by the Participant, shall be evidenced by a non-negotiable promissory note made by the Company which shall not bear interest. Notwithstanding anything to the contrary contained herein, any promissory note made by the Company shall contain the following provision and all payments due hereunder to the Participant shall be subject to the following limitation: "Under no circumstances shall the Company be obligated to pay in the aggregate more than 10% of its EBITDA (as defined in Exhibit I hereto and determined in the sole judgment of the Company's board of directors) to the payee of this Note and the payee of all other promissory notes issued by the Company in consideration of the repurchase by the Company of its stock or phantom units (herein called the "10% limit"). In the event that the 10% limit is exceeded (in the sole judgment of the Company's board of directors), the Company shall be entitled to proportionately reduce the payments (or eliminate such payments entirely) under this Note and the payments made under such other promissory notes so that all of the payments in the aggregate do not exceed the 10% limit. Such payment reductions (or payment eliminations, as the case may be) shall not constitute a default under this Note and, in the event of such reductions (or eliminations, as the case may be), the principal and interest payments (if any) due under this Note shall be extended beyond thirty-six (36) months until the Note is paid in full; however, even during the extended payment period of this Note, in no event may the 10% limit be exceeded.

(d)   Death or Disability. Except as provided in Section 1.5 hereof, in the event of the involuntary termination of the employment of the Participant due to the death or permanent disability of the Participant while employed by the Company or an Affiliate (excluding termination for Cause), the number of Phantom Units which have satisfied the Time Vesting Condition at the date of such death or permanent disability shall be purchased by the Company as provided in Section 1.4(c) above.

(e)   Tax. All payments pursuant to this Section 1.4 shall be subject to applicable foreign, federal, state and local tax withholding as provided in Section 2.3 hereof.

(f)   General. The Participant shall not be entitled to any payment with respect to the Phantom Units except to the extent provided in this Agreement. All decisions as to the amount and form of the consideration due to the Participant hereunder shall be made by the Company and its decision shall be final, binding and conclusive in the absence of clear and convincing evidence that such decision was not made in good faith.

1.5   Forfeiture of Phantom Units Upon Termination of Employment.

(a)   Employment Termination. In the event of the termination of the employment of the Participant (whether voluntary or involuntary) with the Company or an Affiliate, all unvested Phantom Units on the date of such termination shall be deemed to be automatically forfeited, unless the Participant's employment is on that date transferred to the Company or another Affiliate. In the event of the voluntary termination of the employment of the Participant with the Company or an Affiliate or the involuntary termination of the Participant's employment for Cause as defined in Section 1.5(b) hereof, all Phantom Units which have satisfied the Time Vesting Condition on date of such termination shall also be deemed automatically forfeited. If a Participant's employment is with an Affiliate and that entity ceases to be an Affiliate, the Participant's employment will be deemed to have involuntarily terminated when the entity ceases to be an Affiliate unless the Participant transfers employment to the Company or to a remaining Affiliate. In the event of an involuntary termination of the Participant's employment with the Company or an Affiliate without Cause (as defined in Section 1.5(b)), including death or permanent disability, Phantom Units which have satisfied the Time Vesting Condition at the date of employment termination are not forfeited.

(b) Termination With Cause. In the event of the termination of the employment of the Participant for Cause, all Phantom Units (whether or not partially or fully vested) shall be automatically forfeited. The term "Cause" refers to a termination of the employment of the Participant by the Company or an Affiliate for any reason which is commonly viewed as "cause" including, but not limited to, any of the following acts (which are given solely for purposes of illustration only and do not limit the scope of what is deemed to be "Cause"): (i) willful misconduct by the Participant; (ii) failure to abide by written Instructions of the Company or an Affiliate, provided the Participant receives written notice of the failure to abide by such instructions and does not cure such failure within ten (10) days after receiving such written notice; or (iii) indictment of the Participant for a crime which, if convicted, carries a realistic threat of a prison sentence.

1.6 Non-Alienation of Benefits. The Participant shall not have the right to sell, assign, transfer or otherwise convey or encumber in whole or in part the Phantom Units or the right to receive any payment under this Agreement and the Phantom Units and the right to receive any payment hereunder shall not be subject to attachment, lien or other involuntary encumbrance.

1.7 Confidentiality and Non-Interference. In consideration of the award to the Participant of Phantom Units identified herein, the Participant hereby agrees to the confidentiality and non-interference provisions set forth in Attachment A hereto.

ARTICLE II

GENERAL PROVISIONS

2.1   No Right of Continued Employment. The grant of the Phantom Units shall not give the Participant, and nothing in this Agreement shall confer upon the Participant, any right to continue in the employment of the Company or an Affiliate. Nothing in this Agreement shall affect any right which the Company or an Affiliate may have to terminate the employment of the Participant for any reason or for no reason.

2.2   No Rights As A Stockholder. Neither the Participant nor any other person shall be entitled to the privileges of ownership of common stock of the Company or an Affiliate, or otherwise have any rights as a stockholder of the Company or an Affiliate, by reason of the award or vesting of the Phantom Units.

2.3   Tax Withholding Upon Vesting or Payment With Respect to Phantom Units. Upon the vesting or payment with respect to Phantom Units, the Participant is responsible to pay to the Company or an Affiliate all required tax withholding, whether foreign, federal, state or local. All payments under Section 1.4 of this Agreement are subject to withholding of all applicable foreign, federal, state, or local withholding taxes.

2.4   Captions. The captions at the beginning of each of the numbered Sections and Articles herein are for reference purposes only and will have no legal force or effect. Such captions will not be considered a part of this Agreement for purposes of interpreting, construing or applying this Agreement and will not define, limit, extend, explain or describe the scope or extent of this Agreement or any of its terms and conditions.

2.5   Governing Law. THE VALIDITY, CONSTRUCTION, INTERPRETATION AND EFFECT OF THIS AGREEMENT SHALL EXCLUSIVELY BE GOVERNED BY AND DETERMINED IN ACCORDANCE WITH THE LAWS OF THE STATE OF DELAWARE (WITHOUT GIVING EFFECT TO THE CONFLICTS OF LAW PRINCIPLES THEREOF).

2.6   Notices. All notices, requests and demands to or upon the respective parties hereto to be effective shall be in writing, sent by facsimile, by overnight courier or by registered or certified mail, postage prepaid and return receipt requested. Notices to the Company or an Affiliate shall be deemed to have been duly given or made upon actual receipt by the Company. Such communications shall be addressed and directed to the parties listed below (except where this Agreement expressly provides that it be directed to another) as follows, or to such other address or recipient for a party as may be hereafter notified by such party hereunder:

(a) if to the Company or   Family Business Corporation
     an Affiliate:

                                 [Address]

     with a copy to   Frederick D. Lipman, Esq.
                                 Blank Rome LLP
                                 One Logan Square
                                 18th & Cherry Street
                                 Philadelphia, PA 19103-
                                 6998

(b) if to the Participant: to the address for the Participant as it appears on the Company's records.

2.7 Severability. If any provision hereof is found by a court of competent jurisdiction to be prohibited or unenforceable, it shall, as to such jurisdiction, be ineffective only to the extent of such prohibition or unenforceability, and such prohibition or unenforceability shall not invalidate the balance of such provision to the extent it is not prohibited or unenforceable, nor invalidate the other provisions hereof.

2.8 Entire Agreement and Other Provisions. This Agreement constitutes the entire understanding and supersedes any and all other agreements, oral or written, between the parties hereto, in respect of the subject matter of this Agreement, and embodies the entire understanding of the parties with respect to the subject matter hereof. This Agreement may not be amended, supplemented or waived, in whole or in part, except by a written instrument executed by all parties hereto. This Agreement may be executed in one or more counterparts, each of which shall be deemed an original against any party whose signature appears thereon. The rule of construction that ambiguities in a document are construed against the draftsperson shall not apply to this Agreement.

2.9 Binding Agreement. The terms and conditions of this Agreement shall be binding upon the estate, heirs, beneficiaries and other representatives of the Participant to the same extent that such terms and conditions are binding upon the Participant.

2.10 Arbitration. Any dispute or disagreement with respect to any portion of this Agreement (excluding Attachment A hereto) or its validity, construction, meaning, performance, or Participant's rights hereunder shall be settled by arbitration, conducted in Philadelphia, Pennsylvania, in accordance with the Commercial Arbitration Rules of the American Arbitration Association or its successor, as amended from time to time. However, prior to submission to arbitration the Participant will attempt to resolve any disputes or disagreements with the Company over this Agreement amicably and informally, in good faith, for a period not to exceed two weeks. Thereafter, the dispute or disagreement will be submitted to arbitration. At any time prior to a decision from the arbitrator(s) being rendered, the Participant and the Company may resolve the dispute by settlement. The Participant and the Company shall equally share the costs charged by the American Arbitration Association or its successor, but the Participant and the Company shall otherwise be solely responsible for their own respective counsel fees and expenses. The decision of the arbitrator(s) shall be made in writing, setting forth the award, the reasons for the decision and award and shall be binding and conclusive on the Participant and the Company. Further, neither the Participant nor the Company shall appeal any such award. Judgment of a court of competent jurisdiction may be entered upon the award and may be enforced as such in accordance with the provisions of the award.

THE PARTICIPANT HEREBY WAIVES ANY RIGHT TO A JURY TRIAL.

IN WITNESS WHEREOF, the parties hereto, intending to be legally bound hereby, have executed this Agreement as of the day first above written.

Family Business Corporation

By:_____

Name:_____
Title:_____

ACKNOWLEDGEMENT, ACCEPTANCE AND RELEASE AGREEMENT

The undersigned Participant hereby acknowledges receipt of a copy of the foregoing Phantom Unit Agreement (**including Attachment A hereto**), and having read it, hereby signifies his understanding of, and his agreement with, its terms and conditions, including those set forth hereafter. The Participant hereby accepts this Phantom Unit Agreement in full satisfaction of any previous written or verbal promises made to him by Family Business Corporation or any of its Affiliates with respect to stock, stock rights, stock options or phantom unit awards.

_____

NAME OF PARTICIPANT

_____

SIGNATURE OF PARTICIPANT

EXHIBIT I

The Formula Value shall be determined as follows:

1. Compute the net book value of the Company as of the end of the fiscal year immediately prior to the date of employment termination (as defined in Section 1.4(c)) or death or disability (as defined in Section 1.4(d)), as determined under generally accepted accounting principles.

2. Compute the net book value of the Company as of the end of the fiscal year immediately prior to the date of grant, as determined under generally accepted accounting principles.

3. Subtract the result of clause (2) from the result of clause (1). If the result of the subtraction is zero or a minus number, the Formula Value is zero and no payment is due. If the result of the subtraction is a positive number proceed with clause (4) below.

4. Divide the positive result of clause (3) by the number of outstanding shares of common stock of the Company as computed on a fully diluted basis, i.e. inclusive of Common Stock of the Company which may be issued pursuant to options, warrants, convertible securities, Phantom Units or other rights, whether or not similar to the foregoing. This figure constitutes the Formula Value.

5. All decisions as to the computation of the Formula Value shall be made by the Company or its outside accountants and its decision shall be final, binding and conclusive in the absence of clear and convincing evidence that such decision was not made in good faith. Any legal challenge to the computation of the Formula Value by the Participant shall give the Company the right to cause the forfeiture of the award of Phantom Units.

Attachment A

to Phantom Unit Agreement

Confidentiality and Non-Interference.

(a)   The Participant covenants and agrees that, in consideration of the award to the Participant of these Phantom Units, the Participant will not, during the Participant's employment with the Company (as defined herein) or at any time thereafter, except with the express prior written consent of the Company or pursuant to the lawful order of any judicial or administrative agency of government, directly or indirectly, disclose, communicate or divulge to any individual or entity, or use for the benefit of any individual or entity, any knowledge or information with respect to the conduct or details of the Company's business which the Participant, acting reasonably, believe or should believe to be of a confidential nature and the disclosure of which not to be in the Company's interest.

(b)   The Participant covenants and agrees that, in consideration of the award to the Participant of these Phantom Units, the Participant will not, during the Participant's employment with the Company, except with the express prior written consent of the Company, directly or indirectly, whether as employee, owner, partner, member, consultant, agent, director, officer, stockholder or in any other capacity, engage in or assist any individual or entity to engage in any act or action which the Participant, acting reasonably, believe or should believe would be harmful or inimical to the interests of the Company.

(c)   The Participant covenants and agrees that, in consideration of the award to the Participant of these Phantom Units, the Participant will not, for a period of two years after the Participant's employment with the Company ceases for any reason whatsoever (whether voluntary or not), except with the express prior written consent of the Company, directly or indirectly, whether as employee, owner, partner, member, consultant, agent, director, officer, stockholder or in any other capacity, for the Participant's own account or for the benefit of any individual or entity, (i) solicit any customer of the Company for business which would result in such customer terminating their relationship with the Company; or (ii) solicit or induce any individual or entity which is an employee of the Company to leave the Company or to otherwise terminate their relationship with the Company.

(d) The parties agree that any breach by the Participant of any of the covenants or agreements contained in this Attachment A will result in irreparable injury to the Company for which money damages could not adequately compensate the Company and therefore, in the event of any such breach, the Company shall be entitled (in addition to any other rights and remedies which it may have at law or in equity) to have an injunction issued by any competent court enjoining and restraining the Participant and/or any other individual or entity involved therein from continuing such breach. The existence of any claim or cause of action which the Participant may have against the Company or any other individual or entity shall not constitute a defense or bar to the enforcement of such covenants. If the Company is obliged to resort to the courts for the enforcement of any of the covenants or agreements contained in this Attachment A, or if such covenants or agreements are otherwise the subject of litigation between the parties, and the Company prevails in such enforcement or litigation, then the term of such covenants and agreements shall be extended for a period of time equal to the period of such breach, which extension shall commence on the later of (a) the date on which the original (unextended) term of such covenants and agreements is scheduled to terminate or (b) the date of the final court order (without further right of appeal) enforcing such covenant or agreement.

(e) If any portion of the covenants or agreements contained in this Attachment A, or the application hereof, is construed to be invalid or unenforceable, the other portions of such covenant(s) or agreement(s) or the application thereof shall not be affected and shall be given full force and effect without regard to the invalid or enforceable portions to the fullest extent possible. If any covenant or agreement in this Attachment A is held unenforceable because of the area covered, the duration thereof, or the scope thereof, then the court making such determination shall have the power to reduce the area and/or duration and/or limit the scope thereof, and the covenant or agreement shall then be enforceable in its reduced form

(f) For purposes of this Attachment A, the term "the Company" shall include the Company, any successor to the Company and all present and future direct and indirect subsidiaries and other Affiliates of the Company.

[Remaining Appendix Omitted]

Private Company [Sale or IPO Exit] ABC, Inc., 2010 Stock Option Plan

1. Purpose of Plan

The purpose of this 2010 Stock Option Plan (the "Plan") is to provide additional incentive to officers, other key employees, and directors of, and important consultants to, ABC, Inc., a Pennsylvania corporation (the "Company"), and each present or future parent or subsidiary corporation, by encouraging them to invest in shares of the Company's common stock, no par value ("Common Stock"), and thereby acquire a proprietary interest in the Company and an increased personal interest in the Company's continued success and progress.

2. Aggregate Number of Shares

200,000 shares of the Company's Common Stock shall be the aggregate number of shares which may be issued under this Plan. Notwithstanding the foregoing, in the event of any change in the outstanding shares of the Common Stock of the Company by reason of a stock dividend, stock split, combination of shares, recapitalization, merger, consolidation, transfer of assets, reorganization, conversion or what the Committee (defined in Section 4(a)), deems in its sole discretion to be similar circumstances, the aggregate number and kind of shares which may be issued under this Plan shall be appropriately adjusted in a manner determined in the sole discretion of the Committee. Reacquired shares of the Company's Common Stock, as well as unissued shares, may be used for the purpose of this Plan. Common Stock of the Company subject to options which have terminated unexercised, either in whole or in part, shall be available for future options granted under this Plan.

3. Class of Persons Eligible to Receive Options

All officers and key employees of the Company and of any present or future Company parent or subsidiary corporation are eligible to receive an option or options under this Plan. All directors of, and important consultants to, the Company and of any present or future Company parent or subsidiary corporation are also eligible to receive an option or options under this Plan. The individuals who shall, in fact, receive an option or options shall be selected by the Committee, in its sole discretion, except as otherwise specified in Section 4 hereof. No individual may receive options under this Plan for more than 80% of the total number of shares of the Company's Common Stock authorized for issuance under this Plan.

4. Administration of Plan

(a)   Prior to the registration of the Company's Common Stock under Section 12 of the Securities Exchange Act of 1934, this Plan shall be administered by the Company's Board of Directors and, after such registration, by an Option Committee ("Committee") appointed by the Company's Board of Directors. The Committee shall consist of a minimum of two and a maximum of five members of the Board of Directors, each of whom shall be a "Non-Employee Director" within the meaning of Rule 16b-3(b)(3) under the Securities Exchange Act of 1934, as amended, or any future corresponding rule, except that the failure of the Committee for any reason to be composed solely of Non-Employee Directors shall not prevent an option from being considered granted under this Plan. The Committee shall, in addition to its other authority and subject to the provisions of this Plan, determine which individuals shall in fact be granted an option or options, whether the option shall be an Incentive Stock Option or a Non-Qualified Stock Option (as such terms are defined in Section 5(a)), the number of shares to be subject to each of the options, the time or times at which the options shall be granted, the rate of option exercisability, and, subject to Section 5 hereof, the price at which each of the options is exercisable and the duration of the option. The term "Committee", as used in this Plan and the options granted hereunder, refers to the Board of Directors prior to the registration of the Company's Common Stock under Section 12 of the Securities Exchange Act of 1934 and, after such registration, to the Committee; prior to such registration, the Board of Directors may consist of only one director.

(b)   The Committee shall adopt such rules for the conduct of its business and administration of this Plan as it considers desirable.

A majority of the members of the Committee shall constitute a quorum for all purposes. The vote or written consent of a majority of the members of the Committee on a particular matter shall constitute the act of the Committee on such matter. The Committee shall have the right to construe the Plan and the options issued pursuant to it, to correct defects and omissions and to reconcile inconsistencies to the extent necessary to effectuate the Plan and the options issued pursuant to it, and such action shall be final, binding and conclusive upon all parties concerned. No member of the Committee or the Board of Directors shall be liable for any act or omission (whether or not negligent) taken or omitted in good faith, or for the exercise of an authority or discretion granted in connection with the Plan to a Committee or the Board of Directors, or for the acts or omissions of any other members of a Committee or the Board of Directors. Subject to the numerical limitations on Committee membership set forth in Section 4(a) hereof, the Board of Directors may at any time appoint additional members of the Committee and may at any time remove any member of the Committee with or without cause. Vacancies in the Committee, however caused, may be filled by the Board of Directors, if it so desires.

5. Incentive Stock Options and Non-Qualified Stock Options

(a) Options issued pursuant to this Plan may be either Incentive Stock Options granted pursuant to Section 5(b) hereof or Non-Qualified Stock Options granted pursuant to Section 5(c) hereof, as determined by the Committee. An "Incentive Stock Option" is an option which satisfies all of the requirements of Section 422(b) of the Internal Revenue Code of 1986, as amended (the "Code") and the regulations thereunder, and a "Non-Qualified Stock Option" is an option which either does not satisfy all of those requirements or the terms of the option provide that it will not be treated as an Incentive Stock Option. The Committee may grant both an Incentive Stock Option and a Non-Qualified Stock Option to the same person, or more than one of each type of option to the same person. The option price for options issued under this Plan shall be equal at least to the fair market value (as defined below) of the Company's Common Stock on the date of the grant of the option. The fair market value of the Company's Common Stock on any particular date shall mean the last reported sale price of a share of the Company's Common Stock on any stock exchange on which such stock is then listed or admitted to trading, on such date, or if no sale took place on such day, the last such date on which a sale took place, or if the Common Stock is not then listed or admitted to trading on any stock exchange, the average of the bid and asked prices in the over-the-counter market on such date, or if none of the foregoing, a price determined in good faith by the Committee to equal the fair market value per share of the Common Stock.

(b) Subject to the authority of the Committee set forth in Section 4(a) hereof, Incentive Stock Options issued pursuant to this Plan shall be issued substantially in the form set forth in Exhibit I hereof, which form is hereby incorporated by reference and made a part hereof, and shall contain substantially the terms and conditions set forth therein. Incentive Stock Options shall not be exercisable after the expiration of ten years from the date such options are granted, unless terminated earlier under the terms of the option, except that options granted to individuals described in Section 422(b) (6) of the Code shall conform to the provisions of Section 422(c)(5) of the Code. At the time of the grant of an Incentive Stock Option hereunder, the Committee may, in its discretion, amend or supplement any of the option terms contained in Exhibit I for any particular optionee, provided that the option as amended or supplemented satisfies the requirements of Section 422(b) of the Code and the regulations thereunder. Each of the options granted pursuant to this Section 5(b) is intended, if possible, to be an "Incentive Stock Option" as that term is defined in Section 422(b) of the Code and the regulations thereunder. In the event this Plan or any option granted pursuant to this Section 5(b) is in any way inconsistent with the applicable legal requirements of the Code or the regulations thereunder for an Incentive Stock Option, this Plan and such option shall be deemed automatically amended as of the date hereof to conform to such legal requirements, if such conformity may be achieved by amendment.

(c) Subject to the authority of the Committee set forth in Section 4(a) hereof, Non-Qualified Stock Options issued to officers and other key employees pursuant to this Plan shall be issued substantially in the form set forth in Exhibit II hereof, which form is hereby incorporated by reference and made a part hereof, and shall contain substantially the terms and conditions set forth therein. Subject to the authority of the Committee set forth in Section 4(a) hereof, Non-Qualified Stock Options issued to directors and important consultants pursuant to this Plan shall be issued substantially in the form set forth in Exhibit III hereof, which form is hereby incorporated by reference and made a part hereof, and shall contain substantially the terms and conditions set forth therein. Non-Qualified Stock Options shall expire ten years after the date they are granted, unless terminated earlier under the option terms. At the time of granting a Non-Qualified Stock Option hereunder, the Committee may, in its discretion, amend or supplement any of the option terms contained in Exhibit II or Exhibit III for any particular optionee.

(d)   Neither the Company nor any of its current or future parent, subsidiaries or affiliates, nor their officers, directors, shareholders, stock option plan committees, employees or agents shall have any liability to any optionee in the event (i) an option granted pursuant to Section 5(b) hereof does not qualify as an "Incentive Stock Option" as that term is used in Section 422(b) of the Code and the regulations thereunder; (ii) any optionee does not obtain the tax treatment pertaining to an Incentive Stock Option; or (iii) any option granted pursuant to Section 5(c) hereof is an "Incentive Stock Option."

6. Amendment, Supplement, Suspension and Termination

Options shall not be granted pursuant to this Plan after the expiration of ten years from the date the Plan is adopted by the Board of Directors of the Company. The Board of Directors reserves the right at any time, and from time to time, to amend or supplement this Plan in any way, or to suspend or terminate it, effective as of such date, which date may be either before or after the taking of such action, as may be specified by the Board of Directors; provided, however, that such action shall not, without the consent of the optionee, affect options granted under the Plan prior to the actual date on which such action occurred. If an amendment or supplement of this Plan is required by the Code or the regulations thereunder to be approved by the shareholders of the Company in order to permit the granting of "Incentive Stock Options" (as that term is defined in Section 422(b) of the Code and regulations thereunder) pursuant to the amended or supplemented Plan, such amendment or supplement shall also be approved by the shareholders of the Company in such manner as is prescribed by the Code and the regulations thereunder. If the Board of Directors voluntarily submits a proposed amendment, supplement, suspension or termination for shareholder approval, such submission shall not require any future amendments, supplements, suspensions or terminations (whether or not relating to the same provision or subject matter) to be similarly submitted for shareholder approval.

7. Effectiveness of Plan

This Plan shall become effective on the date of its adoption by the Company's Board of Directors, subject however to approval by the holders of the Company's Common Stock in the manner as prescribed in the Code and the regulations thereunder. Options may be granted under this Plan prior to obtaining shareholder approval, provided such options shall not be exercisable until shareholder approval is obtained.

8. General Conditions

(a)   Nothing contained in this Plan or any option granted pursuant to this Plan shall confer upon any employee the right to continue in the employ of the Company or any affiliated or subsidiary corporation or interfere in any way with the rights of the Company or any affiliated or subsidiary corporation to terminate his employment in any way.

(b)   Nothing contained in this Plan or any option granted pursuant to this Plan shall confer upon any director or consultant the right to continue as a director of, or consultant to, the Company or any affiliated or subsidiary corporation or interfere in any way with the rights of the Company or any affiliated or subsidiary corporation, or their respective shareholders, to terminate the directorship of any such director or the consultancy relationship of any such consultant.

(c)   Corporate action constituting an offer of stock for sale to any person under the terms of the options to be granted hereunder shall be deemed complete as of the date when the Committee authorizes the grant of the option to the such person, regardless of when the option is actually delivered to such person or acknowledged or agreed to by him.

(d)   The terms "parent corporation" and "subsidiary corporation" as used throughout this Plan, and the options granted pursuant to this Plan, shall (except as otherwise provided in the option form) have the meaning that is ascribed to that term when contained in Section 422(b) of the Code and the regulations thereunder, and the Company shall be deemed to be the grantor corporation for purposes of applying such meaning.

(e)   References in this Plan to the Code shall be deemed to also refer to the corresponding provisions of any future United States revenue law.

(f)   The use of the masculine pronoun shall include the feminine gender whenever appropriate.

EXHIBIT I

INCENTIVE STOCK OPTION

To:

Name

Address

Date of Grant:

You are hereby granted an option, effective as of the date hereof, to purchase _____ shares of common stock, no par value ("Common Stock"), of ABC, Inc., a Pennsylvania corporation (the "Company"), at a price of $_____ per share pursuant to the Company's Stock Option Plan (the "Plan").

This option shall terminate and is not exercisable after ten years from the date of its grant (the "Scheduled Termination Date"), except if terminated earlier as hereafter provided.

Your option may not be exercised prior to the Scheduled Terminaion Date unless there is an Acceleration Event (as hereafter defined), in which case this option shall become immediately exercisable, except as hereafter provided. An "Acceleration Event" refers to a date which is one year (or such earlier time as the Committee determines) after the earlier of the following: (a) the first closing date for the initial public offering ("IPO") of the Common Stock of the Company (or of a parent corporation) in which the Company (or such parent corporation) raises at least $15 million, or (b) the date of a "Change of Control" (as defined below).

A "Change in Control" shall be deemed to have occurred upon the happening of any of the following events, provided that such event, in addition, unless an exemption is otherwise available, otherwise satisfies the requirements of Section 409A of the Internal Revenue Code of 1986 as amended ("Code") which are set forth in the Appendix to this Agreement:

(i)   The closing of a sale of more than 50% of the outstanding voting stock of the Company to an unaffiliated third party;

(ii)   The closing of a sale of substantially all of the assets of the Company to an unaffiliated third party; or

(iii)   Any other event deemed by the Company in its sole discretion to constitute a "Change in Control" of the Company, provided such event satisfies the requirements of Section 409A of the Code.

An "unaffiliated third party" does not include either (i) an entity which is directly or indirectly controlled by an individual member of the same family that controls the Company or (ii) an individual who is a member of the same family that controls the Company. An individual is considered a member of the same family that controls the Company if such individual is related to the same family that controls the Company by blood, marriage, adoption, not more remote than second cousin. In the event of a dispute as to what constitutes a "Change in Control", the decision of the Company shall be final, binding and conclusive unless there is clear and convincing evidence that it was not made in good faith.

Notwithstanding the foregoing, if on the date of an Acceleration Event, you have not been employed by the Company for a total of at least three (3) years, this option will not be exercisable in full on the date of an Acceleration Event, but instead shall be exercisable as follows: (a) if on the date of an Acceleration Event you have been employed by the Company for a total of two (2) or more years, this option will be exercisable for two-thirds of the total number of shares then subject to this option, and the remaining one-third of the total number of shares then subject to this option will become exercisable after you have been employed by the Company for a total of three (3) years; (b) if on the date of an Acceleration Event you have been employed by the Company for a total of one (1) year or more and less than two (2) years, this option will be exercisable for one-third of the total number of shares then subject to this option and an additional one-third each of the total number of shares then subject to this option shall become exercisable when you have been employed by the Company for two (2) years and three (3) years, respectively; (c) if on the date of an Acceleration Event you have been employed by the Company for a total of less than one (1) year, this option will not be exercisable until you have been employed by the Company for a total of one (1) year, at which time this option will be exercisable for one-third of the total number of shares then subject to this option and an additional one-third each of the total number of shares then subject this option shall become exercisable when you have been employed by the Company for two (2) years and three (3) years, respectively.

In the event of an IPO of the Common Stock of a parent corporation of the Company, and provided such parent corporation assumes the obligations of the Company under this Plan, this option shall thereupon pertain solely to the Common Stock of such parent corporation and the Company shall have no obligation whatsoever hereunder. In the event of an IPO in which the Company or its parent corporation has two classes of Common Stock, only one of which is issued to the public in the IPO, this option shall pertain solely to the class of Common Stock issued to the public in the IPO.

You may exercise your option by giving written notice to the Secretary of the Company on forms supplied by the Company at its then principal executive office, accompanied by payment of the option price for the total number of shares you specify that you wish to purchase. The payment may be in any of the following forms: (a) cash, which may be evidenced by a check and includes cash received from a stock brokerage firm in a so-called "cashless exercise"; (b) (unless prohibited by the Committee) certificates representing shares of Common Stock of the Company, which will be valued by the Secretary of the Company at the fair market value per share of the Company's Common Stock (as determined in accordance with the Plan) on the date of delivery of such certificates to the Company, accompanied by an assignment of the stock to the Company; or (c) (unless prohibited by the Committee) any combination of cash and Common Stock of the Company valued as provided in clause (b). The use of the so-called "attestation procedure" to exercise a stock option may be permitted by the Committee. Any assignment of stock shall be in a form and substance satisfactory to the Secretary of the Company, including guarantees of signature(s) and payment of all transfer taxes if the Secretary deems such guarantees necessary or desirable.

Your option will, to the extent not previously exercised by you, terminate three months after the date on which your employment by the Company or a Company subsidiary corporation is terminated (whether such termination be voluntary or involuntary) other than by reason of disability as defined in Section 22(e)(3) of the Internal

Revenue Code of 1986, as amended (the "Code"), and the regulations thereunder, or death, in which case your option will terminate one year from the date of termination of employment due to disability or death (but in no event later than the Scheduled Termination Date). After the date your employment is terminated, as aforesaid, you may exercise this option only for the number of shares which you had a right to purchase and did not purchase on the date your employment terminated. Provided you are willing to continue your employment for the Company or a successor after a Change of Control at the same compensation you enjoyed immediately prior to such Change of Control, if your employment is involuntarily terminated without cause after a Change of Control, you may exercise this option for the number of shares you would have had a right to purchase on the date of an Acceleration Event. If you are employed by a Company subsidiary corporation, your employment shall be deemed to have terminated on the date your employer ceases to be a Company subsidiary corporation, unless you are on that date transferred to the Company or another Company subsidiary corporation. Your employment shall not be deemed to have terminated if you are transferred from the Company to a Company subsidiary corporation, or vice versa, or from one Company subsidiary corporation to another Company subsidiary corporation.

If you die while employed by the Company or a Company subsidiary corporation, your executor or administrator, as the case may be, may, at any time within one year after the date of your death (but in no event later than the Scheduled Termination Date), exercise the option as to any shares which you had a right to purchase and did not purchase during your lifetime. If your employment with the Company or a Company parent or subsidiary corporation is terminated by reason of your becoming disabled (within the meaning of Section 22(e)(3) of the Code and the regulations thereunder), you or your legal guardian or custodian may at any time within one year after the date of such termination (but in no event later than the Scheduled Termination Date), exercise the option as to any shares which you had a right to purchase and did not purchase prior to such termination. Your executor, administrator, guardian or custodian must present proof of his authority satisfactory to the Company prior to being allowed to exercise this option.

In the event of any change in the outstanding shares of the Common Stock of the Company by reason of a stock dividend, stock split, combination of shares, recapitalization, merger, consolidation, transfer of assets, reorganization, conversion or what the Committee deems in its sole discretion to be similar circumstances, the number and kind of shares subject to this option and the option price of such shares shall be appropriately adjusted in a manner to be determined in the sole discretion of the Committee.

In the event of a liquidation or proposed liquidation of the Company, including (but not limited to) a transfer of assets followed by a liquidation of the Company, or in the event of a Change of Control (as previously defined) or proposed Change of Control, the Committee shall have the right to require you to exercise this option upon thirty (30) days prior written notice to you. If at the time such written notice is given this option is not otherwise exercisable, the written notice will set forth your right to exercise this option even though it is not otherwise exercisable. In the event this option is not exercised by you within the thirty (30) day period set forth in such written notice, this option shall terminate on the last day of such thirty (30) day period, notwithstanding anything to the contrary contained in this option.

This option is not transferable otherwise than by will or the laws of descent and distribution, and is exercisable during your lifetime only by you, including, for this purpose, your legal guardian or custodian in the event of disability. Until the option price has been paid in full pursuant to due exercise of this option and the purchased shares are delivered to you, you do not have any rights as a shareholder of the Company. The Company reserves the right not to deliver to you the shares purchased by virtue of the exercise of this option during any period of time in which the Company deems, in its sole discretion, that such delivery would violate a federal, state, local or securities exchange rule, regulation or law.

Notwithstanding anything to the contrary contained herein, this option is not exercisable until all the following events occur and during the following periods of time:

(a) Until the Plan pursuant to which this option is granted is approved by the shareholders of the Company in the manner prescribed by the Code and the regulations thereunder;

(b) Until this option and the optioned shares are approved and/or registered with such federal, state and local regulatory bodies or agencies and securities exchanges as the Company may deem necessary or desirable;

(c)   During any period of time in which the Company deems that the exercisability of this option, the offer to sell the shares optioned hereunder, or the sale thereof, may violate a federal, state, local or securities exchange rule, regulation or law, or may cause the Company to be legally obligated to issue or sell more shares than the Company is legally entitled to issue or sell;

(d)   Until you have paid or made suitable arrangements to pay (which may include payment through the surrender of Common Stock, unless prohibited by the Committee) (i) all federal, state and local income tax withholding required to be withheld by the Company in connection with the option exercise and (ii) the employee's portion of other federal, state and local payroll and other taxes due in connection with the option exercise; or

(e)   Until you have executed such shareholder agreements as shall be required by the Company. Such shareholder agreements may, at the Company's option, include (among other provisions) provisions requiring you to (i) enter into any "lock-up" agreements required by underwriters, (ii) voting trust agreements, (iii) grant to the Company or its nominees an option to repurchase the stock, (iv) not sell, pledge or otherwise dispose of the stock without the consent of the Company, (v) maintain any Subchapter S elections made by the Company, (vi) grant rights of first refusal to the Company or its nominees with respect to the stock, and (vii) join in any sale of a majority or all of the outstanding stock of the Company.

The following two paragraphs shall be applicable if, on the date of exercise of this option, the Common Stock to be purchased pursuant to such exercise has not been registered under the Securities Act of 1933, as amended, and under applicable state securities laws, and shall continue to be applicable for so long as such registration has not occurred:

(a)   The optionee hereby agrees, warrants and represents that he will acquire the Common Stock to be issued hereunder for his own account for investment purposes only, and not with a view to, or in connection with, any resale or other distribution of any of such shares, except as hereafter permitted. The optionee further agrees that he will not at any time make any offer, sale, transfer, pledge or other disposition of such Common Stock to be issued hereunder without an effective registration statement under the Securities Act of 1933, as amended, and under any applicable state securities laws or an opinion of counsel acceptable to the Company to the effect that the proposed transaction will be exempt from such registration. The optionee shall execute such instruments, representations, acknowledgments and agreements as the Company may, in its sole discretion, deem advisable to avoid any violation of federal, state, local or securities exchange rule, regulation or law.

(b) The certificates for Common Stock to be issued to the optionee hereunder shall bear the following legend:

"The shares represented by this certificate have not been registered under the Securities Act of 1933, as amended, or under applicable state securities laws. The shares have been acquired for investment and may not be offered, sold, transferred, pledged or otherwise disposed of without an effective registration statement under the Securities Act of 1933, as amended, and under any applicable state securities laws or an opinion of counsel acceptable to the Company that the proposed transaction will be exempt from such registration."

The foregoing legend shall be removed upon registration of the legended shares under the Securities Act of 1933, as amended, and under any applicable state laws or upon receipt of any opinion of counsel acceptable to the Company that said registration is no longer required.

The sole purpose of the agreements, warranties, representations and legend set forth in the two immediately preceding paragraphs is to prevent violations of the Securities Act of 1933, as amended, and any applicable state securities laws

It is the intention of the Company and you that this option shall, if possible, be an "Incentive Stock Option" as that term is used in Section 422(b) of the Code and the regulations thereunder. In the event this option is in any way inconsistent with the legal requirements of the Code or the regulations thereunder for an "Incentive Stock Option," this option shall be deemed automatically amended as of the date hereof to conform to such legal requirements, if such conformity may be achieved by amendment. To the extent that the number of shares subject to this option which are exercisable for the first time exceed the $100,000 limitation contained in Section 422(d) of the Code, this option will not be considered an Incentive Stock Option.

Nothing herein shall modify your status as an at-will employee of the Company. Further, nothing herein guarantees you employment for any specified period of time. This means that either you or the Company may terminate your employment at any time for any reason, with or without cause, or for no reason. You recognize that, for instance, you may terminate your employment or the Company may terminate your employment prior to the date on which your option becomes vested or exercisable. You understand that the Company has no obligation to consider or effectuate a public offering of its stock or a Change of Control.

Any dispute or disagreement between you and the Company with respect to any portion of this option (excluding Attachment A hereto) or its validity, construction, meaning, performance or your rights hereunder shall be settled by arbitration in accordance with the Commercial Arbitration Rules of the American Arbitration Association or its successor, as amended from time to time. However, prior to submission to arbitration you will attempt to resolve any disputes or disagreements with the Company over this option amicably and informally, in good faith, for a period not to exceed two weeks. Thereafter, the dispute or disagreement will be submitted to arbitration. At any time prior to a decision from the arbitrator(s) being rendered, you and the Company may resolve the dispute by settlement. You and the Company shall equally share the costs charged by the American Arbitration Association or its successor, but you and the Company shall otherwise be solely responsible for your own respective counsel fees and expenses. The decision of the arbitrator(s) shall be made in writing, setting forth the award, the reasons for the decision and award and shall be binding and conclusive on you and the Company. Further, neither you nor the Company shall appeal any such award. Judgment of a court of competent jurisdiction may be entered upon the award and may be enforced as such in accordance with the provisions of the award.

This option shall be subject to the terms of the Plan in effect on the date this option is granted, which terms are hereby incorporated herein by reference and made a part hereof. In the event of any conflict between the terms of this option and the terms of the Plan in effect on the date of this option, the terms of the Plan shall govern. This option constitutes the entire understanding between the Company and you with respect to the subject matter hereof and no amendment, supplement or waiver of this option, in whole or in part, shall be binding upon the Company unless in writing and signed by the President of the Company. This option and the performances of the parties hereunder shall be construed in accordance with and governed by the laws of the State of Pennsylvania.

In consideration of the grant to you of this option, you hereby agree to the confidentiality and non-interference provisions set forth in Attachment A hereto.

Please sign the copy of this option and return it to the Company's Secretary, thereby indicating your understanding of and agreement with its terms and conditions, **including Attachment A hereto.**

ABC, INC.

By: —————————————————————

I hereby acknowledge receipt of a copy of the foregoing stock option and the Plan, and having read them hereby signify my understanding of, and my agreement with, their terms and conditions, **including Attachment A hereto.** I accept this option in full satisfaction of any previous written or verbal promises made to me by the Company with respect to option grants.

————————————— —————————————

(Signature) (Date)

ATTACHMENT A TO STOCK OPTION

CONFIDENTIALITY AND NON-INTERFERENCE.

(a) You covenant and agree that, in consideration of the grant to you of this stock option, you will not, during your employment with the Company or at any time thereafter, except with the express prior written consent of the Company or pursuant to the lawful order of any judicial or administrative agency of government, directly or indirectly, disclose, communicate or divulge to any individual or entity, or use for the benefit of any individual or entity, any knowledge or information with respect to the conduct or details of the Company's business which you, acting reasonably, believe or should believe to be of a confidential nature and the disclosure of which not to be in the Company's interest.

(b) You covenant and agree that, in consideration of the grant to you of this stock option, you will not, during your employment with the Company, except with the express prior written consent of the Company, directly or indirectly, whether as employee, owner, partner, member, consultant, agent, director, officer, shareholder or in any other capacity, engage in or assist any individual or entity to engage in any act or action which you, acting reasonably, believe or should believe would be harmful or inimical to the interests of the Company.

(c) You covenant and agree that, in consideration of the grant to you of this stock option, you will not, for a period of two years after your employment with the Company ceases for any reason whatsoever (whether voluntary or not), except with the express prior written consent of the Company, directly or indirectly, whether as employee, owner, partner, member, consultant, agent, director, officer, shareholder or in any other capacity, for your own account or for the benefit of any individual or entity, (i) solicit any customer of the Company for business which would result in such customer terminating their relationship with the Company; or (ii) solicit or induce any individual or entity which is an employee of the Company to leave the Company or to otherwise terminate their relationship with the Company.

(d) The parties agree that any breach by you of any of the covenants or agreements contained in this Attachment A will result in irreparable injury to the Company for which money damages could not adequately compensate the Company and therefore, in the event of any such breach, the Company shall be entitled (in addition to any other rights and remedies which it may have at law or in equity) to have an injunction issued by any competent court enjoining and restraining you and/or any other individual or entity involved therein from continuing such breach. The existence of any claim or cause of action which you may have against the Company or any other individual or entity shall not constitute a defense or bar to the enforcement of such covenants. If the Company is obliged to resort to the courts for the enforcement of any of the covenants or agreements contained in this Attachment A, or if such covenants or agreements are otherwise the subject of litigation between the parties, and the Company prevails in such enforcement or litigation, then the term of such covenants and agreements shall be extended for a period of time equal to the period of such breach, which extension shall commence on the later of (a) the date on which the original (unextended) term of such covenants and agreements is scheduled to terminate or (b) the date of the final court order (without further right of appeal) enforcing such covenant or agreement.

(e)   If any portion of the covenants or agreements contained in this Attachment A, or the application hereof, is construed to be invalid or unenforceable, the other portions of such covenant(s) or agreement(s) or the application thereof shall not be affected and shall be given full force and effect without regard to the invalid or enforceable portions to the fullest extent possible. If any covenant or agreement in this Attachment A is held unenforceable because of the area covered, the duration thereof, or the scope thereof, then the court making such determination shall have the power to reduce the area and/or duration and/or limit the scope thereof, and the covenant or agreement shall then be enforceable in its reduced form.

(f)   For purposes of this Attachment A, the term "the Company" shall include the Company, any successor to the Company and all present and future direct and indirect subsidiaries and affiliates of the Company.

[Remaining Appendix Omitted]

EXHIBIT II

NON-QUALIFIED STOCK OPTION FOR OFFICERS AND OTHER KEY EMPLOYEES

To:

Name

Address

Date of Grant:

You are hereby granted an option, effective as of the date hereof, to purchase _____ shares of common stock, no par value ("Common Stock"), of ABC, Inc., a Pennsylvania corporation (the "Company"), at a price of $_____ per share pursuant to the Company's Stock Option Plan (the "Plan").

This option shall terminate and is not exercisable after ten years from the date of its grant (the "Scheduled Termination Date"), except if terminated earlier as hereafter provided.

Your option may not be exercised before the Scheduled Termination Date unless there is an Acceleration Event (as hereafter defined), in which case this option shall become immediately exercisable, except as hereafter provided. An "Acceleration Event" refers to a date which is one year after the earlier of the following: (a) the first closing date for the initial public offering ("IPO") of the Common Stock of the Company (or of a parent corporation) in which the Company (or such parent corporation) raises at least $15 million, or (b) the date of a "Change of Control" (as defined below).

A "Change in Control" shall be deemed to have occurred upon the happening of any of the following events, provided that such event, in addition, unless an exemption is otherwise available, otherwise satisfies the requirements of Section 409A of the Internal Revenue Code of 1986 as amended ("Code") which are set forth in the Appendix to this Agreement:

(iv) The closing of a sale of more than 50% of the outstanding voting stock of the Company to an unaffiliated third party;

(v) The closing of a sale of substantially all of the assets of the Company to an unaffiliated third party; or

(vi) Any other event deemed by the Company in its sole discretion to constitute a "Change in Control" of the Company, provided such event satisfies the requirements of Section 409A of the Code.

An "unaffiliated third party" does not include either (i) an entity which is directly or indirectly controlled by an individual member of the same family that controls the Company or (ii) an individual who is a member of the same family that controls the Company. An individual is considered a member of the same family that controls the Company if such individual is related to the same family that controls the Company by blood, marriage, adoption, not more remote than second cousin. In the event of a dispute as to what constitutes a "Change in Control", the decision of the Company shall be final, binding and conclusive unless there is clear and convincing evidence that it was not made in good faith.

Notwithstanding the foregoing, if on the date of an Acceleration Event, you have not been employed by the Company for a total of at least three (3) years, this option will not be exercisable in full on the date of an Acceleration Event, but instead shall be exercisable as follows: (a) if on the date of an Acceleration Event you have been employed by the Company for a total of two (2) or more years, this option will be exercisable for two-thirds of the total number of shares then subject to this option, and the remaining one-third of the total number of shares then subject to this option will become exercisable after you have been employed by the Company for a total of three (3) years; (b) if on the date of an Acceleration Event you have been employed by the Company for a total of one (1) year or more and less than two (2) years, this option will be exercisable for one-third of the total number of shares then subject to this option and an additional one-third each of the total number of shares then subject to this option shall become exercisable when you have been employed by the Company for two (2) years and three (3) years, respectively; (c) if on the date of an Acceleration Event you have been employed by the Company for a total of less than one (1) year, this option will not be exercisable until you have been employed by the Company for a total of one (1) year, at which time this option will be exercisable for one-third of the total number of shares then subject to this option and an additional one-third each of the total number of shares then subject this option shall become exercisable when you have been employed by the Company for two (2) years and three (3) years, respectively.

In the event of an IPO of the Common Stock of a parent corporation of the Company, and provided such parent corporation assumes the obligations of the Company under this Plan, this option shall thereupon pertain solely to the Common Stock of such parent corporation and the Company shall have no obligation whatsoever hereunder. In the event of an IPO in which the Company or its parent corporation has two classes of Common Stock, only one of which is issued to the public in the IPO, this option shall pertain solely to the class of Common Stock issued to the public in the IPO.

You may exercise your option by giving written notice to the Secretary of the Company on forms supplied by the Company at its then principal executive office, accompanied by payment of the option price for the total number of shares you specify that you wish to purchase. The payment may be in any of the following forms: (a) cash, which may be evidenced by a check and includes cash received from a stock brokerage firm in a so-called "cashless exercise"; (b) (unless prohibited by the Committee) certificates representing shares of Common Stock of the Company, which will be valued by the Secretary of the Company at the fair market value per share of the Company's Common Stock (as determined in accordance with the Plan) on the date of delivery of such certificates to the Company, accompanied by an assignment of the stock to the Company; or (c) (unless prohibited by the Committee) any combination of cash and Common Stock of the Company valued as provided in clause (b). The use of the so-called "attestation procedure" to exercise a stock option may be permitted by the Committee. Any assignment of stock shall be in a form and substance satisfactory to the Secretary of the Company, including guarantees of signature(s) and payment of all transfer taxes if the Secretary deems such guarantees necessary or desirable.

Your option will, to the extent not previously exercised by you, terminate three months after the date on which your employment by the

Company or a Company subsidiary corporation is terminated (whether such termination be voluntary or involuntary) other than by reason of disability as defined in Section 22(e)(3) of the Internal Revenue Code of 1986, as amended (the "Code"), and the regulations thereunder, or death, in which case your option will terminate one year from the date of termination of employment due to disability or death (but in no event later than the Scheduled Termination Date). After the date your employment is terminated, as aforesaid, you may exercise this option only for the number of shares which you had a right to purchase and did not purchase on the date your employment terminated. Provided you are willing to continue your employment for the Company or a successor after a Change of Control at the same compensation you enjoyed immediately prior to such Change of Control, if your employment is involuntarily terminated without cause after a Change of Control, you may exercise this option for the number of shares you would have had a right to purchase on the date of an Acceleration Event. If you are employed by a Company subsidiary corporation, your employment shall be deemed to have terminated on the date your employer ceases to be a Company subsidiary corporation, unless you are on that date transferred to the Company or another Company subsidiary corporation. Your employment shall not be deemed to have terminated if you are transferred from the Company to a Company subsidiary corporation, or vice versa, or from one Company subsidiary corporation to another Company subsidiary corporation.

If you die while employed by the Company or a Company subsidiary corporation, your executor or administrator, as the case may be, may, at any time within one year after the date of your death (but in no event later than the Scheduled Termination Date), exercise the option as to any shares which you had a right to purchase and did not purchase during your lifetime. If your employment with the Company or a Company parent or subsidiary corporation is terminated by reason of your becoming disabled (within the meaning of Section 22(e)(3) of the Code and the regulations thereunder), you or your legal guardian or custodian may at any time within one year after the date of such termination (but in no event later than the Scheduled Termination Date), exercise the option as to any shares which you had a right to purchase and did not purchase prior to such termination. Your executor, administrator, guardian or custodian must present proof of his authority satisfactory to the Company prior to being allowed to exercise this option.

In the event of any change in the outstanding shares of the Common Stock of the Company by reason of a stock dividend, stock split, combination of shares, recapitalization, merger, consolidation, transfer of assets, reorganization, conversion or what the Committee deems in its sole discretion to be similar circumstances, the number and kind of shares subject to this option and the option price of such shares shall be appropriately adjusted in a manner to be determined in the sole discretion of the Committee.

In the event of a liquidation or proposed liquidation of the Company, including (but not limited to) a transfer of assets followed by a liquidation of the Company, or in the event of a Change of Control (as previously defined) or proposed Change of Control, the Committee shall have the right to require you to exercise this option upon thirty (30) days prior written notice to you. If at the time such written notice is given this option is not otherwise exercisable, the written notice will set forth your right to exercise this option even though it is not otherwise exercisable. In the event this option is not exercised by you within the thirty (30) day period set forth in such written notice, this option shall terminate on the last day of such thirty (30) day period, notwithstanding anything to the contrary contained in this option.

This option is not transferable otherwise than by will or the laws of descent and distribution, and is exercisable during your lifetime only by you, including, for this purpose, your legal guardian or custodian in the event of disability. Until the option price has been paid in full pursuant to due exercise of this option and the purchased shares are delivered to you, you do not have any rights as a shareholder of the Company. The Company reserves the right not to deliver to you the shares purchased by virtue of the exercise of this option during any period of time in which the Company deems, in its sole discretion, that such delivery would violate a federal, state, local or securities exchange rule, regulation or law.

Notwithstanding anything to the contrary contained herein, this option is not exercisable until all the following events occur and during the following periods of time:

(g)   Until the Plan pursuant to which this option is granted is approved by the shareholders of the Company in the manner prescribed by the Code and the regulations thereunder;

(h)   until this option and the optioned shares are approved and/or registered with such federal, state and local regulatory bodies or agencies and securities exchanges as the Company may deem necessary or desirable;

(i) During any period of time in which the Company deems that the exercisability of this option, the offer to sell the shares optioned hereunder, or the sale thereof, may violate a federal, state, local or securities exchange rule, regulation or law, or may cause the Company to be legally obligated to issue or sell more shares than the Company is legally entitled to issue or sell;

(j) Until you have paid or made suitable arrangements to pay (which may include payment through the surrender of Common Stock, unless prohibited by the Committee) (i) all federal, state and local income tax withholding required to be withheld by the Company in connection with the option exercise and (ii) the employee's portion of other federal, state and local payroll and other taxes due in connection with the option exercise; or

(k) Until you have executed such shareholder agreements as shall be required by the Company. Such shareholder agreements may, at the Company's option, include (among other provisions) provisions requiring you to (i) enter into any "lock-up" agreements required by underwriters, (ii) voting trust agreements, (iii) grant to the Company or its nominees an option to repurchase the stock, (iv) not sell, pledge or otherwise dispose of the stock without the consent of the Company, (v) maintain any Subchapter S elections made by the Company, (vi) grant rights of first refusal to the Company or its nominees with respect to the stock, and (vii) join in any sale of a majority or all of the outstanding stock of the Company.

The following two paragraphs shall be applicable if, on the date of exercise of this option, the Common Stock to be purchased pursuant to such exercise has not been registered under the Securities Act of 1933, as amended, and under applicable state securities laws, and shall continue to be applicable for so long as such registration has not occurred:

(a) The optionee hereby agrees, warrants and represents that he will acquire the Common Stock to be issued hereunder for his own account for investment purposes only, and not with a view to, or in connection with, any resale or other distribution of any of such shares, except as hereafter permitted. The optionee further agrees that he will not at any time make any offer, sale, transfer, pledge or other disposition of such Common Stock to be issued hereunder without an effective registration statement under the Securities Act of 1933, as amended, and under any applicable state securities laws or an opinion of counsel acceptable to the Company to the effect that the proposed transaction will be exempt from such registration. The optionee shall execute such instruments, representations, acknowledgements and agreements as the Company may, in its sole discretion, deem advisable to avoid any violation of federal, state, local or securities exchange rule, regulation or law.

(b) The certificates for Common Stock to be issued to the optionee hereunder shall bear the following legend:

> "The shares represented by this certificate have not been registered under the Securities Act of 1933, as amended, or under applicable state securities laws. The shares have been acquired for investment and may not be offered, sold, transferred, pledged or otherwise disposed of without an effective registration statement under the Securities Act of 1933, as amended, and under any applicable state securities laws or an opinion of counsel acceptable to the Company that the proposed transaction will be exempt from such registration."

The foregoing legend shall be removed upon registration of the legended shares under the Securities Act of 1933, as amended, and under any applicable state laws or upon receipt of any opinion of counsel acceptable to the Company that said registration is no longer required.

The sole purpose of the agreements, warranties, representations and legend set forth in the two immediately preceding paragraphs is to prevent violations of the Securities Act of 1933, as amended, and any applicable state securities laws.

It is the intention of the Company and you that this option shall not be an "Incentive Stock Option" as that term is used in Section 422(b) of the Code and the regulations thereunder.

Nothing herein shall modify your status as an at-will employee of the Company. Further, nothing herein guarantees you employment for any specified period of time. This means that either you or the Company may terminate your employment at any time for any reason, with or without cause, or for no reason. You recognize that, for instance, you may terminate your employment or the Company may terminate your employment prior to the date on which your option becomes vested or exercisable. You understand that the Company has no obligation to consider or effectuate a public offering of its stock or a Change of Control.

Any dispute or disagreement between you and the Company with respect to any portion of this option (excluding Attachment A hereto) or its validity, construction, meaning, performance or your rights hereunder shall be settled by arbitration in accordance with the Commercial Arbitration Rules of the American Arbitration Association or its successor, as amended from time to time. However, prior to submission to arbitration you will attempt to resolve any disputes or disagreements with the Company over this option amicably and informally, in good faith, for a period not to exceed two weeks. Thereafter, the dispute or disagreement will be submitted to arbitration. At any time prior to a decision from the arbitrator(s) being rendered, you and the Company may resolve the dispute by settlement. You and the Company shall equally share the costs charged by the American Arbitration Association or its successor, but you and the Company shall otherwise be solely responsible for your own respective counsel fees and expenses. The decision of the arbitrator(s) shall be made in writing, setting forth the award, the reasons for the decision and award and shall be binding and conclusive on you and the Company. Further, neither you nor the Company shall appeal any such award. Judgment of a court of competent jurisdiction may be entered upon the award and may be enforced as such in accordance with the provisions of the award.

This option shall be subject to the terms of the Plan in effect on the date this option is granted, which terms are hereby incorporated herein by reference and made a part hereof. In the event of any conflict between the terms of this option and the terms of the Plan in effect on the date of this option, the terms of the Plan shall govern. This option constitutes the entire understanding between the Company and you with respect to the subject matter hereof and no amendment, supplement or waiver of this option, in whole or in part, shall be binding upon the Company unless in writing and signed by the President of the Company. This option and the performances of the parties hereunder shall be construed in accordance with and governed by the laws of the State of Pennsylvania.

In consideration of the grant to you of this option, you hereby agree to the confidentiality and non-interference provisions set forth in Attachment A hereto.

Please sign the copy of this option and return it to the Company's Secretary, thereby indicating your understanding of and agreement with its terms and conditions, **including Attachment A hereto.**

ABC, INC.

By:————————————————————

I hereby acknowledge receipt of a copy of the foregoing stock option and, having read it hereby signify my understanding of, and my agreement with, its terms and conditions, **including Attachment A hereto.**

_____   _____

(Signature)   (Date)

ATTACHMENT A TO STOCK OPTION

CONFIDENTIALITY AND NON-INTERFERENCE.

(a)   You covenant and agree that, in consideration of the grant to you of this stock option, you will not, during your employment with the Company or at any time thereafter, except with the express prior written consent of the Company or pursuant to the lawful order of any judicial or administrative agency of government, directly or indirectly, disclose, communicate or divulge to any individual or entity, or use for the benefit of any individual or entity, any knowledge or information with respect to the conduct or details of the Company's business which you, acting reasonably, believe or should believe to be of a confidential nature and the disclosure of which not to be in the Company's interest.

(b)   You covenant and agree that, in consideration of the grant to you of this stock option, you will not, during your employment with the Company except with the express prior written consent of the Company, directly or indirectly, whether as employee, owner, partner, member, consultant, agent, director, officer, shareholder or in any other capacity, engage in or assist any individual or entity to engage in any act or action which you, acting reasonably, believe or should believe would be harmful or inimical to the interests of the Company.

(c)   You covenant and agree that, in consideration of the grant to you of this stock option, you will not, for a period of two years after your employment with the Company ceases for any reason whatsoever (whether voluntary or not), except with the express prior written consent of the Company, directly or indirectly, whether as employee, owner, partner, member, consultant, agent, director, officer, shareholder or in any other capacity, for your own account or for the benefit of any individual or entity, (i) solicit any customer of the Company for business which would result in such customer terminating their relationship with the Company; or (ii) solicit or induce any individual or entity which is an employee of the Company to leave the Company or to otherwise terminate their relationship with the Company.

(d)   The parties agree that any breach by you of any of the covenants or agreements contained in this Attachment A will result in irreparable injury to the Company for which money damages could not adequately compensate the Company and therefore, in the event of any such breach, the Company shall be entitled (in addition to any other rights and remedies which it may have at law or in equity) to have an injunction issued by any competent court enjoining and restraining you and/or any other individual or entity involved therein from continuing such breach. The existence of any claim or cause of action which you may have against the Company or any other individual or entity shall not constitute a defense or bar to the enforcement of such covenants. If the Company is obliged to resort to the courts for the enforcement of any of the covenants or agreements contained in this Attachment A, or if such covenants or agreements are otherwise the subject of litigation between the parties, and the Company prevails in such enforcement or litigation, then the term of such covenants and agreements shall be extended for a period of time equal to the period of such breach, which extension shall commence on the later of (a) the date on which the original (unextended) term of such covenants and agreements is scheduled to terminate or (b) the date of the final court order (without further right of appeal) enforcing such covenant or agreement.

(e) If any portion of the covenants or agreements contained in this Attachment A, or the application hereof, is construed to be invalid or unenforceable, the other portions of such covenant(s) or agreement(s) or the application thereof shall not be affected and shall be given full force and effect without regard to the invalid or enforceable portions to the fullest extent possible. If any covenant or agreement in this Attachment A is held unenforceable because of the area covered, the duration thereof, or the scope thereof, then the court making such determination shall have the power to reduce the area and/or duration and/or limit the scope thereof, and the covenant or agreement shall then be enforceable in its reduced form.

(f) For purposes of this Attachment A, the term "the Company" shall include the Company, any successor to the Company and all present and future direct and indirect subsidiaries and affiliates of the Company.

[Remaining Appendix Omitted]

EXHIBIT III

NON-QUALIFIED STOCK OPTION FOR DIRECTORS AND IMPORTANT CONSULTANTS

To:

Name

Address

Date of Grant:

You are hereby granted an option, effective as of the date hereof, to purchase _____ shares of common stock, no par value ("Common Stock"), of ABC, Inc., a Pennsylvania corporation (the "Company"), at a price of $_____ per share pursuant to the Company's Stock Option Plan (the "Plan").

This option shall terminate and is not exercisable after ten years from the date of Its grant (the "Scheduled Termination Date"), except if terminated earlier as hereafter provided.

Your option may not be exercised before the Scheduled Termination Date unless there is an Acceleration Event (as hereafter defined), in which case this option shall become immediately exercisable, except as hereafter provided. An "Acceleration Event" refers to a date which is one year after the earlier of the following: (a) the first closing date for the initial public offering ("IPO") of the Common Stock of the Company (or of a parent corporation) in which the Company (or such parent corporation) raises at least $15 million, or (b) the date of a "Change of Control" (as defined below).

A "Change in Control" shall be deemed to have occurred upon the happening of any of the following events, provided that such event, in addition, unless an exemption is otherwise available, otherwise satisfies the requirements of Section 409A of the Internal Revenue Code of 1986 as amended ("Code") which are set forth in the Appendix to this Agreement:

(vii) The closing of a sale of more than 50% of the outstanding voting stock of the Company to an unaffiliated third party;

(viii) The closing of a sale of substantially all of the assets of the Company to an unaffiliated third party; or

(ix) Any other event deemed by the Company in its sole discretion to constitute a "Change in Control" of the Company, provided such event satisfies the requirements of Section 409A of the Code.

An "unaffiliated third party" does not include either (i) an entity which is directly or indirectly controlled by an individual member of the same family that controls the Company or (ii) an individual who is a member of the same family that controls the Company. An individual is considered a member of the same family that controls the Company if such individual is related to the same family that controls the Company by blood, marriage, adoption, not more remote than second cousin. In the event of a dispute as to what constitutes a "Change in Control", the decision of the Company shall be final, binding and conclusive unless there is clear and convincing evidence that it was not made in good faith.

Notwithstanding the foregoing, if on the date of an Acceleration Event, you have not been a director of, or consultant to, the Company or any of its subsidiaries or affiliates for a combined total of at least three (3) years, this option will not be exercisable in full on the date of an Acceleration Event, but instead shall be exercisable as follows: (a) if on the date of an Acceleration Event you have been a director of, or consultant to, the Company or any of its subsidiaries or affiliates for a combined total of two (2) or more years, this option will be exercisable for two-thirds of the total number of shares then subject to this option, and the remaining one-third of the total number of shares then subject to this option will become exercisable after you have been a director of, or consultant to, the Company or any of its subsidiaries or affiliates for a combined total of three (3) years; (b) if on the date of an Acceleration Event you have been a director of, or consultant to, the Company or any of its subsidiaries or affiliates for a combined total of more than one (1) year and less than two (2) years, this option will be exercisable for one-third of the total number of shares then subject to this option and an additional one-third each of the total number of shares then subject to this option shall become exercisable when you have been a director of, or consultant to, the Company or any of its subsidiaries or affiliates for two (2) years and three (3) years, respectively; (c) if on the date of an Acceleration Event you have been a director of, or consultant to, the Company or any of its subsidiaries or affiliates for a combined total of less than one (1) year, this option will not be exercisable until you have been a director of, or consultant to, the Company and the any of its subsidiaries or affiliates for a combined total of one (1) year, at which time this option will be exercisable for one-third of the total number of shares then subject to this option and an additional one-third each of the total number of shares then subject this option shall become exercisable when you have been a director of, or consultant to, the Company or any of its subsidiaries or affiliates for two (2) years and three (3) years, respectively.

In the event of an IPO of the Common Stock of a parent corporation of the Company, and provided such parent corporation assumes the obligations of the Company under this Plan, this option shall thereupon pertain solely to the Common Stock of such parent corporation and the Company shall have no obligation whatsoever hereunder. In the event of an IPO in which the Company or its parent corporation has two classes of Common Stock, only one of which is issued to the public in the IPO, this option shall pertain solely to the class of Common Stock issued to the public in the IPO.

You may exercise your option by giving written notice to the Secretary of the Company on forms supplied by the Company at its then principal executive office, accompanied by payment of the option price for the total number of shares you specify that you wish to purchase. The payment may be in any of the following forms: (a) cash, which may be evidenced by a check and includes cash received from a stock brokerage firm in a so-called "cashless exercise", (b) (unless prohibited by the Committee) certificates representing shares of Common Stock of the Company, which will be valued by the Secretary of the Company at the fair market value per share of the Company's Common Stock (as determined in accordance with the Plan) on the date of delivery of such certificates to the Company, accompanied by an assignment of the stock to the Company; or (c) (unless prohibited by the Committee) any combination of cash and Common Stock of the Company valued as provided in clause (b). The use of the so-called "attestation procedure" to exercise a stock option may be permitted by the Committee. Any assignment of stock shall be in a form and substance satisfactory to the Secretary of the

Company, including guarantees of signature(s) and payment of all transfer taxes if the Secretary deems such guarantees necessary or desirable.

Your option will, to the extent not previously exercised by you, terminate three months after the date on which you cease for any reason to be a director of, or consultant to, the Company or a subsidiary corporation (whether by death, disability, resignation, removal, failure to be reappointed, reelected or otherwise, or the expiration of any consulting arrangement, and regardless of whether the failure to continue as a director or consultant was for cause or without cause or otherwise), but in no event later than ten years from the date this option is granted. After the date you cease to be a director or consultant, you may exercise this option only for the number of shares which you had a right to purchase and did not purchase on the date you ceased to be a director or consultant. Provided you are willing to continue your directorship or consultancy for the Company or a successor after a Change of Control at the same compensation you enjoyed immediately prior to such Change of Control, if your directorship or consultancy is involuntarily terminated without cause after a Change of Control, you may exercise this option for the number of shares you would have had a right to purchase on the date of an Acceleration Event. If you are a director of, or consultant to, a subsidiary corporation, your directorship or consultancy shall be deemed to have terminated on the date such company ceases to be a subsidiary corporation, unless you are also a director of, or consultant to, the Company or another subsidiary corporation, or on that date became a director of, or consultant to, the Company or another subsidiary corporation. Your directorship or consultancy shall not be deemed to have terminated if you cease being a director of, or consultant to, the Company or a subsidiary corporation but are or concurrently therewith become a director of, or consultant to, the Company or another subsidiary corporation.

In the event of any change in the outstanding shares of the Common Stock of the Company by reason of a stock dividend, stock split, combination of shares, recapitalization, merger, consolidation, transfer of assets, reorganization, conversion or what the Committee deems in its sole discretion to be similar circumstances, the number and kind of shares subject to this option and the option price of such shares shall be appropriately adjusted in a manner to be determined in the sole discretion of the Committee.

In the event of a liquidation or proposed liquidation of the Company, including (but not limited to) a transfer of assets followed by a liquidation of the Company, or in the event of a Change of Control (as previously defined) or proposed Change of Control, the Committee shall have the right to require you to exercise this option upon thirty (30) days prior written notice to you. If at the time such written notice is given this option is not otherwise exercisable, the written notice will set forth your right to exercise this option even though it is not otherwise exercisable. In the event this option is not exercised by you within the thirty (30) day period set forth in such written notice, this option shall terminate on the last day of such thirty (30) day period, notwithstanding anything to the contrary contained in this option.

This option is not transferable otherwise than by will or the laws of descent and distribution, and is exercisable during your lifetime only by you, including, for this purpose, your legal guardian or custodian in the event of disability. Until the option price has been paid in full pursuant to due exercise of this option and the purchased shares are delivered to you, you do not have any rights as a shareholder of the Company. The Company reserves the right not to deliver to you the shares purchased by virtue of the exercise of this option during any period of time in which the Company deems, in its sole discretion, that such delivery would violate a federal, state, local or securities exchange rule, regulation or law.

Notwithstanding anything to the contrary contained herein, this option is not exercisable until all the following events occur and during the following periods of time:

(g)   Until the Plan pursuant to which this option is granted is approved by the shareholders of the Company in the manner prescribed by the Code and the regulations thereunder;

(h)   Until this option and the optioned shares are approved and/or registered with such federal, state and local regulatory bodies or agencies and securities exchanges as the Company may deem necessary or desirable;

(i)   During any period of time in which the Company deems that the exercisability of this option, the offer to sell the shares optioned hereunder, or the sale thereof, may violate a federal, state, local or securities exchange rule, regulation or law, or may cause the Company to be legally obligated to issue or sell more shares than the Company is legally entitled to issue or sell;

(j)   Until you have paid or made suitable arrangements to pay (which may include payment through the surrender of Common Stock, unless prohibited by the Committee) (i) all federal, state and local income tax withholding required to be withheld by the Company in connection with the option exercise and (ii) your portion of other federal, state and local payroll and other taxes due in connection with the option exercise; or

(k) Until you have executed such shareholder agreements as shall be required by the Company. Such shareholder agreements may, at the Company's option, include (among other provisions) provisions requiring you to (i) enter into any "lock-up" agreements required by underwriters, (ii) voting trust agreements, (iii) grant to the Company or its nominees an option to repurchase the stock, (iv) not sell, pledge or otherwise dispose of the stock without the consent of the Company, (v) maintain any Subchapter S elections made by the Company, (vi) grant rights of first refusal to the Company or its nominees with respect to the stock, and (vii) join in any sale of a majority or all of the outstanding stock of the Company.

The following two paragraphs shall be applicable if, on the date of exercise of this option, the Common Stock to be purchased pursuant to such exercise has not been registered under the Securities Act of 1933, as amended, and under applicable state securities laws, and shall continue to be applicable for so long as such registration has not occurred:

(a) The optionee hereby agrees, warrants and represents that he will acquire the Common Stock to be issued hereunder for his own account for investment purposes only, and not with a view to, or in connection with, any resale or other distribution of any of such shares, except as hereafter permitted. The optionee further agrees that he will not at any time make any offer, sale, transfer, pledge or other disposition of such Common Stock to be issued hereunder without an effective registration statement under the Securities Act of 1933, as amended, and under any applicable state securities laws or an opinion of counsel acceptable to the Company to the effect that the proposed transaction will be exempt from such registration. The optionee shall execute such instruments, representations, acknowledgments and agreements as the Company may, in its sole discretion, deem advisable to avoid any violation of federal, state, local or securities exchange rule, regulation or law.

(b) The certificates for Common Stock to be issued to the optionee hereunder shall bear the following legend:

"The shares represented by this certificate have not been registered under the Securities Act of 1933, as amended, or under applicable state securities laws. The shares have been acquired for investment and may not be offered, sold, transferred, pledged or otherwise disposed of without an effective registration statement under the Securities Act of 1933, as amended, and under any applicable state securities laws or an opinion of counsel acceptable to the Company that the proposed transaction will be exempt from such registration."

The foregoing legend shall be removed upon registration of the legended shares under the Securities Act of 1933, as amended, and under any applicable state laws or upon receipt of any opinion of counsel acceptable to the Company that said registration is no longer required.

The sole purpose of the agreements, warranties, representations and legend set forth in the two immediately preceding paragraphs is to prevent violations of the Securities Act of 1933, as amended, and any applicable state securities laws.

It is the intention of the Company and you that this option shall not be an "Incentive Stock Option" as that term is used in Section 422(b) of the Code and the regulations thereunder.

Nothing herein guarantees your term as a director of, or consultant to, the Company for any specified period of time. This means that either you or the Company may terminate your relationship with the Company at any time for any reason, with or without cause, or for no reason. You recognize that, for instance, the Company may terminate your relationship with the Company prior to the date on which your option becomes vested or exercisable. You understand that the Company has no obligation to consider or effectuate a public offering of its stock or a Change of Control.

Any dispute or disagreement between you and the Company with respect to any portion of this option (excluding Attachment A hereto) or its validity, construction, meaning, performance or your rights hereunder shall be settled by arbitration in accordance with the Commercial Arbitration Rules of the American Arbitration Association or its successor, as amended from time to time. However, prior to submission to arbitration you will attempt to resolve any disputes or disagreements with the Company over this option amicably and informally, in good faith, for a period not to exceed two weeks. Thereafter, the dispute or disagreement will be submitted to arbitration. At any time prior to a decision from the arbitrator(s) being rendered, you and the Company may resolve the dispute by settlement. You and the Company shall equally share the costs charged by the American Arbitration Association or its successor, but you and the Company shall otherwise be solely responsible for your own respective counsel fees and expenses. The decision of the arbitrator(s) shall be made in writing, setting forth the award, the reasons for the decision and award and shall be binding and conclusive on you and the Company. Further, neither you nor the Company shall appeal any such award. Judgment of a court of competent jurisdiction may be entered upon the award and may be enforced as such in accordance with the provisions of the award.

This option shall be subject to the terms of the Plan in effect on the date this option is granted, which terms are hereby incorporated herein by reference and made a part hereof. In the event of any conflict between the terms of this option and the terms of the Plan in effect on the date of this option, the terms of the Plan shall govern. This option constitutes the entire understanding between the Company and you with respect to the subject matter hereof and no amendment, supplement or waiver of this option, in whole or in part, shall be binding upon the Company unless in writing and signed by the President of the Company. This option and the performances of the parties hereunder shall be construed in accordance with and governed by the laws of the State of Pennsylvania.

In consideration of the grant to you of this option, you hereby agree to the confidentiality and non-interference provisions set forth in Attachment A hereto.

Please sign the copy of this option and return it to the Company's Secretary, thereby indicating your understanding of and agreement with its terms and conditions, **including Attachment A hereto.**

ABC, Inc.

By:————————————————————

I hereby acknowledge receipt of a copy of the foregoing stock option and, having read it hereby signify my understanding of, and my agreement with, its terms and conditions, **including Attachment A hereto.**

————————————————   ————————————————
(Signature)   (Date)

ATTACHMENT A TO STOCK OPTION

CONFIDENTIALITY AND NON-INTERFERENCE.

(a)   You covenant and agree that, in consideration of the grant to you of this stock option, you will not, during your term as a director of, or a consultant to, the Company or at any time thereafter, except with the express prior written consent of the Company or pursuant to the lawful order of any judicial or administrative agency of government, directly or indirectly, disclose, communicate or divulge to any individual or entity, or use for the benefit of any individual or entity, any knowledge or information with respect to the conduct or details of the Company's business which you, acting reasonably, believe or should believe to be of a confidential nature and the disclosure of which not to be in the Company's interest.

(b)   You covenant and agree that, in consideration of the grant to you of this stock option, you will not, during your term as a director of, or a consultant to, the Company, except with the express prior written consent of the Company, directly or indirectly, whether as employee, owner, partner, member, consultant, agent, director, officer, shareholder or in any other capacity, engage in or assist any individual or entity to engage in any act or action which you, acting reasonably, believe or should believe would be harmful or inimical to the interests of the Company.

(c)   You covenant and agree that, in consideration of the grant to you of this stock option, you will not, for a period of two years after your term as a director of, or a consultant to, the Company ceases for any reason whatsoever (whether voluntary or not), except with the express prior written consent of the Company, directly or indirectly, whether as employee, owner, partner, member, consultant, agent, director, officer, shareholder or in any other capacity, for your own account or for the benefit of any individual or entity, (i) solicit any customer of the Company for business which would result in such customer terminating their relationship with the Company; or (ii) solicit or induce any individual or entity which is an employee of the Company to leave the Company or to otherwise terminate their relationship with the Company.

(d)   The parties agree that any breach by you of any of the covenants or agreements contained in this Attachment A will result in irreparable injury to the Company for which money damages could not adequately compensate the Company and therefore, in the event of any such breach, the Company shall be entitled (in addition to any other rights and remedies which it may have at law or in equity) to have an injunction issued by any competent court enjoining and restraining you and/or any other individual or entity involved therein from continuing such breach. The existence of any claim or cause of action which you may have against the Company or any other individual or entity shall not constitute a defense or bar to the enforcement of such covenants. If the Company is obliged to resort to the courts for the enforcement of any of the covenants or agreements contained in this Attachment A, or if such covenants or agreements are otherwise the subject of litigation between the parties, and the Company prevails in such enforcement or litigation, then the term of such covenants and agreements shall be extended for a period of time equal to the period of such breach, which extension shall commence on the later of (a) the date on which the original (unextended) term of such covenants and agreements is scheduled to terminate or (b) the date of the final court order (without further right of appeal) enforcing such covenant or agreement.

(e)   If any portion of the covenants or agreements contained in this Attachment A, or the application hereof, is construed to be invalid or unenforceable, the other portions of such covenant(s) or agreement(s) or the application thereof shall not be affected and shall be given full force and effect without regard to the invalid or enforceable portions to the fullest extent possible. If any covenant or agreement in this Attachment A is held unenforceable because of the area covered, the duration thereof, or the scope thereof, then the court making such determination shall have the power to reduce the area and/or duration and/or limit the scope thereof, and the covenant or agreement shall then be enforceable in its reduced form.

(f)   For purposes of this Attachment A, the term "the Company" shall include the Company, any successor to the Company and all present and future direct and indirect subsidiaries and affiliates of the Company.

[Remaining Appendix Omitted]

Notes

Introduction

1. D. Mattioli, "Recession Spells Ed for many Family Businesses," *The Wall Street Journal*, October 6, 2009; *Family Business Statistics*, American Management Services, Inc., http://www.amserv.com.com/familystatistics.html
2. Ronald C. Anderson and David M. Reeb, *Founding-Family Ownership and Firm performance: Evidence from the S&P 500*, 58 J. FIN. 1301, 1302 (2003).
3. J. Lee, "Impact of Family Relationships on Attitudes of the Second Generation in Family Business," *Family Business Review*, vol. XIX, no. 3, September 2006, p. 175.
4. Hutcheson J. O. (2002). "Tales from the Family Crypt: Are you guilty of believing any of these widespread myths about family businesses?" *Financial Planning*, Oct 1, pp. 119–120.
5. Ronald W. Masulis, Peter Kien Pham and Jason Zein, Pyramids: Empirical Evidence on the Costs and Benefits of Family Business Groups around the World, *European Corporate Governance Institute (ECGI) 2009, http://ssrn.com/abstract_id=1363878*
6. Gersick, Davis, Hampton, Lansberg "Generation To Generation: Life Cycles of the Family Business" (Harvard Business School Press—1997).
7. G., Muske and M Fitzgerald, "A Panel Study of Copreneurs In Business: Who Enters, Continues, and Exits?" *Family Business Review*, vol. XIX, no. 3, September 2006, p. 193.
8. Some have suggested that there should be a sixth category called the "Family Syndicate." However, on analysis, the family syndicate is generally nothing more than a cousin consortium consisting of more distant cousins and possibly other relatives.
9. R. Chittoor and R. Das, "Professionalization of Management and Succession Performance A Vital Linkage," *Family Business Review* (Vol. XX, No. 1, March 2007).

1   Succession Planning

1. Kets and Vries, M.F.R. (1993), "The Dynamics of Family Controlled Firms; the Good News and the Bad News," *Organizational Dynamics*. 21, Winter, 59–71; Ward, J.L. (1987), *Keeping the Family Business Healthy*, San Francisco, CA: Jossey-Bass. Matthews, C., Moore, T.W. Fialko, A.S. (1999), Succession in family firm: A cognitive categorization perspective, *Family Business Review*, 12(2): 159–169.

2. Perricone et al. Patterns of Succession and Continuity in Family-Owned Businesses: Study of an Ethnic Community; *Family Business Review*, Vol. 14, No. 2 (2001).
3. J. Ward, "Perpetuating the Family Business: 50 Lessons Learned from Long-Lasting, Successful Families in Business," (Palgrave MacMillan 2004).
4. R. Chittoor and R. Das, "Professionalization of Management and Succession Performance A vital Linkage," *Family Business Review* (Vol. XX, No. 1, March 2007).
5. Stéphanie Brun de Pontet, Carsten Wrosch and Marylene Gagne, "An Exploration of the Generational Differences in Levels of Control Held among Family Businesses Approaching Succession." *Family Business Review*, Vol. XX, no. 4, December 2007, p. 337; Handler, W.C. (1990), Succession in Family firms: A mutual role adjustment between entrepreneur and next-generation family members, *Entrepreneurship, Theory and Practice*, 15, 37–51.
6. Bracci, Enrico, A Knowledge Framework for Understanding Small Family Business Succession Process (July 29, 2008). Available at SSRN: http://ssrn.com/abstract=1184620
7. "Wiseguy: Ronald Perelman," Men.Style.com, October 2006, http://men.style.com/details/wiseguy/full?id=content_4986
8. Francesco Chirico, "The Accumulation Process of Knowledge in Family Firms," Electronic Journal of Family Business Studies (EJFBS) Issue 1, Volume 1, 2007.
9. Frank Hoy, Nurturing The Interpreneur, *Electronic Journal of Family Business Studies*, Issue 1, Vol. 1 (2007).
10. John James Cater, III and Robert T., Justis, "The Development of Successors From Followers to Leaders in Small Family Firms: An Exploratory Study," *Family Business Review*, June 2009, Vol. 22, No. 2.
11. Id.
12. M. Paisner, "Sustaining the Family Business: An Insider's guide to Managing Across Generations," Perseus Books 1999.
13. J. Martel, "The Dilemmas of Family Wealth," Bloomberg Press, 2006.
14. J. Ward, "Perpetuating the Family Business," Palgrave MacMillan 2004.
15. Barach, J.A., Ganitsky, J., Carson, J.A. and Doochin, B.A. 1988. Entry of the Next Generation: Strategic Challenge for Family Business, Journal of Small Business Management, Vol. 26, No. 2, pp. 49–56.
16. Maria Panaritis, "How he rescued Boscov's," The Philadelphia Inquirer, November 27, 2009, p. A1.
17. Arthur Andersen/MassMutual, *American Family Business Survey* (Springfield, MA: MassMutual, 1997).
18. Randel S. Carlock and John L. Ward, *Strategic Planning for the Family Business: Parallel Planning to Unify the Family and Business* (Palgrave 2001).
19. Pietro Mazzola, Gala Marchisio and Joe Astrachan, "Strategic Planning in Family Business: A Powerful Development Tool for the Next Generation", *Family Business Review* (September 2008) Vol. XXI, no. 3, p. 2 39.
20. T. Blumentritt, "The Relationship Between Boards and Planning in Family Businesses," *Family Business Review*, vol. XIX, no. 1, March 2006, p. 65.
21. J. Ward, "Keeping the Family Business Health: How to Plan for Continuing Growth, Profitability, and Family Leadership," (Jossey-Bass Publishers 1987), p. 12.
22. Judy Martel, *The Dilemmas of Family Wealth: Insights on Succession, Cohesion, and Legacy* (Bloomberg Press 2006), p. 41.
23. Edward Monte, a therapist and family business consultant, quoted in Shel Horowitz, "Father and Sons, Mothers and Daughters," Family Business Center,

University of Massachusetts Amherst. (http://www.umass.edu/fambiz/articles/successors/fathers_sons.html)

24. Id.

25. H. Van Auken and J. Werberl, "Family Dynamics and Family Business Financial Performance: Spousal Commitment," *Family Business Review*, vol. XIX, no. 1, March 2006, p. 49.

26. K. Cappuyns, "Women Behind the Scenes in Family Businesses," Electronic Journal of Family Business Studies (EJFBS) Issue 1, Volume 1, 2007. See also Hampton Book Review, Book Review Vol. 22, Number 4, December 2009.

27. *Woods v. Wells Fargo Bank Wyoming*, 90 P3d 724 (Wyo 2004).

28. *Thomas James v. Jerry James*, 768 So. 2d 356; (Supreme Court of Alabama 2000).

29. Finch, Nigel, Identifying and Addressing the Causes of Conflict in Family Business (May 2005). Available at SSRN: http://ssrn.com/abstract=717262

30. C. Aronoff, Ph.D. and J. Ward, Ph.D., "Family Business Values: How to Assure a Legacy of Continuity and Success," Family Enterprise Publishers 2001 (2nd Printing).

31. Johan Lambrecht and Jozef Lievens, "Pruning the Family Tree: An Unexplored Path to Family Business Continuity and Family Harmony" *Family Business Review* 2008: 21: 295.

32. James Olan Hutcheson, "The End of a 1,400-Year Old Business," *BusinessWeek* (April 16, 2007).

2 Family Employee Agreements and Shareholder Agreements

1. Coauthored by Norman S. Heller, Esq., Blank Rome LLP, New York, NY.

2. Larry and Laura Colin, "Family, Inc.: How to Manage Parents, Siblings, Spouses, Children, and In-Laws in the Family Business" (The Career Press, Inc. 2008) p. 39.

3. Lynda Livingston, "Control Sales in Family Firms," *Family Business Review*, March 2007, Vol. XX, no. 1, p. 49; Schultze, W.S. et al., "Exploring the agency consequences of ownership dispersion among the directors of private family firms". *Academy of Management Journal* (2003), 45, 179–194.

4. Id.

5. S. Nelton "When Widows Take Charge" *Family Business Source Book* 3rd ed., Family Enterprise Publishers (2005), 494.

6. Braver, S., and D. O'Connel (1998). *Divorced Dads*. New York: Tarcher-Putnam.

7. Larry & Laura Colin, "Family, Inc.: How to Manage Parents, Siblings, Spouses, Children, and In-Laws in the Family Business" (The Career Press, Inc. 2008) p. 162.

8. "Antenuptial (Premarital) Agreements in Connecticut" (Connecticut Judicial Branch Law Libraries 2001–2008) http://www.jud.ct.gov/lawlib/Notebooks/Pathfinders/AntenuptialAgreements/antenup.htm

9. *Friezo v. Friezo*, 281 Conn. 166, 204, 914 A.2d 533 (2007).

10. *Jardine v. McVey, 2009 WL 48213 (Supreme Court of Nebraska, Jan. 9, 2009).*

3 Governance Structures for Family Businesses

1. S. Lane et al., "Guidelines for Family Business Boards of Directors," *Family Business Review*, vol. XIX, no. 2, June 2006, 147.

2. Deborah A. DeMott, *Guest at the Table? Independent Directors in Family-Influenced Public Companies*, Duke Law School (2007) http://ssrn.com/abstract=1010732

3. T. Blumentritt, "The Relationship Between Boards and Planning the Family Business," *Family Business Review*, vol. XIX, no. 1, March 2006, 65.

4. Poza, E. J. (2004), *Family Business*. Ohio; Thompson, South-Western Publishing.

5. Aronoff, C . E. and Ward, J. L. (1996), *Developing Family Business Policies: Your Guide to the Future*, Mareitta, GA: Family Enterprise Publishers; Schwartz, M. C. and Barnes, L. B. (1991), "Outside Boards and Family Businesses: Another look." *Family Business Review*. 4: 269–285.

6. Ehrlich S. and Bianchi C., "Winners Make It Happen; Losers Let It Happen: An Interview With Leonard Lavin, Founder, Alberto-Culver Corporation." *Family Business Review*, vol. XIX, no. 4, December 2006, 335.

7. Aronoff C., PhD, and Ward J., PhD, "Family Business Governance: Maximizing Family and Business Potential," Family Enterprise Publishers (1996) (5th Printing).

8. John Ward is the Wild Group Professor of Family Business at IMD (Lausanne, Switzerland) and also a professor at the Kellogg School of Management at Northwestern University.

9. Ward J. (2005), "Unconventional Strategy: Why Family Firms Outperform," in *Unconventional Wisdom: Counterintuitive Insights for Family Business Schools*. New York: John Wiley & Sons, Ltd. (2005).

10. *Lois Grato et al v. Louis Grato et al.*, 272 N.J. Super. 140; 639 A.2d 390; 1994, Superior Court of New Jersey, Appellate Division.

11. Tillet, G. (2001), *Resolving Conflict: A Practical Approach*, Melbourne: Oxford University Press.

12. Van der Heyden, L., Blondel, C., and Carlock, Randel S., "Fair Process for Justice in Family Business." *Family Business Review*, Vol. 18, No. 1: 1–21 (March 2005.) Available at SSRN: http://ssrn.com/abstract=727284

13. Finch, Nigel, Identifying and addressing the causes of conflict in family business.

14. Finch, Nigel, The Role of Non-Family Managers in Promoting Business Continuity in Family Owned Enterprises: Practical Conflict Resolution Techniques for Independent Managers and Non-Executive Directors (2005). Available at SSRN: http://ssrn.com/abstract=902790

15. Finch, Nigel, Identifying and Addressing the Causes of Conflict in Family Business (May 2005). Available at SSRN: http://ssrn.com/abstract=717262

16. *Warehime v Warehime*, 563 Pa 400, 761 A.2d 1138 (2000); *Warehime v Warehime*, 860 A.2d 41 (Pa. 2004).

17. Edward Lewine, "Ratifying the Family Constitution," *N.Y. Times,* Jan. 26, 2006.

18. Stephen R. Covey, *The 7 Habits of Highly Effective Families,* 93, 142 (1997).

19. Jeffrey Abrahams, *The Mission Statement Book: 301 Corporate Mission Statements from America's Top Companies 8* (Ten Speed Press 1999).

20. Id; See also Linda C. McClain, "Family Constitutions and the (New) Constitution of the Family," 75 *Fordham Law Review,* 833 (2006).

21. *Strategic Planning for the Family Business, p. 81.*

22. T. Hubler, "The Soul of Family Business," Family Business Review, Vol. 22, No. 3, September 2009.

23. Id, pp. 82–83.

24. Habbershon, T. G., and Pistrui, J. 2002. "Enterprising Family Domain: Family-Influenced Ownership Groups in Pursuit of Transgenerational Wealth," Family Business Review, Vol. 15, No. 3, 223–238; Daily, C.M. and Dollinger, M.J. 1993 "Alternative Methodologies for Identifying Family versus Non-family Managed Businesses." *Journal of Small Business Management*, Vol. 31, No. 2, 70–90.

4 Worst Practices: What We Can Learn from Family Disasters

1. *Thorndike v. Thorndike*, 910 A2d 1224 (NH 2006).
2. *Rosenthal v. Rosenthal et a.l*, Decision No. 4763, law Docket No. KEN-87–175, Supreme Judicial Court of Maine, 543 A.2d 348; 1988 Me. LEXIS 152.
3. *Elizabeth Trimarco, et al. v. Ann Trimarco, et al.*, Superior Court of New Jersey, Appellate Division, 396 N.J. Super. 207; 933 A.2d 621; 2007 N.J. Super. LEXIS 318; 26 I.E.R. Cas. (BNA) 1650.
4. *Johnson v. Johnson*, 720 NW2d 20 (2006).
5. *Franchino v. Franchino*, 2004 WL 1698711 (Mich App July 29, 2004).
6. *Rocco Guarnieri et al v. Louis Guarnieri et al* 104 Conn. App. 810; 936 A.2d 254 2007 Conn. App. LEXIS 445.

5 Compensating Family Members

1. Larry and Laura Colin, *Family, Inc.: How to Manage Parents, Siblings, Spouses, Children, and In-Laws in the Family Business* (The Career Press, Inc. 2008) p. 34.
2. C. Aronoff, S. McClure, and J. Ward, *Family Business Compensation* 2nd ed., (FBCG Publications 2009).
3. Ibid.

6 Creating Phantom Equity Incentives for Key Employees, Both Family and Non-Family

1. Co-authored by Barry L. Klein, Esq., Partner at Blank Rome LLP.
2. F. Hoy, "Nurturing the Interpreneur," Electronic Journal of Family Business Studies (EJFBS) Issue 1, Volume 1, 2007; Chua, J. H., Chrisman, J. J., and Sharma, P. 2003. "Succession and Nonsuccession Concerns of Family Firms and Agency Relationships with Nonfamily Managers," *Family Business Review*, vol. 16, pp. 89–107; Ibrahim, A.B., and Ellis, W.H., 2004, *Family Business Management—Concepts and Practice*, Kendall/Hunt, 2nd Ed., Dubuque, Iowa, USA; Schultzendorff, D. v. 1984. Fremdmanager in Familienunternehmen—Eine empirische Analyse. Dissertation No. 922, Hochschule St. Gallen, Switzerland.
3. Antonio Carrasco-Hernandez and Gregorio Sanchez-Marin, "The Determinants of Employee Compensation in Family Firms: Empirical Evidence," *Family Business Review*, Vol. XX, no. 3, September 2007, p 215.

7 Dealing with Inactive Minority Shareholders

1. Miguel A. Gallo and Kristin Cappuyns, *Family Members Who Do Not Work in The Family Business: How to Enhance Their "Unity" and "Commitment"*. University of Navarra (September, 2004); Blondel, Ch., Carlock, R.S. & Van de Heyden, L. (2000) Fair Process: Striving for Justice in Family Businesses. 11th Annual F.B.N. World Conference, Proceedings, London; Carlock, R. & Ward, J. (2001) *Strategic Planning for the Family Business, Parallel Planning to Unify the Family and Business*, New York; Palgrave. Gallo, M.A., Corbetta, G. Dyer, G., Tomaselli, S., Montemerlo, D. & Cappuyns, K. (2001) Success as a Function of Love, Trust and Freedom in Family Businesses, IESE, Chair of Family Business, *Monograph No. 4*.

2. Jodi Wilgoren, "$900 Million Accord Enables Breakup of Pritzker Dynasty". *The New York Times*, January 7, 2005.
3. Once a family business has more than 500 shareholders of record and more than $10 million of assets, the family business entity must register under the Securities and Exchange Act of 1934 and provide periodic reports and other information.
4. *Schumacher v. Schumacher*, 469n.w.2d 793 (Supreme Court of North Dakota 1991) *Crosby v. Beam*, 548 N.E.2d 217 (Supreme Court of Ohio 1989); *Thomas James v. Jerry James* 768 So. 2d 356 (Supreme Court of Alabama, Rel. January 28, 2000).
5. *Crosby v. Beam*, 548 N.E. 2d 217 (Supreme Court of Ohio 1989).
6. *Margaret B. Ford et al v. William K. Ford et al*, 941 A.2d 138 (Superior Court of Pennsylvania 2005).
7. *Gottfried et al. v. Gottfried et al.*, Supreme Court, Special Term, New York County, Part VI, 73 N.Y.S.2d 692; 1947 N.Y. Misc. LEXIS 3108.
8. Id.
9. *O'Neal and Thompson's, Close Corporations and LLCs: Law and Practice* 3rd ed. (Eagan MN: Thomson Reuters/West, June 2009) §9:20.
10. *Dodge v. Ford Motor Co.*, 204 Mich., 459, 170 N.W. 668, 3 A.L.R. 413 (1919); 20 Colum. L. Rev. 93 (1920); 17 Mich. L. Rev. 502 (1919); 28 Yale L.J. 710 (1919).
11. *Aiello v. Aiello*, 447 Mass. 388, 852 N.E. 2d 68 (2006).

8 Eliminating Minority Shareholders

1. Co-authored by Alan L. Zeiger, Esq., Blank Rome LLP, Philadelphia, PA.
2. See *Judith Lawton, et al., Plaintiffs v. Robert Nyman, et al. Defendants and Jeffrey Nyman, Plaintiff v. Robert Nyman, et al. Defendants*, C.A. No. 98–288-T C.A. No. 02–290-T, U.S. District Court for the District of Rhode Island, 357 F. Supp. 2d 428; 2005 U.S. Dist. LEXIS 2373; See also *Lawton v. Nyman*, 2002 U.S. Dist. LEXIS 17398, C.A. No. 98–288-T, 2002 WL 221621 (D.R.I. January 17, 2002); See also *Kiepler v. Nyman*, 2002 U.S. Dist. LEXIS 19630, C.A. No. 98–272-T, 2002 WL 221622 (D.R.I. January 17, 2002).
3. *Gerald M. Kelly, et al., v. The Wellsville Foundry Inc.* (Ohio 2000).
4. *In the Supreme Court*, State of Wyoming, *Suzanne W. Brown, individually: Suzanne W. Brown, as Successor Trustee of the Marie Arp Schroeder Testamentary Trust; and Suzanne W. Brown, as Successor Trustee of the Catharine S. Holmes Trust v. Arp and Hammond Hardware Company*, 2006 WY 107.
5. See *Achey v. Linn County Bank*, 261 Kan. 669, 931 P2d 16 (1997).
6. *Gerald M. Kelly, et al., v. The Wellsville Foundry Inc.* (Ohio 2000)·
7. Id. 5.

9 Family Businesses in Financial Distress

1. Raymond L. Shapiro, Esq. and Joel C. Shapiro, Esq., Blank Rome LLP, Philadelphia office contributed to this chapter.
2. J. Lee, "Family Firm Performance: Further Evidence", *Family Business Review, vol. XIX, no. 2, June 2006, p. 103.*
3. Determination of whether a debtor is a "small business debtor" requires application of a two-part test. First, the debtor must be engaged in commercial or business activities (other than primarily owning or operating real property) with total non-contingent liquidated secured and unsecured debts of $2,190,000 or less. Second,

the debtor's case must be one in which the U.S. trustee has not appointed a creditors' committee, or the court has determined the creditors' committee is insufficiently active and representative to provide oversight of the debt. 11 U.S.C. § 101 (51D)
4. 11 U.S.C. §1126(c).
5. http://en.wikipedia.org/wiki/Boscov's

10 Selling a Family Owned Business

1. Thomas M. Zellweger and Joseph H. Astrachan, "On the Emotional Value of Owning a Firm", *Family Business Review* (2008) Vol. 21, p. 347.
2. F. Visscher, C. Aronoff and J. Ward, "Financing Transitions: Managing Capital and Liquidity in the Family Business", Family Business Leadership Series No. 7 (Business Owner Services 1995), p. 29.

11 Preserving and Transferring Family Wealth

1. Co-authored by Lawrence S. Chane, Esq., Blank Rome LLP, Philadelphia, PA.

12 Family Businesses Going Public

1. S. Ehrlich and C. Bianchi, "Winners Make It Happen; Losers Let It Happen: An Interview With Leonard Lavin, Founder, Alberto-Culver Corporation". *Family Business Review*, vol. XIX, no. 4, December 2006, p. 335.
2. Ronald C. Anderson & David M. Reeb, *Founding-Family Ownership and Firm Performance: Evidence form the S&P 500*, 58 J. FIN. 1301, 1302 (2003); Jim Lee, "Family Firm Performance: Further Evidence", *Family Business Review*, Vol. XIX, no. 2, June 2006, p. 103.
3. Belén Villalonga & Raphael Amit, *How Do Family Ownership, Control, and Management Affect Firm Value?* 80 J.FIN. ECON. 385 (2006).
4. Laporta, R., Lopez-de-Silanes, F., & Shleifer, A. (1999), Corporate ownership around the world, *Journal of Finance*, 54, 4/1–517; D. Miller and I. LeBreton-Miller, "Family Governance and Firm Performance: Agency, Stewardship, and Capabilities", *Family Business Review*, vol. XIX, no. 1, March 2006, p. 73.
5. D. Miller and I. LeBreton-Miller, "Family Governance and Firm Performance: Agency, Stewardship, and Capabilities", *Family Business Review*, vol. XIX, no. 1, March 2006, p. 73.
6. Ravasi, Davide and Marchisio, Gaia,Family Firms and the Decision to Go Public: A Study of Italian IPOs(March 2001). SDA BOCCONI, Research Division Working Paper No. 01–45. Available at SSRN: http://ssrn.com/abstract=278237 or DOI: 10.2139/ssrn.278237; Arkebauer, K.R., (1991), Cashing Out. New York: Harper Business.
7. Jones, R.G., (1979), Analyzing Initial and Growth Financing for Small Businesses, Management Accounting, 30–38.
8. Judy Martel, *The Delemas of Family Wealth: Insights on Succession, Cohesion, and Legacy* (Bloomberg Press 2006) p. 60.
9. Perrini, F., (1999a), Capitale di Rischio e Mercati per le PMI, Metodologie e Canali di Accesso al Capitale per lo Sviluppo. Milano: egea.

10. Ravasi, Davide and Marchisio, Gaia,Family Firms and the Decision to Go Public: A Study of Italian IPOs(March 2001). SDA BOCCONI, Research Division Working Paper No. 01–45. Available at SSRN: http://ssrn.com/abstract=278237 or DOI: 10.2139/ssrn.278237.
11. See www.SharkRepellent.net
12. Henrik Cronqvist & Mattias Nilsson, *Agency Costs of Controlling Minority Shareholders*, 38 J., FIN. & QUANT.ANALYSIS 695 (2003).
13. Asjeet Lamba & Geof Stapledon, *The Determinant of Corporate Ownership Structure: Australian Evidence* (2001).
14. Randall P. Morck et al., *Inherited Wealth, Corporate Control, and Economic Growth: The Canadian Disease?*, in CONCENTRATED CORPORATE OWNERSHIP 319, 327–329.
15. Hsu, Scott H.C, Reed, Adam V. and Rocholl, Joerg,The New Game in Town: Competitive Effects of IPOs(March, 20 2009). Journal of Finance, Forthcoming. Available at SSRN: http://ssrn.com/abstract=1365940
16. S. Ehrlich and C. Bianchi, "Winners Make It Happen; Losers Let It Happen: An Interview With Leonard Lavin, Founder, Alberto-Culver Corporation". *Family Business Review*, vol. XIX, no. 4, December 2006, p. 335.
17. *Benihana of Tokyo Inc. v. Benihana, Inc.*, 906 A.2d 114 (Del. 2006).
18. Id.

Index